T0374207

We R2B1

By Teaching Biblical Truth

To God be the glory,
great things He has done!

Gary Buchanan

WESTBOW
PRESS®
A DIVISION OF THOMAS NELSON
& ZONDERVAN

WestBow Press books may be ordered through booksellers or by contacting:

WestBow Press
A Division of Thomas Nelson & Zondervan
1663 Liberty Drive
Bloomington, IN 47403
www.westbowpress.com
1 (866) 928-1240

ISBN: 978-1-9736-1685-6 (sc)
ISBN: 978-1-9736-1686-3 (hc)
ISBN: 978-1-9736-1684-9 (e)

Library of Congress Control Number: 2018901023

Print information available on the last page.

WestBow Press rev. date: 3/20/2018

Contents

APPRECIATION

God is good, all the time. When asked why his book *The Five Love Languages* was so successful, Gary Chapman responded "God - from first to last and all in between." God provided <u>everything</u> needed to prepare this book (time, ideas, Scripture insight, life's lessons, computer skills, a supportive wife, amazing interviews, great reviewers and editors); to Him be the glory. The following is an adaptation of a note in Howard Hendricks's Bible. When I write, I fail. When I trust, He succeeds. This book is a product of the provision of God. I must mention a portion of those blessings. Great thanks go to my wife Peggy for her prayers, patience, and participation. She was so cooperative through the months of my hogging our computer. She read, corrected and commented on the rough, rough draft to get it ready for peer reviews. The reviews provided by Carolyn Dennison, Sam Nalley, and Rev. Sam Harris were instrumental in producing a message that could be understood by readers. Don't blame WestBow Pres for this work not meeting writing standards, I didn't use their editing service.

I interviewed nineteen leaders of various churches who provided great insights into how we can conquer our differences. I also want to thank the pastor who refused an interview after reading one chapter. His comments changed the attitude displayed in this book. I am humbly grateful to them all. The proceeds I receive from this book will be used to support the WeR2B1.com website, or given to charity.

INTRODUCTION

"Alone we can do so little; together we
can do so much." - Helen Keller

The 2001 edition of the *World Christian Encyclopedia* reveals
there are 33,830 Christian denominations worldwide.[1]
WOW! According to the 2010 edition of the *Handbook
of Denominations in the United States,* there are 211
denominations (with more than 5,000 members) that consider
themselves to be Christians.[2] Added to that are thousands
of non-denominational churches. In spite of that buffet of
belief opportunities, Christianity is on the decline in North
America, Europe, Australia and other places in the world. Is
this fractured face of Christianity a major deterrent to the
spread of the gospel and contributing to the decline of western
Christianity? "Every kingdom divided against itself is laid
waste, and a divided household falls" (Luk 11:17).

It is as though Jesus was a "religious big bang" and the
theological universe is still expanding. Is that what He
intended? Samuel G. Dawson, claims that conflicting doctrinal
beliefs within the professed Christian community provide the
strongest argument atheists and skeptics can use. It has
inhibited the spread of the gospel more than all the militant
atheists put together![3] Nonbelievers dismiss Christians as
another splintered form of human religious expression. We
have broken up into denominations and fight each other much
like the branches of Islam do. Why would an unbeliever see us
any differently? When the lost hear all our different theologies,
we sound like a room full of people all talking at once. Most
do not really listen to any of us. We should be speaking
with one voice. This book deals with all religions that claim
Jesus as their Savior. Some are considered cults, because
others contend their beliefs violate perceived essentials of the
Christian faith. They will all be referred to as denominations,
though some would not use that term.

On Christmas morning 2014, the wonderful world of Twitter was treated to the viewpoint of astrophysicist and cosmologist Neil deGrasse Tyson. Mr. Tyson, to put it mildly, was not a believer. Among the many tweets he sent to his 2.8 million followers was this: "On this day long ago, a child was born who, by age 30, would transform the world. Happy Birthday Isaac Newton b. Dec 25, 1642." The date of Sir Isaac Newton's birth is actually in some dispute. However, Sir Isaac Newton's beliefs are quite different from Tyson. Newton said, "This most beautiful system of the sun, planets, and comets, could only proceed from the counsel and dominion of an intelligent being.... This being governs all things, not as the soul of the world, but as Lord over all; and on account of His dominion He is wont to be called 'Lord God.'"[4] Why does Tyson, an anti-Christian, have such a great following?

This book deals with several questions related to unity. How are denominations addressed in the Bible? Have the centuries of constructionist theology led to the contemporary practice of interpreting Scripture however needed to support a particular worldview? Why are non-denominational churches on the rise, and many affiliated with a denomination changing their name to avoid those labels? Why is the church growing in Africa, Asia, and South America? Christianity would be growing in other areas if the effort and resources directed toward arguing theology and denominational squabbles were applied to discipleship, ministry and seeking the lost.

The objective of this initiative was not to publish a theological document, rather to pursue an environment where we can grow back together and present a more unified body to the lost public. A foundational point for this book is if two differ on the requirements for salvation, at least one is wrong. Biblical guidance for teaching, in addition to the causes and consequences of false teaching are thoroughly examined. Finally, recommended steps for the body to begin to grow back together top down and bottom up are presented.

Target audiences are those in leadership and everyone who teaches anything about Christianity. The latter applies to those sharing their faith with others - family, friends, co-workers, etc. Those writing on denominational and theological topics are especially intended readers. Many voices in today's tsunami of opinions tell us what is wrong with denominations. They provide much less in the way of suggestions for how, and just as importantly why, we should strive to be one body in Christ. This work provides both. It is not a call to "come over to our side." The contested theology examined involves my denomination.

The first great commandment is to "love the Lord with all your heart, soul, and mind; the second is to love your neighbor as yourself" (Mat 22:37-39). The great commission is to "make disciples". Our conduct is the most important expression in doing those three "great" objectives. Teaching would be second. There is a wide spectrum of teaching by people claiming to be Christians. Some provide great insights into God's Word, while others are more like many US judges. Their interpretation tends to drift to match the prevailing values of the people, like the tail wagging the dog.

Some say Jesus taught on money more than any other topic. That may be true, but the topics of preaching, teaching, and discipleship show up directly or indirectly throughout the New Testament (abbreviated as NT). Parents teach more in day-to-day situations than any other influence on our children. Our conduct and the values shared to friends, relatives and coworkers reveal almost everything about our beliefs.

I learned how to teach through great effort and a lot of trial and error. I read some topical books, such as working with youth that contained subject matter content and tips on teaching techniques, but less on the critical matter of being faithful to the Bible. This book covers vital guidance every teacher needs to know and follow.

Many contemporary school history textbooks do not contain the full truth of the motives for the founding of the United

States just a few centuries ago. When considering the primitive times and materials used, preservation of the Bible from 2000 years ago, and older, is a great miracle. Our ability to see the text inspired by the Holy Spirit in reputable translations is a great blessing. Secular history, archeology and human experience continue to prove the validity of this miracle. Scripture was the primary source for this book. Quotes and references from others were included to illustrate the biblical concepts. The phrase "reputable translation" describes those widely accepted in Christianity and have not fallen into the distortions mentioned in chapter 11.

This book targets a wide spectrum of biblical familiarity; consequently, ample Scripture was included and referenced. Some authors use a phrase from the Bible and expect all readers to know the source. When reading theological books, I often pass over cited Scripture and move on to the author's next concept. By including the text, the reader can fully consider the reference.

> Psa 119:11, 105, 130 [11]I have stored up your word in my heart, that I might not sin against you.... [105] Your word is a lamp to my feet and a light to my path.... [130] The unfolding of your words gives light; it imparts understanding

What Scripture has to say is far more important than my words of mortar holding the bricks of truth in place. The Word must be the basis for our thinking, talking and writing. In most cases when stating a spiritual position, we should be able to support it with Scripture or keep it to ourselves.

> Col 4:5-6 Walk in wisdom toward outsiders, making the best use of the time. [6] Let your speech always be gracious, seasoned with salt, so that you may know how you ought to answer each person.

God's nature does not change - Mal 3:6, and Jas 1:17. Concepts referenced in the Old Testament (abbreviated as

OT) should be true today unless changed in the NT. Two or more witnesses are required for valid testimony - Deu 19:15. At least two passages of Scripture support key points. Referenced Scripture was displayed with a dash - Jhn 3:16, and quoted Scripture was indented or shown in parenthesis after the passage (Jhn 3:16). Over 50% of the content in this book was directly or indirectly from Scripture. Readers must at least say this book is not half bad.

On a recent trip, we saw a warning sign - do not disturb geological artifacts. It is difficult to analyze and draw conclusions about a fossil out of the context of the discovery location. That makes great sense. I placed a high priority on using Scripture in harmony with the context. Unless annotated otherwise, Scripture references are from the English Standard Version (ESV). This was not an endorsement of that translation over others.

Why read a book by a layman? Dwight L. Moody never went to seminary "Except to go in one door and out the other,"[5] but was considered the most prolific evangelist of the 19th century. Lack of seminary training is where the comparison ends. God can do things of great value through anyone.

The first Great Awakening in the United States turned our nation toward God in a significant way. It reshaped the religious, social and moral landscape of early America from 1727 to 1747. The 1857 Revival started when the North Dutch Reformed Church of Manhattan decided to stay downtown and reach out to the lost masses of people who surrounded them. To accomplish this, they employed a 48-year old businessman, Jeremiah Lanphier, as missionary to the inner city. Secular historians rarely mention this revival today, but it had an amazing impact. During the winter of 1857–58, revival swept across the land with such power it was estimated 50,000 conversions occurred weekly. We do not see that level of conversion in the United States today with over 10 times the population. In the period 1857-59, approximately one million people, in a population of less than thirty million, became believers.[6] Eleven million people would come to faith in a comparable movement today. Is that not worth refining our theology and teaching where appropriate? It would be wonderful if one of those who came to faith was a person you have been praying about for years. What if one of the people accepting Jesus was a prolific opponent of Christianity like the Apostle Paul was; and then they began to use their talents to promote Jesus? We need another great revival. Will you be one to help ignite a revival in western Christianity?

I have had a burden to pursue this work for about 20 years, compiling Scripture and other reference information. Being an engineer by education and occupation, I felt inadequate to be a writer. God used some uneducated authors to write portions of the Bible. Three technology giants achieved great success without college degrees - Bill Gates, Steve Jobs, and Michael Dell. They founded companies and became multi-billionaires. I have been a teacher of youth and adults for over 35 years, attended thousands of Bible studies, heard thousands of sermons on Moody radio, and that many more in person. I have read many books on the Christian faith. Thanks to the Lord, I had phenomenal online research tools like the Blue Letter Bible site. I am vastly experienced, "the splendor of old men is their gray hair" or lack thereof. However, I am not out of touch, I would never admit to licking my finger to turn the page on an e-reader.

We can miss God's overarching emphasis on a particular topic when mentioned in a few verses in many books of the Bible. This is especially true if we read many books instead of reading the Bible. As we read the NT, we see many concepts presented. When we pull together everything those letters and epistles have to say about a specific topic, we see a broadly compelling emphasis on that issue or behavior. This is far different from the beliefs some draw from isolated verses. Reading Scripture topically is like walking through a park, camera in hand, looking for a gorgeous scene, a new bird, a beautiful flower, or a stunning sunset. We consider everything in detail. Aimless reading of Scripture can be like one jogging through the park with our thoughts far away; we do not see the forest *or* the trees. When organized topically, Scripture provides an even clearer perspective to edify us. I read the Bible cover to cover several times looking for answers and guidance related to unity and teaching.

We need to get some terminology defined before starting. It is amazing how definitions change circumstantially over time just as the interpretation of Scripture has. Those producing dictionaries also exhibit an agenda at times. The definition used for denominations is an adaptation of the American Heritage Dictionary of the English Language: a group of religious congregations united under a common faith and name and organized under a single administrative and/or legal hierarchy. Many will say, "We aren't a denomination," and by some definitions they are correct. Those claiming the name of Christ cast a shadow of influence on the world, and should read this book.

The term Christian is losing its meaning. During the 2016 US election coverage, the media consistently used the term evangelicals. They never gave a definition. Wikipedia limited their definition of evangelicals to Protestants. The National Association of Evangelical's definition was too general - Evangelicals take the Bible seriously and believe in Jesus Christ as Savior and Lord. The following is a good definition for evangelicals - believers who emphasize Christian unity, the unique authority of Scripture, salvation by grace through faith, and evangelism.[7] I searched at length for a succinct definition of Christian and did not find a good one. Some said you had to read the whole New Testament to understand. I have used the term Christian to refer to someone who claims Jesus as his or her Lord and Savior. Their life should confirm it - Mat 3:8-10, 7:21; Mar 3:35, 4:20; Luk 3:8-9; Act 26:20; Heb 6:7-9; 1Jn 2:4,10, 3:9 and Jas 2:17-18.

The title pastor applies to the teachers from all faith groups - bishop, minister, preacher, priest, lay leader, etc. The term church is generic for all Christian bodies. The first definition for cult from the Miriam Webster dictionary would never work, it describes all people of religion - "formal religious veneration: worship." The first definition offered by Google was also far too generic. The second alternative describes "cult" as used in this book - "a group with misplaced or excessive admiration for a particular person or thing."

I looked at several definitions for the word "essential", like the one that makes the acrostic DOCTRINE.[8] Most listed specific elements rather than giving a description. The definition used for a Christian essential is - "a basic, indispensable, or necessary element to be saved." Most confession statements contain doctrines that are not an essential as used in this book. These definitions are included in the Glossary at the end of this book for reference as you read.

Denomination names are seldom mentioned. I did not want to offend anyone; the Holy Spirit can use these words to touch whom He chooses; that will be much more effective than accusations. If I offend someone anyway, please be assured my objective was to move us toward unity, not to affront. The humor you encounter was an intended reward for reading this diatribe; it may also help keep your bones healthy - Pro 17:22. Be assured it was not sarcasm; many theological writers use an overdose of that. Perhaps they feel it makes them seem more intelligent and authoritative. "Does a spring pour forth from the same opening both fresh and salt water" (Jas 3 11)? Excessive sarcasm says a lot about the heart and spiritual maturity of the author and gives reason to consider their words with great caution. Writing is likely the most powerful form of teaching; treat it with the most respect.

You may be thinking that one book by a rank amateur will not blunt this denominational quagmire. You are not the first to have that reaction. My response is "If God is your partner, make your plans BIG!" - D. L. Moody

1. A BURNING PLATFORM

Holy Father, keep them in your name, which you have given me, that they may be one, even as we are one. Jhn 17:11

Our unity is important to Jesus. He again calls us to be one in the following passages, repeating it twice for emphasis. He adds a second motivation for unity, "so the world will believe." Our unity has a bearing on our evangelism. John records the same message from our Lord in Jhn 10:16 and 13:34-35.

> Jhn 17:20-23 "I do not ask for these only, but also for those who will believe in me through their word, ²¹ that they may all be **one**, just as you, Father, are in me, and I in you, that they also may be in us, so that the world may believe that you have sent me. ²² The glory that you have given me I have given to them, that they may be **one** even as we are one, ²³ I in them and you in me, that they may become perfectly **one**, so that the world may know that you sent me and loved them even as you loved me.

There is a non-denominational association of churches that uses Jhn 13:34 as a mission statement. How can we expect a lost and dying world to believe we are peddling the truth when we cannot agree on the requirements for salvation in Scripture (i.e. the essentials)? We frequently treat each other with harsh criticism and worse. Paul contended with divisions between Jewish and Gentile Christians - Eph 3:6 and Gal 3:27-28. Would he view denominationalism any differently?

> Eph 2:14-16 For he himself is our peace, who has made us both one and has broken down in his flesh the dividing wall of hostility ¹⁵ by abolishing the law of commandments expressed in ordinances, that he might create in himself one new man in place of the two, so making peace, ¹⁶ and might reconcile us both

1

to God in one body through the cross, thereby killing the hostility.

Eph 4:1-6 I therefore, a prisoner for the Lord, urge you to walk in a manner worthy of the calling to which you have been called, [2] with all humility and gentleness, with patience, bearing with one another in love, [3] eager to maintain the unity of the Spirit in the bond of peace. [4] There is one body and one Spirit—just as you were called to the one hope that belongs to your call - [5] one Lord, one faith, one baptism, [6] one God and Father of all, who is over all and through all and in all.

Paul continues the emphasis Jesus placed on unity. This passage seems more like a command than a suggestion.

Eph 4:11-16 And he gave the apostles, the prophets, the evangelists, the shepherds and teachers, [12] to equip the saints for the work of ministry, for building up the body of Christ, [13] until we all attain to the unity of the faith and of the knowledge of the Son of God, to mature manhood, to the measure of the stature of the fullness of Christ, [14] so that we may no longer be children, tossed to and fro by the waves and carried about by every wind of doctrine, by human cunning, by craftiness in deceitful schemes. [15] Rather, speaking the truth in love, we are to grow up in every way into him who is the head, into Christ, [16] from whom the whole body, joined and held together by every joint with which it is equipped, when each part is working properly, makes the body grow so that it builds itself up in love.

There are more examples where Paul mandates unity - "together you may with one voice glorify the God and Father of our Lord Jesus Christ" (Rom 15:6), "to agree in the Lord" (Phl 4:2), "there are many parts, yet one body." (1Co 12:20), "there may be no division in the body, and "to which indeed you were called in one body" (Col 3:15). His letters were written to all believers in towns that apparently had some divisive dynamics as he mentions this issue in five different letters.

> 1Co 12:12-13 For just as the <u>body is one</u> and has many members, and <u>all the members of the body</u>, though many, <u>are one body</u>, so it is with Christ. [13] For in one Spirit we were all <u>baptized into one body</u>--Jews or Greeks, slaves or free--and all were made to drink of one Spirit.

To make it completely clear, Paul supports the call for unity with condemnations of divisions - "<u>watch out for those who cause divisions</u> and create obstacles contrary to the doctrine that you have been taught" (Rom 16:17). David knew unity was well worth seeking, "Behold, how good and pleasant it is <u>when brothers dwell in unity</u>!" (Psa 133:1); also 2Ch 30:12.

Paul includes an appeal, "that there be no divisions among you" (1Co 1:10). Avoid divisive people in leadership. Time and time again, ungodly leaders have commandeered organizations to their downfall. Paul cautions the Galatians that "the works of flesh are evident: ... strife, jealousy, fits of anger, rivalries, dissensions, divisions" (Gal 5:19-20). Do we see that today? Church splits, law suits between churches, and enough ink to reach the bridles of the horses has been applied to arguments about contested beliefs. Jude rounds out the discussion with a strong condemnation for the divisive.

> Jde 1:19 It is these who <u>cause divisions</u>, worldly people, <u>devoid of the Spirit</u>.

Think about how the world sees us. Instead of working for unity in Christ, we turn the church into alphabet soup. Every abbreviation on the cover represents groups in the US professing the Christian faith. Does our promoting the divisions in the body cause the blaspheming of God?

> Rom 2:23-24 You who boast in the law dishonor God by breaking the law. [24] For, as it is written, "The name

3

of God is blasphemed among the Gentiles because of you."

This book does not promote the "coexist" concept that all roads lead to heaven, because they do not. Some claim positions that conflict with Scripture. The Bible speaks clearly about turning from the teaching it provides - Rev 22:18. A big surprise awaits those who describe the Bible as a buffet of ideas from which we can pick and choose what we want to believe. My hope is the Bible believing denominations can grow back together, and clear the fog of 33,800 denominations so people can recognize and hear from the real body of Christ.

There are some churches that focus on the essentials of the Christian faith and waste little time dealing with non-essential differences like those in chapter 11; praise God. If two bodies differ on a matter that either side deems to be an essential, they likely consider each other a cult. We should rigorously compare contested conclusions in our belief documents to the whole of Scripture and see if they are upheld or brought into question. Chapter 10 contains an example review. Some writers commend denominations for their zeal in attempting to get it right. Does God give participant trophies for heartfelt wrong doctrine?

The various denominations are like brands of allergy medicine. They all claim to be the best, and all have side effects. Some side effects sound worse than the allergies. If there was one best medicine, everyone would buy it and the others would go out of business. We, too, have our side effects and imperfections, or the "perfect" church would have risen to the top and all the others faded - Act 2:47, and 6:7.

Many Christian bodies have placed the cult label on the denominations that do not accept the doctrine of the Trinity as fully accurate. Chapter 11 explores biblical teaching related to the Trinity. There are other denominations, considered Christian, with adherents who deny equally relevant beliefs. Cult is a subjective and dangerous term to use indiscriminately. There are probably groups that would consider my denomination to be a cult.

Will we ever stop being "tossed to and fro by the waves and carried about by every wind of doctrine" (Eph 4:14)? The devil has been trying to mislead humanity since the garden. False doctrine harms our testimony, example, and effectiveness. It is logically impossible that our differing essentials are all valid. We likely all have religious beliefs that are wrong in the eyes of God. This is not new, 2Ch 13:11 and 28:6 describe Judah and Israel killing each other, both claiming to have the only true worship. In reality, neither faction had true worship. They both had plenty of sin, including distorted religious practices. Sadly, we value distinctions over obedience and full congruity with all Scripture. We diminish our influence as we fracture into smaller and smaller bodies.

Instead of pasting a selected verse in a PowerPoint slide, I pasted the whole template from the Blue Letter Bible website. The gospel is often lost in our disjointed messages.

Some will say the lost are unaware of our denominations. A lot of our dirty laundry appears on secular news - splits, infighting, clergy abuses, evolving standards, etc. We frequently hear the term "good Muslim" thrown around in the media.

The public asks, "Why are they not standing up against the radical terrorist Muslims?" It seems most of the unchurched paint all Christians with the same brush, wondering why we do not do something about those who beat their son to death in church, protest at the funeral of fallen military personnel, or molest children. Is that not what Scripture calls for?

If part of the body (true or in name only) is weak or sick, we all suffer - 1Co 12:26. Bad press drags us all down. If we had one true Christian organization, we could denounce such behavior as non-Christian and back it up with Scripture and an affiliation too big to ignore. The media is not likely to quote a statement from one of our 33,830 fractured voices.

Christianity is Declining in America

What does the future hold for Christianity in America? Canada has passed laws regarding hate speech that applies to the messages spoken in their pulpits. We have already seen attempted challenges to the content of sermons in America. Some cell phone software providers have removed selected Christian apps from their app stores. The definition of marriage took a complete reversal in an incredibly brief period. At one point, laws in 32 states defined marriage as one man and one woman. Reaching 38 states would prompt an Article V Constitutional Convention to consider an amendment. Just five years later, the Supreme Court ruled those laws unconstitutional and now marriage is open to any two people (so far). Where could this lead if Christianity continues to decline? Here are a few burdens likely to occur. It could become Illegal to promote religion in public. Our phone, text, and email communication searched for what the world considers hate speech. Sites could be blocked from access by web searches based on its objectionable Christian content, while viewing obscenity and murder is accessible to all. Websites might be banned for their Christian content. Where will it end? Many will say God is in control. Yes He is. However, He usually inspires His people and supports their initiatives as opposed to doing it for us - 2Ch 7:14.

If a church were doing what it should, God would usually bless it with success in ministry and growth - Act 16:5. There are a few reasons He might not for a short period. When some groups do not get the desired success, they continue to reinvent the church. Sometimes new approaches draw nonbelievers into the church. Other times it is wrong, unjustifiable in Scripture. For example, a denomination has voted at least three times at the highest level to make premarital sex not a sin, a classic example of lowering the bar to meet societal norms. "Whoever wishes to be a friend of the world makes himself an enemy of God." (Jas 4:4). The Bible is clear on this for about a dozen consequential reasons. God was not trying to steal our fun. He was trying to guide us through life with the greatest overall joy and fulfillment, and the least pain and misfortune.

The development of the Apostles creed in the 4th century emphasized the importance of "one catholic (universal) church." Over 50% of the people professing Christianity use that confession. We just cannot agree on who is in the one body. The myriad of books, blogs, and articles that support our assorted theologies do not make them right. Scripture clearly mandates unity in the church. We need doctrine fully based on Scripture to become **one**.

The Impact of Our Division

Scripture says the people will know Him through our unity. What does our disunity tell the lost? Is obeying Jesus important? John's gospel tells us obeying Jesus and abiding in His love is the measure of our belief - Jhn 14:12, 14:21, and 15:10.

Surely, there is an acceptable list of essential tenets that all believers could adopt. Those who say no stand a great chance of being disobedient on unity, likely wrong about some doctrine, and are perpetuating the impediment to reaching the lost. Why are 4,000 churches closing their doors every year in America? Why are 80% of the 250,000 Protestant churches in America either stagnant or declining?[1] A 2012 global poll reports 59% of the world's population is religious, and 36% are not religious, including 13% who are atheists, with a 9% decrease in religious belief from 2005.[2] The other 5% was not described; they likely gave no response. Why are so many drifting toward nihilism? In 2010, Christianity was the largest religion in the world with 2,168,330,000 claiming that label; compared to Islam with 1,599,700,000.[3] The 2001 edition of the *World Christian Encyclopedia* identifies 10,000 distinct religions worldwide, of which 150 have over one million followers. Their data shows immense global shifts in the religious affiliation of the world population between 1900 and 2000. Though Christianity became the first truly universal religion in terms of geography, it lost some market share. Second-ranked Islam expanded considerably and Hinduism somewhat, while Buddhism declined. Chinese and other folk religions dropped precipitously, as did Judaism.[4]

The European countries that produced the likes of Zwingly, Tindell, Huss, Luther, Calvin, and the Wesley brothers have been declining in professing Christians for over a century. The proportion of Europeans who professed Christianity dropped from 95% in 1910 to 76% in 2010. The basis for that data was a country-by-country analysis of about 2,400 data sources; including censuses and nationally representative population surveys.[5] Those sources tend to include people who are Christian in name only. Based on surveys of church attendance and spiritual influence, the number of true Christians is significantly less. The Anglican Church's annual pew count reports an average of 1.4 percent of the population of England attends services on Sunday. The 2010 euro barometer poll showed just 18% of the Swedish population said they believed in a personal God.[6] A missionary from the Czech Republic told me he met adults that have never talked to a Christian.

The following appeared in The Wall Street Journal in June 2015. "The closing of Europe's churches reflects the rapid weakening of the (Christian) faith in Europe, a phenomenon that is painful to both worshipers and others who see religion as a unifying factor in a disparate society. By example, the Netherlands is expected to close two-thirds of its Roman Catholic Churches in the next decade."[7]

Another good indication of the direction a person is going in their beliefs is how religious they consider themselves. This table indicates an extremely disturbing pattern.

DROP IN SELF DESCRIBED RELIGIOSITY INDEX[8]

Country	2005	2012	% Change in Religiosity
Global Average	77%	68%	-9%
Vietnam	53%	30%	-23%
Ireland	69%	47%	-22%
Switzerland	71%	50%	-21%
France	58%	37%	-21%
South Africa	83%	64%	-19%
Iceland	74%	57%	-17%
Ecuador	85%	70%	-15%
United States	73%	60%	-13%
Canada	58%	46%	-12%
Austria	52%	42%	-10%

SHARE OF "I AM RELIGIOUS" AND "NOT RELIGIOUS"
From respondents in these faith groups.[8]

Religious	"I am Religious"	"Not Religious"
Christians (all denominations)	81%	16%
Muslims	74%	20%
Jews	38%	54%
Hindus	82%	12%

It is interesting to note the "undecided" was least among the Christians at 3%. The study identified two correlations to this decline - wealth and education.[8] Scripture supports that conclusion - Mat 19:24, and Pro 26:12. It would be great to see the next survey ask if the cacophony of battling Christian denominations is a reason some do not believe. The list of the 10 most religious countries shows a correlation to evangelism and the lack of denominational hostility. Scripture would predict that, too - Rom 10, and Psa 9:9.

In 2000, Barna published the results of interviews with 22,000 adults and over 2,000 teenagers in 25 separate surveys. Sixty percent of the 20-somethings who were involved in a church during their teen years are already gone.[9] According to the *Yearbook of American and Canadian Churches,* the total membership in affiliated Christian churches in America and Canada peaked in 2004 at 163,498,911 and has declined by over 2% by 2010.[10] Research by Pew Forum on Religion and Public Life in 2012 found that 20% of Americans claim no religious identity, marking "none" on surveys. They number 25% in the United Kingdom.[11] Roughly 60 percent of Americans, raised as Catholics, are no longer practicing Catholics. Half of them have left the church entirely and half remain nominally Catholic; they rarely take any part in the life of the church.[12]

The Republican Party promoting moral values has had an impact on younger Americans who have come to equate Christianity with "Republican," and have turned away from Christianity. A 2010 study showed the intensity of the religion of Milllennials to be the lowest of the last 5 generations, which have declined, in chronological order. Fully one-in-four members of the millennial generation -- so called because they came of age around the year 2000 -- do not profess any particular faith. Indeed, Milllennials are significantly more unaffiliated than members of Generation X were at a comparable stage in their life cycle (20% in the late 1990s) and twice as unaffiliated as Baby Boomers were as young adults (13% in the late 1970s).[13]

From 1990 to 2000, the combined membership of all Protestant denominations in the US declined by almost 5 million members (9.5 percent), while the US population increased by 24 million (11 percent).[14] Pew Research studies from 2007 and 2014 provided the alarming results for Christianity in America shown in the table below.[15]

Demographic	2014 % in US*	Change*
Unaffiliated	22.8	+6.7
Non-Christian**	5.9	+ 1.2
Evangelical Protestant	25.4	-0.9
Catholic	20.8	-3.1
Mainline Protestant	14.7	-3.4

* - Data is in percent of the US population.
** - Includes Jews, Muslims, Buddhists, Hindus, other world religions and other faiths.

The Christian share of the US population fell from 78.4% to 70.6%, driven by declines among mainline Protestants and Catholics. The unaffiliated (Atheists, Agnostics, and "nothing") experienced the most growth. Jehovah's Witness and "other Christian" were the only groups to grow, both by 0.1% of the US population.

Over the same period, the proportion of Americans who say they are "absolutely certain" God exists dropped from 71% to less than 67%. The share of US adults who say they believe in God declined from 92% to 89%.[16] Interestingly, there is about 20% that are not certain. I recently read that North America has 95% of the world's youth workers while only having 5% of the youth. A 2014 Pew Research survey of the general public compared to the "Next Generation Left" found its biggest difference in survey responses, 53% vs. 91%, on the following question: is it necessary to believe in God in order to be moral and have good values?[17]

A 2005 article on the house church movement in America opined that within a few years it would help to restore the simplicity of the NT church. They are effective in countries where organized churches are not allowed.[18] They are vulnerable to the same challenges non-denominational churches face and more. Ten years later, they are still underground and survey results indicate Christianity continues to decline.

This is old news. What have we done about it? Not much, the trends continue like a runaway train gaining speed. To keep doing what we have been doing with greater effort is a popular definition of insanity. What is causing this decline?

Could the reason many of our churches are not growing be related to our broken spiritual mirror? We are not taking a true look at how we do church, so God has to do it for us.

> 1Co 11:31-32 But if we judged ourselves truly, we would not be judged. [32] But when we are judged by the Lord, we are disciplined so that we may not be condemned along with the world.

I asked several dozen pastors and elders why they think Christianity is on the decline in America. The answers fell into five general groups.

- The most common answer was lack of discipleship.
- The second and third was sin and satan.
- The next largest group placed the blame on external forces like the rise of liberalism and biblical criticism, government, societal corruption, removal of religion from schools, one even said it is the fulfillment of prophecy - Scripture says there will be a falling away.
- The last group, expanding on the first, placed the blame squarely on believers. The failings included - complacency, lack of discipleship and evangelism, how we raised our children, watered down preaching, doing church our way not God's way, our message not tailored to the audience, not sharing, too many distractions (idols), and becoming increasingly secular.

The most interesting reply was - there is really no decline. There are proportionally as many true Christians today as there were 60 years ago. The apparent decline is the falling away of people claiming to be Christian because it is no longer a societal norm; they were Christians in name only. I asked if this also applied to Europe where Christianity has almost disappeared. Interestingly, he cited many of the reasons provided above for the decline in Europe.

Declines are due to all these causes and others working in concert. The failings of the church led to the problems in all five replies. Amazingly, no one mentioned denominations directly. When asked specifically if denominations harm the spread of the gospel, they all said "Yes" and gave great reasons. I read seven articles about missionaries leaving the field. Eliminating the natural causes (retirement, health, etc.), disputes with other believers was among the top five in every article, and the number one reason in several.

A poll, conducted by Thom S. Rainer, identified several reasons Christians are leaving denominations. He found we have developed a negative reputation - excessive infighting and politics, many are too liberal, too bureaucratic, not good stewards of their financial resources, and no perceived benefit to belonging to denominations. The world identifies us by what we are against rather than what we are for.[19]

Another cause contributing to all areas is the decline in those who say the Bible is the inspired, inerrant Word of God. Saying the Bible is flawed is like turning off the earth's magnetic field. There is no longer a true North to provide a reference for navigation. This gives credence to anyone's opinion of where North is. Beyond the obvious, the loss of the magnetic field would lead to the dissipation of the atmosphere that supports life itself. Our planet is an amazing gift from God and so is the Bible. Without it, we reduce theological discussion to an endless diatribe of opinions. Many say the Bible is no longer relevant today. Would the infinite intellect of our God who created everything give us guidance with a shelf life? According to a 2017 Gallop poll, 24% of Americans believe the Bible is the literal word of God. About 26% of Americans view the Bible as secular stories and history, up from 21% in 2014.[20]

Has our extreme and conflicting interpretations of the Bible caused this? The question of the accuracy of the Bible was not a major issue until the 19th century; similar in time to the start of the denominational explosion.[21] Most put the majority of the blame for this drift squarely on Christian academia. That was the case in this excerpt from <u>The Battle for the Bible</u> written in 1976.

> The situation has worsened in the last 40 years. If history has any lesson to teach, it is that defection from inerrancy generally takes place in the educational institutions then spreads from there.[21]

Consider the quandary for God when He decided what to put in Scripture; I could only give it a limited guess. He could not put everything in it, as it would be bigger than any library could hold and no one would read it. Scripture teaches He gave us all the guidance we need for life in this world and how to join Him for eternity.

> 2Pe 1:3-4 His divine power has granted to us all things that pertain to life and godliness, through the knowledge of him who called us to his own glory and excellence, 4 by which he has granted to us his precious and very great promises, so that through them you may become partakers of the divine nature, having escaped from the corruption that is in the world because of sinful desire.

"The Bible was not given for our information but for our transformation."[22] - D. L. Moody

"The faith will totter if the authority of the Holy Scriptures loses its hold on men. We must surrender ourselves to the authority of Holy Scripture, for it can neither mislead nor be misled." - Augustine.[23]

Religion usually provides significant input to the moral law of a society. Some say it is wrong for laws to dictate morality, directly or indirectly. Most laws direct the morality of the people in a democracy or republic. The same would be true for totalitarian governments; the laws are a dictator's morality. Otherwise, we revert to survival of the fittest. The Bible instructs God's creation with the best way to live; pursuing laws consistent with Scripture is faithful. This does not mean to merge religion and the state. That has been a problem for centuries.

People were shocked that the Supreme Court rejected the biblical definition of marriage. We brought that on ourselves. First, "Christians" discredited the sanctity of marriage by amassing a divorce rate of over 50%, comparable to the unchurched. You may say the number is much less among evangelical Christians. Remember that our attackers usually paint us with the same brush. Secondly, we should have kept the institution of marriage in the church. When Christians were in the majority, we allowed the act of marriage (a concept given by God) to be incorporated into the fabric of state laws. We should not have been alarmed when they decided to change it. You may lament that the Supreme Court, rather than Congress, did it. Public support for gay marriage was approaching 60%. Congress would have done it eventually. The separation of church and state has always been a double-sided issue. When you sleep with dogs, you usually get fleas (no malice intended to the canine version).

The Bible has shown repeatedly, that if we turn away from God and His values, He will often turn away from us. What are the consequences of our divisions? We are all familiar with 2Ch 7:14, but we seldom refer to the preceding verse. We know God can remove any of our challenges. However, we do not like to recall that He sends some of our challenges - Eze 14:15-16 and many others.

> 2Ch 7:13 When I shut up the heavens so that there is
> no rain, or command the locust to devour the land, or
> send pestilence among my people.

Beginning with the periods of blessings and discipline described in the OT, God's grace on humanity has displayed a cyclical pattern. There are periods of blessings and growth, decline, spiritual drought, and finally persecution. This has also been true from the resurrection to the present. Jesus started the gospel of Christianity in the Middle East, and it spread from there. Peter's letters are to churches that were in the current day Turkey, as were the seven churches in Revelation. Very few Christians remain in these areas today. Over the centuries the "center of Christianity" moved to northern Africa and then to Rome. Then Europe became a Christian stronghold for centuries and the cradle of the Protestant movement. Some contend God sent the Black plague, killing almost 33% of the European population from 1347-1350, in response to the split papacy in 1305 and the subsequent corrupt period known as the church's Babylonian captivity.[24] The church did not turn around quickly. In 1409, the council of Pisa rejected the French and Roman Pope and elected a new Roman Bishop. Each of the three popes excommunicated the followers of the other two popes.[24] How does God feel about denominational battles?

> Isa 9:21 Manasseh devours Ephraim, and Ephraim
> devours Manasseh; together they are against Judah.
> For all this his anger has not turned away, and his
> hand is stretched out still.

Currently the percentage of church going Christians in European countries are in single digits, some are approaching zero. The US was predominately a Christian nation for 250 years; now <10% go to church on a regular basis.

> Mat 23:37 "O Jerusalem, Jerusalem, the city that kills
> the prophets and stones those who are sent to it! How
> often would I have gathered your children together as a

hen gathers her brood under her wings, and you were not willing!

Christianity is on the rise in parts of Africa, Asia, and South America. Why does the church grow dramatically for generations then decline during others? Atheism and other religions rise to fill the void. Some pastors contend Islam flourishes when the faith of God's people decline. That is consistent with Israel and surrounding nations in the OT. It seems the church grows when God's people share Christianity in its basic gospel form. It grows by the thousands every day just like described in Acts. However, Christianity frequently declines in these areas after long periods. In some places it ceases to exist. Why does this happen? What is the difference between the growing church in the mission areas of the world and the dying church in the established areas? Several things come to mind. Most places where the church is growing are far less affluent. They do not have all the distractions we do. They frequently face persecution; I have always heard the church grows under persecution. The areas where the church is well established seem to develop several problems. Complacency, getting caught up in doing religion, arguing about theology, and denominational squabbles are common challenges.

There is a natural cycle in human endeavors - initiation > vitality > complacency > decay > failing. We see it in business, sports, government, and religious organizations. Dr. Elmer L. Towns described a similar cycle for denominations - sect > institution > denomination > deterioration. Sadly, the spread of the gospel to many areas progressed as follows:

1. proclaimed to those who had not heard
2. they enthusiastically accept the good news
3. later generations intellectually assume these beliefs while individual religious fiefdoms form
4. succeeding generations neglect or rebel against God's teaching
5. atheism or other religions fill the void

We should not see this in the church of the living God; He has no grandchildren. There are businesses that have flourished for many centuries. What is the difference? How can we turn this trend around? It is similar to an athletic coach emphasizing the importance of being solid on the basics and fundamentals? Christianity is growing where people focus on emulating Jesus - meet people's needs and share the gospel. How do we get back to the basics?

A 2015 survey asked what the most influential book in history is. The Bible received 58% of the responses. The next closest answers were the Quran and Origin of Species at 5% each.[25] We are forever in a war for the minds of the next generation. Another way of looking at it is a spiritual and cultural tug of war. We know God has already won the war and if we all pull together, we can win the battle for this generation. Otherwise, our impact on western Christianity will likely decline as we fight each other instead of the enemy.

We toured Northern Ireland in 2014. "The Troubles" are still quite evident in their art, history and politics even three decades after Christians stopped the war against each other (Catholics against Protestants). Most Christian battles of today stew in the courts of law and public opinion. How can we claim to worship the same Savior when our behavior often tells a different story? "Men never do evil so completely and cheerfully as when they do it from religious conviction" - Blaise Pascal.[26]

Christian denominations squabbling over theological non-essentials and mysteries instead of worrying about the lost is much like the rebels in the Syrian Civil War of 2010 - 2018+. Their objective was to remove their abusive dictator Assad. As they made progress, they began to worry who would be in charge following victory. This led to them fighting each other, while Assad sat by and watched in appreciative amusement. The devil likely feels the same way when we squabble over doctrinal matters instead of seeking the lost. The Syrian rebel infighting allowed ISIS to evolve and take over vast areas of Syria and Iraq, killing and torturing thousand of Christians and Muslims.

Gal 5:15 But if you bite and devour one another, watch out that you are not consumed by one another.

According to a 2012 Gallop poll, 10% of Republicans would not support a Mormon for President.[27] Surveys show that non-voting Christians could have changed the outcome of the 2012 presidential election. That is hard to understand, as Romney's moral values were consistent with Christianity. If we can find so much to dislike about other denominations and religions, imagine how the non-believers feel. We generate their doubt and opposition for them. God told Ezekiel He wanted the exiled and divided kingdom to be one.

Eze 37:15-17, 22 The word of the LORD came to me: [16] "Son of man, take a stick and write on it, 'For Judah, and the people of Israel associated with him'; then take another stick and write on it, 'For Joseph (the stick of Ephraim) and all the house of Israel associated with him.' [17] And join them one to another into one stick, that they may become one in your hand. [22] And I will make them one nation in the land, on the mountains of Israel.

In 1453, all that remained of Constantine's Eastern Empire was the city of Constantinople. As they were about to be overrun by Muslims, the Roman Catholics and Eastern Christians worshiped together in the Church of Holy Wisdom and shared the Lord's Supper. Following the conquest, that building remained a Muslim mosque until 1930s when it became a museum.[28] During tough times we forget our petty differences and come together to meet the challenges. A pastor friend visited Egypt in November 2015 and saw Christianity growing. He commented that radical pressures have brought unity among the Protestant, Orthodox and Catholic churches. Several Christian denominations banded together to prevent the building of a mosque that would tower over the Church of the Annunciation in Nazareth as they already do the Church of the Nativity in Bethlehem and the Church of the Holy Sepulcher in Jerusalem. We visited a small Nazarene church in Oregon. The pastor began the service with prayer for each of the other two congregations in town by name; they were of different denominations. If western Christianity continues to decline, we will likely grow closer to those in other denominations as we go from a super majority to a super minority. It may approach the situation in Jer 34:7 when the cities of Lachish, Azekah, and Jerusalem were the only fortified cities that Babylon had not conquered. We know how that story ends. Some may say this will never happen to Christianity in America. Talk to someone who was around in the 1950s; they can relate how far we have already fallen.

We Must Help End the Decline

Are we going to wait until we have to identify each other with a secret Ichthys symbol (∝) as the early church did during periods of persecution? Regardless of the date of your reading, there are Christians being killed or persecuted somewhere in the world. We can make a difference there, and help prevent that from spreading. Would you rather expend the effort to evangelize and have more Christians among us, or let the decline continue? That would result in eroded values, a terrible environment to raise our children, God's punishment for not obeying, and likely persecution - Jhn 16:2.

Many areas of Christianity are in a spiritual recession or depression. Dealing with the causes is no small task. Some of the issues are outside our direct control. Those we can control will take focused effort. Growing back together could be the most effective option we have. Will God hold us accountable if we do not? How long we stay in this decline depends on God and us. Revival usually takes Sprit led initiative from His people. Then the Lord provides His support to make it successful. God wants His people to "rend your hearts and not your garments." (Joe 2:13). We are on a burning platform, doing nothing is almost the worst option. He is waiting to support us in a mighty way if we just humble ourselves, admit our sins, pray for His leading and provision, and then roll up our sleeves and work to make it better.

20

2. THE PROBLEM

For I fear that perhaps when I come I may find you not as I wish, and that you may find me not as you wish-- that perhaps there may be quarreling, jealousy, anger, hostility, slander, gossip, conceit, and disorder. 2Co 12:20

Internet searches with the phrase - "denominations harm the gospel"; found 22,900,000 hits. I did not read them all. The vintage of the old scanned articles, papers, etc. was amazing. The oldest one I saw was 1789. The following is an excerpt from an 1847 article titled Condition of Society and Its Only Hope, is Obeying the Everlasting Gospel.[1]

If the facts herein set forth, do not arouse the honest reader to a different course of action, from that pursued by the world around him, we fear that neither reason nor revelation can do him any good.

These very old statements prove several passages of Scripture are true - nothing new under the sun, and are we to continue in sin. A person I interviewed said the devil is using denominations to hamper the work and growth of the kingdom of God. My immediate reaction was that could not be. After thinking about it, I realized satan uses any deterrent he can to impede the gospel. This would include the wasted efforts, confusion, and adverse image of Christianity that denominationalism has produced at times. There were many articles on denominational splits. Some bashed specific or all other denominations. A few even praised denominations. Many base their doctrinal extremes on one or two isolated passages in the Bible. It almost looks like some are striving to be different, to create a defensible uniqueness. Christian author Phillip Yancey spoke at our General Assembly several years ago. He asked what Jesus thinks about PCUSA, PCA, EPC, OPC, ARPC, BPC, CPC, RPCNA, and SCPC (all Presbyterian denominations). He paused for a moment of conviction and said, "PU", an expression for it stinks.

One excellent article on the impact of denominations was a compilation of information from other sites with links to the source. David Pratt contended, "If we really want to please God, however, we must forsake what we want and practice what He wants."[2] We are all in favor of applying this concept when looking at the sins of others. However, when it comes to our own teaching sins, we doggedly hang on to our beliefs. We do not know for sure whether we are right or not. God wants unity; will you pursue what God wants over what you want? We often pray, "Your will be done," do we mean it?

Howard Gunter, described as a blog reader, provided this excellent perspective about denominations. "When a tradition and its accompanying practices become MORE important to the following than basic Bible doctrines, that denomination becomes a constraint rather than a blessing. I especially adhere to that specializing in a single or few practices derived from Scripture may rob the following of a full teaching of the Christian life as set before us by the ONE EXAMPLE: Jesus the Christ and in some cases encourage an attitude of eliteness." One solution offered in the article was from the pastor of a Baptist church that was being intentionally inter-denominational by emphasizing essential theology,[2] certainly a good start.

In the spring of 2013, Pope Francis said, "The church is the body of Christ, but when Catholics fight among themselves or Catholics and other Christians are in conflict with one another, they make Christ's body suffer."[3] Man has been altering religion since God first presented the concept. It appears that adulterating God's truth is another part of our Adamic sin nature. Christian faith groups formed quickly generating creeds as early as 170 A.D. We experience division and prejudice naturally. The Bible is full of it - Judah vs. Israel, Jews vs. Samaritans, and Jews vs. Christians. The Pharisees and Sadducees differed on many beliefs, primary of those was the Sadducee's belief that there is no life after death - Act 23:8. Some Judaizers did not think the Gentiles should come into the kingdom of God even though they received an anointing with the Holy Spirit - Act 11:1-4. Since Christ ascended, there has been more quarreling and fighting than any soap opera could offer - Catholics vs. Protestants, Catholics and Protestants vs. Anabaptists, Presbyterians vs. Presbyterians, churches divided against each other; and untold numbers of turf battles between and within denominations and congregations.

Unraveling History

Divisions have harmed God's people almost from the beginning. Israel split in 930 BC. This, along with their associated sin, led to the conquest of the divided nations in 722 and 586 BC. The early church had similar problems. In addition to contested theology, there were wars between Christian bodies. The Sassanid Persian and Byzantine Roman empires were militarily and economically exhausted from decades of fighting one another. Most historians agree the early success of the Islamic conquest was the result of the weakened and dissatisfied condition of these Christians from years of fighting each other. Others point to the ideological (i.e. religious) coherence and mobilization as a primary reason why the Muslim armies so quickly established the largest pre-modern empire until that time. From 622 through 750 AD, Islam conquered lands from modern day Afghanistan into southeast Europe, the Arabian Peninsula, all the Middle East, major portions of northern Africa, Portugal and most of Spain.[4] Unity was a key factor for the victor and lack of unity for the vanquished.

1Co 10:6 Now these things took place as examples for us, that we might not desire evil as they did.

This church history timeline shows the split of the Eastern Orthodox and Roman Catholic Churches in 1054 when Pope Humbert excludes Patriarch Michael from fellowship with Roman Catholics.[5] The schism actually began in 196 when Pope Victor excommunicated Eastern Christians for celebrating Easter during Passover.[6] This illustration of the unraveling time line depicts the major splits. Imagine one with 33,800 groups.

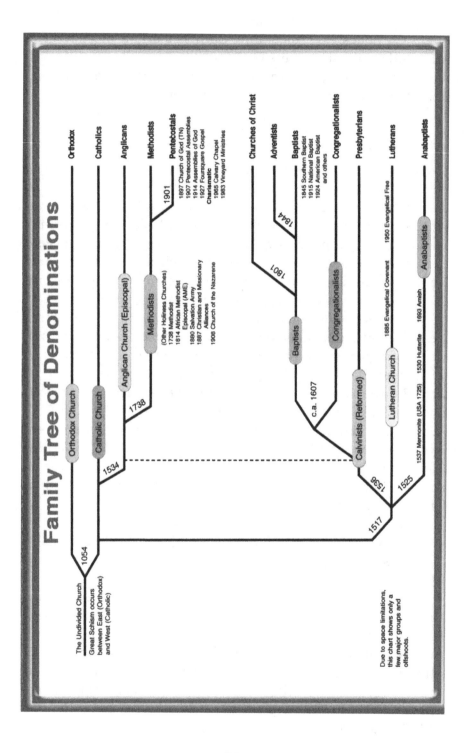

Family Tree of Denominations

The Undivided Church

1054 Great Schism occurs between East (Orthodox) and West (Catholic)

Due to space limitations, this chart shows only a few major groups and offshoots.

Orthodox Church — Orthodox

Catholic Church — Catholics

1534 — Anglican Church (Episcopal) — Anglicans

1738 — Methodists — Methodists

(Other Holiness Churches)
1738 Methodist
1814 African Methodist Episcopal (AME)
1880 Salvation Army
1887 Christian and Missionary Alliances
1908 Church of the Nazarene

1901 — Pentecostals

1897 Church of God (TN)
1907 Pentecostal Assemblies
1914 Assemblies of God
1927 Foursquare Gospel
Charismatic
1965 Calvary Chapel
1983 Vineyard Ministries

Churches of Christ

1801 — Baptists — 1844 — Adventists

c.a. 1607 — Baptists

1845 Southern Baptist
1915 National Baptist
1924 American Baptist and others

Congregationalists — Congregationalists

1536 — Calvinists (Reformed) — Presbyterians

1885 Evangelical Covenant — 1950 Evangelical Free

1525 — Lutheran Church — Lutherans

1517

1537 Mennonite (USA 1725) — 1530 Hutterite — 1693 Amish

Anabaptists — Anabaptists

24

In spite of that history, six different Christian denominations contend to control the space in the Church of the Holy Sepulcher, in Jerusalem. A dispute over who can make changes to the facility has resulted in a ladder resting against an upper window since 1757. Upon the pontifical orders of Pope Paul VI in 1964, the ladder was to remain in place until such a time as the Catholic Church and the Orthodox Church reach a state of ecumenism.[7] WOW!

We have been worshiping our theological pride and egos for centuries and He has given us what we asked for, a spiritual tower of Babel. Many churches have dozens of other fellowships within five miles of them and hardly speak to each other.

> Psa 106:14-15 But they had a wanton craving in the wilderness, and put God to the test in the desert; [15]he gave them what they asked, but sent a wasting disease among them.

There have been great manipulations to promote one faith over another. Gift giving at Christmas evolved when it was made a US national holiday in 1870. The Jews moved gift giving from Purim to Hanukkah in the late 19th century to combat the popularity of Christian gift giving at Christmas.[8] News sources show people killed for changing from Islam to Christianity, or just being a Christian. It is almost as bad for people leaving some Christian denominations. A good friend said his family was not welcome to his grandparent's Christmas gathering because they attended a different Christian denomination. Really?!

All human institutions are flawed; just look at world governments. They have evolved over the centuries. The US government is one of the best on the planet - good, worthwhile, yet still not perfect. We should not move toward anarchy because we cannot have a perfect government. Problems with previous attempts to establish the universal body of Christ is no reason to give up. Our continued march toward ecclesiastical anarchy is harming the kingdom. Imagine the

United States as 50 different countries. Our national history would have been dramatically different. There were significant problems with only 13 colonies before the Constitution was developed. They had 13 different currencies, nine different navies, trade disputes among many colonies and rampant protests in the streets. In many ways, we have been a nation under God. Recall the great things the United States has done in the past. Would those things have happened if we were 50 individual countries? It is more likely we would have been the origin of wars as Europe has been than the one to come in and restore peace and civil liberties. The multitude of denominations has similarly impacted the effectiveness of the Church. Must we become dhimmi before we start to grow back together?

> Ecc 4:12 And though a man might prevail against one who is alone, two will withstand him--a threefold cord is not quickly broken.

Catholics, Orthodox, and Protestants are the three major strands of Christianity. All three have unraveled over the centuries. How did we get to 33,800 Christian denominations? Some use these numbers to say the Protestant Reformation was a miserable failure and not from God, since He clearly wants one church. It is hard to argue with their logic. The *Handbook of Denominations in the United States* lists 211 Christian denominations in the 19 major groups shown in Appendix A.[9]

The denominations in these groups are clear in some cases and somewhat subjective in others as some have characteristics of more than one group. In some cases, the *Handbook of Denominations in the United States* moved bodies from one group to another from one edition to the next. They use the word denomination generically to represent any organized body, association, alliance, etc. They included anybody that professes Christianity. Most will likely not agree that they are all Christian denominations. Not all new bodies were included. Beginning with the 12th edition they generally did not include a body in their book until they had 5,000 in membership, so some would appear in one or more editions after they formed.

The number of Christian denominations grew from 202 to 211 in the period between the 2005 and 2010 editions. Even more compelling is that the increase of nine was actually 22 additions and 13 deletions. The list from the 13th edition (2010) is included in Appendix A. These changes were from a variety of causes - splits, mergers, dissolving, widened definition of Christian by the authors, etc. Those dropped from the list dissolved, merged with another body, or dropped below the 5,000 threshold for inclusion. Their data illustrates the constant state of change and the growing number of bodies even as Christianity continues to decline in America. It is a telling indication of the great flux of identities in the body of Christ. This should be far more stable if we are obeying God. Two large sources of change are not very evident in the data from this book. Reported membership has seen decline in most denominations over the last 20 years. Somewhat related to that is the establishment and growth of non-denominational churches. The Yellow Pages for Chattanooga, TN contained churches with Christian, or a directly related term in their title, that did not fit in any of the faith groups listed in Appendix A. Peggy and I gave a study Bible translated into Japanese to some Buddhist friends that were moving back to Japan, having lived in the US for four years. We suggested they talk to a Christian pastor in Japan if they had questions. There are websites for almost as many Christian flavors in Japan as there are here. That does not provide a good witness for the validity of our message.

The October 2015 Evangelical Leaders Survey reports that 84 percent agree that American Evangelical churches and Christians are less divided over doctrinal distinctives than they were 25 years ago.[10] Organizational statistics do not support that. If it is true among evangelical churches, it is definitely NOT true among all who claim to be Christian. The book, *God the Evidence* by Patrick Glynn, talked about religious tribalism. It spoke of our putting trivial battles between denominations above walking the walk.[11] We argue in every medium about whose theology, soteriology, and eschatology are best. In God's perspective, we look like five year olds arguing whose dad can beat up the other.

Fights over internal issues split congregations. This can be good in that it forms new fellowships and bad in that it harms the reputation of the Church. The hard feelings linger so they miss the opportunity to share activities between congregations. On several occasions, visitors from other denominations have come to our door. I tell them I am an elder in the Presbyterian Church and yet some continue promoting their denomination. Is their motive to just to get more contributing members or do they really believe that Presbyterians are not going to heaven? This behavior is a major obstacle to unity in the body of Christ. We should love our brothers and sisters because we are one in Jesus - Jhn 15:11-12, 1Th 3:12, and 1Pe 1:22.

Why do we have so many denominations today? The primary reason is that we can. The divergence accelerated when King Charles of England allowed denominations other than the Church of England to form. Religious freedom in the American colonies continued this trend as did the protections provided in the First Amendment to the US Constitution. This is good and bad, no one wants a state prescribed religion; and God does not want over 33,800 denominations giving such a confused face to the body of Christ. Some would say we have traded one Pope for a pope in every pulpit.

Early in my driving career, I was traveling down a country road for the first time in the dark. To display my abundant wisdom, I did not have my bright lights on. I encountered a sharp curve, over shot and went into the ditch. However, due to my great reflexes I was able to get the car back into the road. My inexperience again came into play. I swerved several times and ended up in the ditch on the other side. In many ways, the Protestant movement was like my driving experience. They were so anxious to get out of the ditch they felt the Catholic Church was in; they overshot and went into the ditch on the other side. Yes, the Catholic Church had several problems. Some they have resolved, and some contested issues are not essentials. Protestants, on the other hand, are so proud of their newfound differences that we have become obsessed with some of them. We are a part of the problem, keeping the body of Christ from being one.

Some Protestant denominations have drifted farther from biblical beliefs than the Catholic Church ever did. The denominational explosion of the last 500 years created an environment for the formation or transformation of groups that call themselves Christian even though they do not believe Jesus is God. In some ways, the great reformation has become a great dispersion. We have distorted Scripture into the theology of us. It is not logical that God would inspire theology that is contrary to other passages in His Word. Many people who call themselves Christians are living this verse.

Pro 14:12 There is a way that seems right to a man, but its end is the way to death.

With over 33,800 Christian voices saying what is right, adding another opinion seems like the right thing to do. You may be saying this does not apply to us, our theology is fully correct. That calls to mind an old saying - I was conceited, but now I am perfect. If you think you have it all right, at a minimum you are likely guilty of pride, and you need to hear about judging others. Have you ever taught a study of other denominations and only dealt with what was wrong with the others without objectively looking at your own? Early on, I believed my denomination was completely right.

Luk 18:11 The Pharisee, standing by himself, prayed thus: 'God, I thank you that I am not like other men, extortioners, unjust, adulterers, or even like this tax collector.

Is our condemnation of other denominations somewhat like the Jews hating and killing the Christians even though the latter had a much better handle on truth? We are all guilty.

> Rom 2:1 Therefore you have no excuse, O man, every one of you who judges. For in passing judgment on another you condemn yourself, because you, the judge, practice the very same things.

Religious elitism and bigotry have been around since Cain resented Abel's worship. It shows up throughout the Bible, and continues to the present. It is apparently yet another strand of DNA in our fallen nature. God corrected Peter for this in a dream.

> Act 10:28 And he said to them, "You yourselves know how unlawful it is for a Jew to associate with or to visit anyone of another nation, but God has shown me that I should not call any person common or unclean.

> Mat 7:2 For with the judgment you pronounce you will be judged, and with the measure you use it will be measured to you.

Homosexuality is an especially divisive topic in the body of Christ. It is not one of the seven things God hates - Pro 6:16-19. Some say this sin meets the description for "feet that make haste to run to evil", but so would a number of other sins that we do not condemn as severely. How we respond to them could easily get us on that list of seven. We allow those who are repentant from other serious sins to be pastors in many denominations. We do not have such a disdain for adulterers, swindlers, and drug dealers why homosexuals? A possible explanation is their defiant position that they were born that way and it is not wrong. Jesus loved people where they are, but never left them there. Our congregations are 100% sinners; we should welcome sinners including homosexuals. We would likely have more cases of people turning away from those feelings; perhaps changing the widely held opinion they were born that way.

Our theological judgementalism will not help people with flawed beliefs consider biblical truth. Our judging frequently spills over into how we relate to society. A Barna study released in February 2016 found nearly half of non-religious adults perceive Christians to be extremists. The following survey description of Christian behavior indicates the public paints all believers with the same brush.

> Using religion to justify violence, refusing standard medical care for children, and refusing to serve a customer whose lifestyle conflicted with their beliefs (supported by >80% of responders).[12]

We bring much of this condemnation on ourselves. I am not saying opposition to evil is bad, Scripture calls us to that. It is not so much what we oppose but how we go about it. Our judgmental spirit discredits the Bible we reference for our condemnations. Judging can be an unintended inoculation, preventing the understanding of the gospel. The Bible says the world will hate us, but we should not provoke them. Scripture also tells us to win people over with our good behavior. Jesus seldom set an example of judging, quite the contrary; He told us we would be judged in the same way we judge others - Mat 7:2.

Religious snobbery destroys the interest of potential Christians. We met a shuttle driver who carried a grudge against a church that decades before would not let neighborhood kids play on their outdoor basketball courts. Theological condemnation of lay people in other denominations can make huge barriers to unity.

A news article reported a group petitioning a city council to place an exhibit recognizing satan in a park next to a nativity scene. When asked if they were satanists, they said, "No," they just wanted to oppose the Christians. We have all seen many examples of this resentment toward Christians. A popular radio pastor recounted an experience sharing his faith early in his Christian walk. He confronted a non-believer very aggressively. After weeks of heated discussion, the non-believer said, "you may have won the debate but I won't believe your religion because I despise you." We must admit our behavior has prompted a lot of the push back we experience.

Creeds, Covenants, and Catechisms

From the creeds of the second century to the catechisms and other extra-biblical documents of today, we display our need to document what we believe. To a point, that is a good thing; but as with most human endeavors, we tend to overdo it. The Jews accumulated the Talmud over a period of about 1,000 years. They shared scholarship orally; the Talmud represents the written record of an oral tradition. It became the basis for many rabbinic legal codes and customs, and successor documents such as the Mishneh Torah and the Shulchan Aruch. The following is an excerpt from Wikipedia and is consistent with several other sources.

> The entire Talmud consists of 63 tractates, and in standard print is over 6,200 pages long. It is written in Tannaitic Hebrew and Aramaic, and contains the teachings and opinions of thousands of rabbis (dating from before the Christian Era through the fifth century CE) on a variety of subjects, including Halakha (law), Jewish ethics, philosophy, customs, history, lore and many other topics. Its final redaction probably belongs to the end of the 4th century, but the individual scholars who brought it to its present form cannot be fixed with assurance.[13]

There are translations of the Talmud in many other languages including several in English. The original language is cryptic and hard to understand. Beginning in the 11th century various commentaries augmented interpretation. There is extensive research and debate over the accuracy of the current versions.

Textural critics range from those who claim it is fully accurate to the reformers who claim it has had extensive changes from the original forms.[13] That sounds familiar.

The Talmud did not contain a concise list of the commands in the Torah. A 12th century rabbi named Moshe ben Maimon (Rambam), better known to the secular world as Maimonides, compiled the list of 613 commandments (mitzvoth) contained in the Mishneh Torah. Rambam's list is probably the most widely accepted list, but it is not the only one. The requirements of the 613 commandments needed further explanation to enable full compliance. For example it contains 39 types of work that is not permitted on Shabbat (the Sabbath).[14] Of course the rebellious nature of humans identified technicalities to get around these limitations, which led to further specificity.

The early Christian church was led by oral tradition until God's word was documented in various epistles and letters generated during the first century. Copying and sharing these documents took time. Collections of writing similar to the NT content were circulating by around 200 AD. The influence of oral tradition continued until the NT canon was widely accepted in the late fourth century. The Eastern Church (Orthodox) adopted the current canon in 500 AD. Some disputed the content into the 16th century. A key concept of the test of the inspiration of a document for the NT canon was the basis for its Apostolic origin. This has resulted in an emphasis on apostolic teaching, including oral traditions.

The term tradition has at least three religious definitions. Some use the word tradition to describe a church body instead of using denomination. The second use describes worship styles and musical preferences, etc. Thirdly, there is the oral tradition including what some consider inspired guidance from God and later recorded in various documents. Some are considered essentials of faith and are called capital T Traditions. These groups support the use of oral traditions with the following Scripture passages as well as Luk 10:16; Jhn 21:25, Acts 2:42, 1Co 15:3, 11; 1Pe 1:25 and Mat 28:19.

> 1Co 11:2 Now I commend you because you remember me in everything and maintain the traditions even as I delivered them to you.

> 2Th 2:15 "hold to the traditions that you were taught by us, either by our spoken word or by our letter"

> 2Ti 2:2 and what you have heard from me in the presence of many witnesses entrust to faithful men who will be able to teach others also.

Jesus told the Pharisees some of their traditions were causing followers to break the commandments of God.

> Mat 15:3 He answered them, "And why do you break the commandment of God for the sake of your tradition?

Could that be the case with some traditions today? Some will make a case for their importance by contending that oral tradition is the source for the canon of Scripture. We cannot know that for sure. It is just as likely that the writings of the apostles were treasured, copied and available when the Bible was assembled. The Quran is a compilation of oral traditions; it is not inspired by God. Either the Bible is the guidance God intended for us to have or it is not. All of Scripture makes a clear case for the former. Can you think of a reason God would not have led the canonization of Scripture to be what He wanted it to contain, including previous oral tradition? It seems Paul was God's instrument to provide that teaching for us - 1Th 4:2. He incorporates additional quotes from Jesus - Acts 20:35 and other Christian teaching - Eph 5:14.

We should not advocate the abolition of all tradition; Scripture speaks to it. Some tradition has brought good to the body of Christ. However, as warned in Scripture, we should use it very carefully. There have been many heresies introduced into various bodies through oral tradition.

Col 2:8-10 <u>See to it that no one takes you captive by philosophy and empty deceit</u>, according to <u>human tradition</u>, according to the elemental spirits of the world, and not according to Christ. [9] For in him the whole fullness of deity dwells bodily, [10] and you have been filled in him, who is the head of all rule and authority.

The US government attempts to control people with laws and regulations. In a two-year project, the Department of Justice compiled a list of approximately 3,000 criminal offenses, which by the 1980s was scattered among 50 titles and 23,000 pages of federal law.[15] Churches are a lot like governments, the longer they exist the more problems and questions they encounter. They attempt to deal with them by establishing more laws, regulations and policies. The newer denominations and non-denominational churches have much fewer and smaller doctrinal statements.

We visited a new movement church that had a fairly standard statement of belief, but included their position on the timing of the rapture. I asked the pastor why they included such a disputed concept that has little impact on how we live our lives day to day. He said it was included because people wanted to know. As questions arise, we address them in our documents.

The Catholic Church has been around for almost 2,000 years. They have a long history of documents that were coalesced into the *The Catechism of the Catholic Church* (CCC), first published in 1992. The second revised edition, published in 1994, is available in several languages. Pope John Paul II said the catechism will make an important contribution to renewing the whole life of the Church and is a sure norm for teaching the Faith. Joseph Cardinal Ratzinger, later Pope Benedict XVI, said the catechism is an authentic expression of the Church's Faith. The CCC contains elements from the Catechism of the Council of Trent (1566): the Apostles' Creed, the Sacraments, the Ten Commandments, and the Lord's Prayer.[16] It has four sections with 2,865 articles covering 756 pages. The forward, from John Paul II, describes it as a systematic presentation of Sacred Scripture, the living Tradition in the Church, the authentic Magisterium (the authority to lay down what is the authentic teaching of the Church), and the spiritual heritage of the Fathers. Additionally, the Catholic Church has their Canon Law to regulate its external organization and government and to order and direct the activities of Catholics toward the mission of the Church.[17]

The Orthodox Church also dates back to the apostolic times. The original form of the Nicene Creed is central to the Orthodox Church faith in most of its branches. It is the long tradition of the church, not the pronouncements of individual theologians or canon law that defines orthodoxy. The tradition includes the decisions of the seven Ecumenical Councils as well as the tradition of the Divine Liturgy itself. The Holy Canons are the basis of the Church's canonical tradition. They stem from three main sources: Ecumenical Synods (representing the universal Church), Local Synods (subsequently ratified by the Ecumenical Synods as representing the tradition of the universal Church), and the Fathers of the Church. All of these canons, which number about one thousand, are contained in several collections. The one most widely used today in the Greek-speaking Orthodox Churches is the Pedalion (Rudder), which takes its name from the metaphor of the Church depicted as a ship.[18] This document is 1,011 pages with 855 canons, covering various matters of the church.[19]

Jan Huss (1369-1415) was a Czech priest, philosopher, Christian reformer and Master at Charles University in Prague. He challenged several published church traditions stating that a Christian's supreme duty is to the Scriptures and God. He often stated, "We ought to obey God rather than men." His writings led to his excommunication in 1411 and he was burned at the stake in 1415.[20] Today's more civil treatment of differing theological positions is much appreciated.

The doctrinal documents for Protestant denominations vary as much as their theology. The Evangelical Presbyterian Church (EPC), founded in 1981, endorses the Westminster Confession of Faith, Longer Catechism, and the Shorter Catechism. They have a Book of Order that provides guidance for worship, government, and discipline.

It would be great if all these denominational theology books evolved toward full agreement with Scripture. Most of the changes are going the other way, with denominational splits and organizations choosing to take positions not clearly supported by all of Scripture. In some ways, theology follows a similar path as energy. Entropy is a function of thermodynamic variables. It is a measure of the energy that is **not** available for work during a thermodynamic process. A closed system evolves toward a state of maximum entropy (useless energy). It seems that Christian theology is tending toward a state of maximum doctrinal entropy; they have become quite turgid.

> 1Co 10:23 "All things are lawful," but not all things are helpful. "All things are lawful," but not all things build up.

God's first words in Job 38:2 would be surprisingly appropriate for portions of our denominational distinctions; "Who is this that darkens counsel by words without knowledge?" We should confess as Job did, "Surely I spoke of things I did not understand, things too wonderful for me to know," (Job 42:3). I hope I do not hear in heaven what God said to Job's three friends, "Because you have not spoken of me what is right..."(Job 42:7).

There are quite a number of issues in Christian doctrine that people consider important enough to place in a belief statement. They must be very important, almost an essential, to cause denominational splits, and promote extensive criticism and debate in the media. Recall essential doctrine, as used in this book, is a requirement for salvation. Some will still claim that all their doctrine is essential. One would likely not go to war over anything less than a political essential. The American Civil War is a great example. What were the contested essentials there? Some would say state's rights, those are important. They have been a topic of debate from the founding fathers preparing the Constitution through today. The desired amount of states' rights is a personal preference based on experience, situation, and other parameters. Others would say the war was primarily over slavery. Some would have said that is an essential. Again, our position on slavery would have been in large part based on our situation. Surely, Americans today feel slavery is absolutely wrong. However, about 150,000 Southerners died for that cause. Almost every man of fighting age in the south fought in that war. Would you be willing to die for ALL of your doctrinal beliefs?

The 45 tenets presented in Appendix F are from a sample of 20 belief statements. They came from churches, denominations, Bible colleges, or associations; most are from the last 200 years. Some statements contained as few as seven items while others filled a volume. They did not specify what was required for salvation. However, many require acceptance of their doctrine for membership. Their content was a product of their emphasis. None of the 45 beliefs was found in all 20 statements. I would have expected to see at least some of the first 10 accepted by all. Most of those beliefs have two main alternatives while some have three. In reality, there are more than two options for each. For example, there are many variations of support for the accuracy of Scripture. Some claim only non-verbal plenary inerrancy; or Scripture is only accurate in concepts, not every word. Doing the math, there are over 79 trillion possible combinations of just these 45 Christian beliefs. That is enough possible combinations to have the religion of me for many generations to come. Unfortunately, we would be alone in that church.

The Westminster Confession of Faith (WCF) circulated in 1647. The London Baptist Confession of Faith (LBCF) followed in 1689. Some say much of the LBCF preceded the WCF.[21] It is amazing how similar they were in their original form and how different they have evolved today. Has God provided new revelation? Have modern theologians found new Scripture truth not recognized in the 17th century? Are we generating differences that God never intended? Some denominational differences are crucial; they address apostasy in other groups. However, the ink, time, and words spent on the non-essential issues are substantial. If the non-essential disputes were not clouding the issue, we might see more progress in resolving essential differences.

Peggy can always tell when I am putting off a challenging task. It can be any of several reasons: vulnerable, difficult, do not know where to start, or just something I would rather not do. I get very busy doing things that are far less important than the issue I am procrastinating. All too often, God's people get into long debates, discussions, and book writing about doctrinal non-essentials, etc. rather than focusing on God's clear call to evangelism and ministry. In a way, it is religious procrastination. An obsession with theology to the neglect of evangelism is analogous to an obsession with knowledge to the neglect of our body. The body will soon atrophy and die, taking all the knowledge with it.

"Doctrine and Orthodoxy are a means to ministry not a means to the end" - Kenneth Priddy. In preparing this book, the following passage was more relevant to me than ever before. It is a testimony of Solomon's intelligence and God's inspiration. One could read books related to Christian doctrine for a lifetime and never finish.

> Ecc 12:11-12 The words of the wise are like goads, and like nails firmly fixed are the collected sayings; they are given by one Shepherd. [12] My son, beware of anything beyond these. Of making many books there is no end, and much study is a weariness of the flesh.

Impact of Division

One of my bosses loved this analogy on life - we are all drillers, bailers, pluggers, rowers, or riders. It was not sophisticated but quite profound. We are all in this boat together. Those drilling holes in the boat are consuming the time of others to bail the water or plug the holes. Some are just along for the ride, leaving few to make real progress rowing. With regard to growth of the kingdom and unity in the body, which role(s) do you usually play? Remember, our mission is to save those who are drowning in disbelief.

The Bible compares our relationship to God as a marriage in at least 15 passages - 2Co 11:2, and Rev 19:7. There are many parallels. The groom asks the bride to marry him. Regardless of the intensity of her love, marriage usually does not occur until the groom asks, or at least agrees. Once the marriage has taken place, the bride must be faithful to the groom for the marriage to be successful (groom too, but that does not fit the analogy). God describes Israel's unfaithfulness in the OT as adultery in a dozen places. Why all this imagery if our relationship with God is not similar? There are many self serving marital behaviors that do no good and may even harm human marriages. When we promote a theology that is not true, we harm our relationship with the Lord. It may not be spiritual adultery as described in Jdg 2:17 and 8:27 but it is clear they harm our marriage to Jesus. Jesus frequently referred to the Jewish leaders as adulterous - Mat 12:39. Are we being adulterous in our teaching?

In Act 23:5-10 Paul started a shouting match between the Pharisees and Sadducees at his trial in Jerusalem. All he had to do was mention the resurrection then stand back and watch the fireworks. Paul was amused, just as the devil is when we argue minutia and misguided interpretations. At times, we are just as sensitive about our beliefs today. Denominational arguments and put downs harm our evangelism. Atheists, agnostics, Muslims and even Jews use our denominationalism as their reason for not considering the

40

biblical truth about Jesus. The media uses our differences against us to demonstrate our lack of unity in thought or purpose.

The small size of many churches makes effective ministry extremely difficult. In 2011, the median church (half bigger and half smaller) had 75 members. The published mean (average) is much higher due to the mega churches. A church of 75 members usually equates to a staff of one pastor, the smaller ones may have a layperson leading. Ninety percent of the churches in America have less than 350 members.[22] Unless those fellowships have a narrow demographic, there is not enough talent for effective ministry for children, teens, families, singles, seniors, choir, etc. They likely do not have the staff or volunteers that have the gifts and expertise to meet the needs of all those groups. Some fellowships have sister churches close enough to share in ministry, but many do not. It would be great if they had relationships with the other area churches to share gifts and resources to minister to their flock and promote the kingdom to a lost world.

Not effectively ministering to youth leads to one of several bad outcomes. They become part of the 59% of Christian youth that turn from their faith in their 20s and never come back. J. Werner Wallace posted a blog titled "Are Young People Really Leaving Christianity?" with compiled statistics from several books regarding the exodus of young people from the church.[23] The following are a couple of examples.

> Church youth already are lost in their hearts and minds in elementary, middle and high school – not in college as many assume.[24]

> Nearly three out of every five young Christians disconnect from their churches after the age of 15. A 2010 study found 29% of young Christians said, "Churches are afraid of the beliefs of other faiths," and feel they have to choose between their friends and their faith.[25]

Some may not think youth ministry is an urgent need today. A Barna study reported in January 2016 found 71% of teens (13-18) view porn once or more a month. While only 32% of those, ages 13-24, felt it was wrong.[26] A 1999 Barna survey focused on finding out how teen beliefs differ from their parents found the following.[27]

- 63% don't believe Jesus is the Son of the one true God
- 58% believe all faiths teach equally valid truths
- 51% don't believe Jesus rose from the dead
- 65% don't believe satan is a real entity
- 68% don't believe the Holy Spirit is a real entity
- 70% don't believe a moral absolute truth exists

A Google search found at least 40 re-publications of these Barna survey results followed by the statement "In order to show you the most relevant results, we have omitted some entries very similar to the 40 already displayed." Thus, there were undoubtedly many more. Are we just going to talk and write about this tragedy or do something to improve it? Our churches must have access to an effective youth program.

Some Separation is Needed

There are groups that call for the end to all denominationalism in the body of Christ. That is not the purpose of this book. Since we will likely never turn away from denominations, let's maximize the benefits and minimize the impacts. Chapter 12 discusses some ideas to do just that.

Some will counter that the Bible says there will be divisions.

> Luk 12:51-53 Do you think that I have come to give peace on earth? No, I tell you, but rather division. [52] For from now on in one house there will be five divided, three against two and two against three. [53] They will be divided, father against son and son against father, mother against daughter and daughter against

mother, mother-in-law against her daughter-in-law and daughter-in-law against mother-in-law."

Luke is talking about the division between believers and non-believers. There are other examples.

2Ti 3:7-8 "always learning and never able to arrive at a knowledge of the truth. [8] Just as Jannes and Jambres opposed Moses, so these men also oppose the truth, men corrupted in mind and disqualified regarding the faith."

Teaching the truth today is critical in both presentation and understanding; yet, false teaching is as bad as ever.

2Co 6:14, 17 Do not be unequally yoked with unbelievers. For what partnership has righteousness with lawlessness? Or what fellowship has light with darkness? ... [17] Therefore go out from their midst, and be separate from them, says the Lord, and touch no unclean thing; then I will welcome you,

This concept of valid separation also appears in Jhn 7:43, 9:16, and 10:19. Again, these divisions are between Christians and non-Christians. According to a 2014 Evangelical Leadership Survey, nearly 60% of evangelical leaders have changed denominations since childhood.[28] The sheep in the flocks move around as well. We are looking for the perfect church and it does not exist. There are bodies that are clearly not committed to our Lord. Some faithful Christian churches stay in a denomination that is drifting away from the Bible because they will lose their building and property if they leave. Do not emulate the frog boiled to death in a pan of water gradually heated on the stove. We need to draw a clear line between Christians and those who only claim the name.

Sectarianism is denominationalism on steroids. They identify themselves as the only valid Christian body, contending the rest are going to hell. This is separation to an extreme.

Promoting isolated bodies of Christianity is making it hard for the unbelievers to identify the true Christians.

Independent is Not the Answer

Denomination affiliation appears to be declining in importance; 50% of marriages in 2007 were to someone who was from a different religious denomination. This was approximately 12% a century ago. A bit less than one third of all marriages remain mixed denominations today, as one or both have converted to the same religion. Those leaving the faith of their parents grew from 19% in 1890 to 27% in 1980.[29]

From 1972 to 2014, the five main faith groups considered evangelical (Baptist, Methodist, Presbyterian, Lutheran, Episcopal) have all declined as a percent of the American population. In that same period the membership in non-denominational churches that consider themselves evangelical has grown by over 400%. There is a move away from denominations across the country. Non-denominational churches now represent over 25% of the total identified as evangelical. Studies have shown the source of their membership is around 40% dechurched and unchurched people.[30] They are not just stealing people from established denominations.

The Hartford Institute of Religious Research in 2010 found over 35,000 independent or non-denominational churches representing more than 12,200,000 adherents. These churches are present in every state and in 2,663 out of the total of 3,033 counties in America.[31] The USAChurches.org directory listed 2,602 independent churches in November 2017; that is up by 133 from November 2015.[32]

Why are many churches changing their names to avoid denominational association? Two large churches near us have done so in the last few years. The Baptist General Conference changed their name to Convergence. They experienced success in planting churches. Some churches remain in their denomination but remove the labels from publications. Many attendees at Saddleback Church do not know they are in a Southern Baptist Convention church until they attend the new member's class.

Non-denominational churches do provide the fresh start that people find attractive without the baggage. They do not have volumes of do's and don'ts that go beyond biblical teaching. However, non-denominational churches are not the answer. In a way, it is like the urban flight. The problem is farther away, but not solved. They are more vulnerable to pastors going on a tangent in their teaching and no structure to hold them accountable. Like Jim Jones, David Koresh, and Terry Jones (2010 planned Quran burning[33]) to mention a few. "Some of these men and women become so powerful that no one can tell them no" - H. B. London. We see prolific pastors continue to fall into financial or sexual scandals. People are abused in non-denominational churches, too. The abuse rate in non-denominational churches as a whole is similar to the rate in large denominations. For example, the US gets a lot more press about our murder rate than Latvia, but the rates were almost the same in 2009. If there were one body of Christ, there would be strong opposition to starting a new denomination. However, having 33,800 denominations just begs for another.

A blog by Jason Helopoulos stated that denominations can provide their membership the following needs far better than an independent fellowship: accountability, safeguarding the Pastorate, safeguarding the congregation, safeguarding the Pastor, unified confession, coordinated mission, unified voice, theological precision, fellowship, mutual encouragement and support, education of clergy, and financial accountability.[34] If the move to different networks, fellowships, and independent churches does spell the end of denominations we definitely need an association of some type to provide these important services.

Ecumenical Initiatives

There are already dozens of groups promoting ecumenical objectives. The Ecumenical Councils have served to document a history of the heresies they were dealing with. There has and always will be false teachers. There is a lot we can do to limit false teaching, the first is - DON'T ADD TO IT! Some will not see the need to promote unity; the ecumenical movement has been unsuccessful in uniting the body of Christ in 1700 years of attempts. Seven Ecumenical Councils from 325 to 787 AD failed to achieve much agreement between the Catholic Church and the Orthodox Church. They fought over matters of theology like Nestorianism (disunion between the human and divine natures of Jesus). The Catholic Church held other Ecumenical Councils beginning in 869 AD to deal with differences within their body. In spite of those efforts, the Protestant Reformation resulted. Several bodies split off from the church. Thomas Edison tried over 1,000 configurations for a light bulb before finding the one that he patented as the incandescent light. Great things are attainable if we just commit to doing it.

Attempts have been made in the past to reconcile differences in the body of Christ like the plan devised by Queen Elizabeth I, called Middle Church. In addition to trying to find middle ground on various contested positions, she wanted the church to be under her control.[35] Any plan to unite the body of Christians must not have personal agendas, public or private. Another attempt was the Westminster Assembly from 1643 to 1648 during a civil war between the Protestants and Catholics that killed 8-10 million people. They came up with a plan to develop a uniformly acceptable ecclesiastical system for the Churches of England, Scotland and Ireland addressing all areas of religious life. The efforts of dozens of ministers for five years were swept away when King Charles II took the throne in 1660.[36] We have many examples from history of what not to do. How would Jesus deal with this?

Some described the cross-denominational camp meetings held in the late 18th century in America as the second great awakening. Unfortunately, this period of unity and growth produced more denominations. Many feel the beginning of the modern ecumenical movement was the Eastern Orthodox Ecumenical Patriarch Germanos of Constantinople, suggesting in 1920, "To the Churches of Christ Everywhere" a "fellowship of churches" similar to the League of Nations.[37] The Faith and Order conference after WW I reached 85% agreement on doctrinal issues. In 1925, ninety-one liberal groups took a different approach. Their Life and Work Conference focused on social reform. Maybe, they seem to have thought, If we downplay doctrine, we can achieve complete unity.[38] There have been similar two steps forward and three steps back since. Can we agree that biblical truth and caring for the unfortunate are both important? Can we come together committed to address both sides of Christian expression without neglecting one to an over emphasis of the other?

Various organizations have worked for Christian Unity in the last 100 years. Appendix E provides a sample of these bodies, their membership and mission. Most ecumenical organizations (EO) have an element in their mission to solve or mitigate theological differences. They have achieved limited success in that area. In 1960, the Consultation on Church Union (COCU) began an initiative to merge 10 major Protestant bodies into one super church to occur in 1970. Conflicts with existing denominational practices arose and participants were not willing to change or work for a consensus. A gradual decline in scope resulted in the publication of "Churches in Covenant Communion" in 1989.[39] Three churches had problems with the ministry requirements in that document. In 2002, the organization became the Churches Uniting in Christ. They set an objective to target "full reconciliation of ministries, as well as resolution of any remaining challenges." They sought to meet that objective by the Week of Prayer for Christian Unity in 2007.[40] Subsequently, their priorities have evolved to focus on racial justice issues.

Many denominations have refused to participate in interfaith initiatives; some even discipline those in their organization who do. Denominations who are members of ecumenical bodies like WCC have churches in their body that refuse to participate. They are not willing to give the appearance of compromising their doctrinal tenets for the inclusion of other Christians. Most would agree the influence of many of these organizations has peaked and is on the decline much like Christianity has in the areas where the member denominations operate. How would Jesus approach this dilemma?

Most websites of active ecumenical groups were quite impressive. However, websites are often like campaigning politicians; they paint a much rosier picture than the reality behind the words. A sample publication from one organization presented the latest thoughts and ideas on religious trends. The article was a Scrabble player's dream with such words as communiterians, metanarriative, faitheism, and consequentialist. This creative vocabulary was exceeded in shock value by the news that an atheist was selected as one of the interfaith scholars at a Protestant college in the US.[41] The six page article did a great job describing the explosion in attitudes of what religion should be in a person's life. The author attributed all these changes and weird ideas to God, making an analogy to Jacob wrestling an angel.

Why do we need so many ecumenical groups? They tend to form along the lines of the involved faith groups. Not all members of a particular faith group have the same political inclination. New organizations have spawned to meet this additional dimension of diverse focus and priority. These bodies do display unity among some churches and denominations. However, there are so many, with largely different positions and agendas, they serve to amplify the disunity seen in the body of Christ.

Most EOs have failed to make progress on theological differences. Repeated opposition to tolerance, cooperation, or any change, has blunted attempts to resolve or mitigate these differences. Most of them now focus on ministry rather than on unification of the whole body of Christ. The natural step beyond care for human needs is political advocacy.

The National Council of Churches has endeavored to promote cooperation and unity within the body of Christ. They have 36 member denominations, representing 17% of those professing Christ in America. There seems to be a committee, working group, task force, commission, etc. for every issue we see in the news of the day. Reading through the histories of these organizations showed a lot of bumps and setbacks along the way. Most of the ecumenical groups have evolved, similar to denominations. There are many name changes, metamorphosis, and new startups. Most longstanding organizations have seen decline for years. The National Association of Ecumenical and Interreligious Staff has a long history in working for the ecumenical movement. They have not documented a meeting on their website since 2011.[42]

These groups spread themselves too thin trying to solve every problem confronting humanity. This focus of time, talent, and treasures on social and political issues leaves minimal initiatives to resolve theological differences, which is the key to greater unity. Declining participation and resources from supporting churches has resulted in many devolving into a blog for articles and photos.

Sadly, the only ecumenical successes cited in a Wikipedia article on that topic are the introduction of the Christian flag and the increasing number who display it, and the 1930s initiative to have a World Communion Sunday. Chapter 12 contains other ecumenical progress.

Do all these challenges and setbacks mean the unity of the body emphasized by Scripture is no longer important? No, it is just hard for humans to do. Obstacles to a unified body of Christ include pride, complacency, indifference, and insufficient knowledge of one another.[43]

Sounds too tough, let's just give up. The great Christians of history faced much tougher circumstances and thankfully did not give up; neither should we. There are many objections to pursuing unity. Denominational structures provide blessings and cause problems. Some help manage the trend of ever changing beliefs. We need the anchor of a larger body, a more revered document to set a spiritual standard to withstand wayward leaders who want to change our beliefs to match their own. It is just far too easy for them to say, "God has told me ..."

Some denominations say they do not participate in EOs because of criticism and condemnation. Those claims are often valid, we can be harsh critics. We must come with an open mind regarding our spiritual flaws and a tender heart for theirs, and pray for the Lord's leading to identify which is which. This one body should be a no condemnation zone. Jesus did not come to the world to condemn it - Jhn 3:17, and 12:47. Scripture tells us not to condemn them either - Luk 6:35-38. Faithfully pursued, we will determine how much of our doctrine is solid rock and what may be unstable sand.

There are growing churches with great ministry that feel they do not need this. They could see several benefits.

*   their fellowship grows and ministers to even more of those in need
*   knowing they helped to begin a revival of the true body of Christ
*   their accurate beliefs adopted by others
*   see beliefs and practices they need to set aside, if there are any

The decline of Christianity in America today is a compelling motivation for us to close ranks for the spread of the gospel. As Ben Franklin said at the signing of the Declaration of Independence "We must all hang together, or assuredly we shall all hang separately." Every denominational split is similar to a divorce. The departing party likely has valid grievances. They also have contributed to the problem, and their strained feelings have caused them to see problems worse than the reality. God calls us all to strive to work together. He did provide criteria in which a denominational divorce can occur, but He did not say divorce is required when the criteria occurred. He would rather we work it out by emulating our marriage relationship with our Savior Jesus Christ. Scripture asserts that He wants one body of believers. Do not be quick to bail or to point others to the door. Work hard to achieve the unity commanded by the Lord.

Family members get mad at each other and do not speak for years. This includes parent, child, brother, sister, etc. I have a friend who changed his last name for personal reasons. His dad has hardly spoken to him for over 30 years. There is no way this is better! They should have worked to restore the relationship with a blend of discussions, shared understanding, apologies, forgiveness, forgetting differences, and live and let live. Is that how we should operate within our Christian family?

We usually fight most with those in denominations closely associated with ours. They often have the same denomination group in their name (Baptist, Methodist, Presbyterian, Lutheran, etc.) and we are concerned they will give us all a bad name. It is like fighting within our genetic family; familiarity breeds contempt. We hear of siblings that fight all the time. The only time they fight harder than with each other is when someone else is hurting their sibling. Why can't we muster that loyalty for our Christian brothers and sisters, and help them fight the evil one who is attacking us all? Instead, we often choose to display our dirty laundry, perceived self-righteousness and judgmental spirits for the unchurched to see.

To compound the problem, we often take the opposite position on non-theological issues as well. Many take the other side on political issues just to be different from those we disagree with theologically. For example, many evangelicals rail about environmental preservation initiatives. There are some that appear to be overkill or too aggressive for the situation. In general, we need to protect and preserve this island of provision in an otherwise vastly bleak universe.

We complain about people with agendas that are not consistent with Scripture taking control of our denominations and EOs. Why is this happening? We are certainly more spiritual, why are they more motivated, involved and effective? Yes, some of the EOs have adopted geopolitical policies that we do not agree with. Many villainize Christians for taking political positions seen to be against the poor or the immigrant. We are supposed to be the champion of both of those causes. The EOs are not perfect. Those seeking to unite Christians in beliefs and deeds consistent with the Bible are far better than those doing nothing.

Yet another problem with turning our back on unity is we have significantly turned away from any initiative to seek and receive the blessings the Lord will provide as we work to become one body. Ecumenism is dying at the local level as well. We live in the buckle of the Bible belt; we had an area ministerial association twenty years ago. Pastors would fellowship together and we had cross-denominational meetings for occasions like Thanksgiving. Some groups still meet, but they are narrower in their participation. In his book, *A Healthy Church*, Stephen A Macchia devotes a chapter to networking across denominations in the body of Christ. Yet many of the pastor fellowships he described have ceased to exist. We continue to split, not close ranks.

We recently had a fundraiser for a non-denominational Christian initiative to place Bible teachers in schools. There were representatives from 10 churches. Two were independent, the others represented six denominations. Several preachers spoke and we sang together, it was a real taste of heaven. The blessings these united initiatives bring to this objective and to the participants are well worth the effort. Unfortunately, too many consider ecumenical initiatives with the attitude of John.

> Luk 9:49 John answered, "Master, we saw someone casting out demons in your name, and we tried to stop him, because he does not follow with us."

Was Jesus more concerned with unity or peripheral theology? There is great agreement in what it means to be a Christian. Most differences are about non-essential doctrine. We need to approach those differences with the attitude of Jesus in verse 50 - "But Jesus said to him, 'Do not stop him, for the one who is not against you is for you.'" We need to come together in the shared love for the Father, Son and Holy Spirit, the acceptance of the Holy Bible as the Word of God, and commit to one body of Christ. The focus would be to celebrate areas of agreement, put non-essential areas of differences on the back burner in our teaching and resource allocations, and show the world what Christianity is really all about.

In 1974 representatives from 150 countries adopted The Lausanne Covenant with 15 statements about their shared beliefs regarding God, Jesus, the Holy Spirit, evangelism, the Church and ministry partnerships.[44] That document contains a general theology that anyone calling himself Christian should be able to support. The call to ministry reflects the priorities that our Lord gives us in Scripture. There is more than a lifetime of challenges to pursue. The text of the covenant is available at www.lausanne.org. This excerpt from the Lausanne covenant is targeting the areas of the world that need to hear the gospel. It would work equally well in reaching the lost in our own neighborhoods.

> Yet we who share the same biblical faith should be closely united in fellowship, work and witness. We confess that our testimony has sometimes been marred by a sinful individualism and needless duplication. We pledge ourselves to seek a deeper unity in truth, worship, holiness and mission. We urge the

development of regional and functional cooperation for the furtherance of the Church's mission, for strategic planning, for mutual encouragement, and for the sharing of resources and experience.

Their requested cooperation for the furtherance of the Church's mission has had limited impact. They held the Second International Congress on World Evangelization in Manila, Philippines in 1989. The result was the Manila Manifesto, an elaboration of the Lausanne Covenant. The manifesto dealt with the growing strain between evangelism and social concern. We all know they are both relevant. Jesus made it clear through His teaching and the teaching He shared through the NT writers; we are to take care of the down and out. What we do not see in Scripture is the mandate to argue about theological nuances to the neglect of evangelism and social concerns. Instead of fighting over the believers with doctrinal banter, we should all be working together and fighting for the lost with the essentials of the gospel. This chapter may have rambled on too long; but without compelling motivation, change will not occur.

3. EVOLUTION OF DENOMINATIONS

And then many will fall away and betray one another
and hate one another. [11] And many false prophets
will arise and lead many astray. Mat 24:10 -11

The title verse is Jesus speaking about the end times. Many
say we are close to the return of our Lord. This prophecy is
discouragingly true today. How did we end up with 33,800
Christian denominations in the world, largely in the last 500
years? Most, if not all, are man's handiwork. It is puzzling why
denominations and independent churches are forming when
Christianity is declining in America. Most new movements
have formed out of existing denominations. We look at these
new splits and formations with our arms folded in judgment
and think they just want to be different, or worse, they
are just wrong. Granted, some of the splits are the result
of theological migration, usually away from the Bible. The
driver in many of the new bodies has been problems with
the previous expressions of faith. We have either become
stale in our Christian expression or deviated from Scripture,
usually some of both. Much of the blame lies with those who
walked before us not being adequately faithful to Scripture
and committed to unity. So what are we going to do about it?

We saw repeated passages in chapter 1 where God wants us
to be one. When we create new denominations and churches,
we are moving away from His desire. Iron sharpens iron. If we
work together with an open mind we can make both sides of
our differences better and seek unity. The table below is my
summary of the motives for formation of new Christian bodies
in America described in the *Handbook of Denominations in the
United States*.[1] These codes appear in the second table that
follows. Are all these reasons acceptable to God or would He
have expected us to work it out?

Code	Reason for Denomination Change
A	**Association** of independent bodies formed, or changed membership
E	Group formed to minister to an specific **ethnic** group or immigrant group
L	Split off to pursue **less biblical agenda**
M	Formed by **missions** from another continent for other than ethnic reasons
N	**New** body formed for other reasons, such as different theology
R	Split along **racial** lines
T	Separated for **theological** purity and practice (e.g. baptism, Sabbath)
U	two or more bodies **united** (merger)
S	Split off to **avoid a merger**
Z	Split for **other causes**: government, administration, ministries, missions, language used in worship, lifestyle, history of the group, or political activism

The second table provides the primary motivation for the formation of new denominations in each faith group using the codes in the table above.

Motivation For The Formation Of New
Bodies In The 19 Major Faith Groups

Reason Codes→ Faith Group↓	A	E	L	M	N	R	T	U	S	Z	Tot
Orthodox, Oriental Orthodox		10		5			1				16
Catholic		3	4		1		3				11
Episcopal and Anglican			1	1			4				6
Lutheran	1	1		1				2	5		10
Reformed, Congregational, Presbyterian		4	1	1		1	5	2	3		17

56

Reason Codes→ Faith Group↓	A	E	L	M	N	R	T	U	S	Z	Tot
Mennonite and Anabaptist	1	3		1			4	1		1	11
Friends (Quaker)	2						1				3
Brethren and Pietistic		2	1				4			4	11
Baptist	7	1	2	2		2	6	1	1	9	31
Methodist		1				3	1	1	2	3	11
Native American			1								1
Holiness	1		1				5	2		3	12
Christian and Restorationist (Stone-Cambellite Tradition)	1						3			1	5
Adventist and Sabbatarian (Hebraic)					1		8				9
Pentecostal	2	1	4		9	1	1	7		1	26
Fundamentalist and Bible					1		7	3			11
Community and New Paradigm			1		2			1			4
Latter Day Saints - Mormon			1		1					1	3
Others - Christ or Catholic in their name4			1		2		1				4
Total	15	26	16	13	17	7	54	20	11	23	202

By far the biggest driver for division is theological, with 54 splitting to preserve theological positions, 26 leaving to pursue less biblical objectives, and most of the 17 new bodies were for theological differences. The second largest driver would be race and ethnicity. What part of Gal 3:28 is not clear? Our segregated bodies are not a good testimony to the public. Why can't we grow back together based on essential beliefs and continue our worship preferences in individual churches?

The Israelites and Samaritans argued about religion and ethnicity for centuries. They worshiped on different mountains - Jhn 4:21-22. The Samaritans rejected all Scripture after the Pentateuch. Jesus had some strong words for them. Much of the theological debate is our responding to our natural need to be spiritual, described by Blaise Pascal (1623-62).[2] "There is a God shaped vacuum in the heart of every person which cannot be filled by any created thing, but only by God, the Creator, made known through Jesus." We fill that spiritual need in a variety of ways, from being faithful to Scripture, to satanism, and everything in between.

One way we meet that spiritual need is by obsessing, arguing, and debating theology. Sometimes good comes from this questioning, such as the Protestant Reformation. Harm can also come from it, such as the Protestant Reformation. There appears to be no end to the creation of new denominations, or sects, claiming to be Christian; some are faithful to truth and some not. Humanity will counterfeit anything of value - money, art, music, movies, clothing, food (look up counterfeit olive oil), and yes, religion. Every major religion in the world has a version of the Golden Rule in their teaching, even Satanism.[3] One pastor said we do not have a copyright on the name Christian so anyone can use it. That is true, so what do we do? Just like our bank notes, we need to keep most all of them authentic and it will be easier to detect the frauds. If a large percentage of our paper money were counterfeit, people would quickly lose confidence in it and go to some other form of currency. All bodies will claim to have the authentic theology; all the rest will disagree with them.

In stark contrast to today's trends, some of the giants of faith did not want separate names for followers. Charles Spurgeon did not want people referring to themselves as Baptists, "I look forward with pleasure to the day when there will not be a Baptist living! I hope that the Baptist name will soon perish, but let Christ's name last forever."[4] John Wesley did not want his followers to call themselves Methodists.[5] Martin Luther had similar feelings; he told his followers to call themselves Christians not Lutherans.[6]

Historically the majority of people accepted the faith system they are first taught. Concentrations of religious affiliation in various parts of the world have existed for millennia. The information age has changed this some.

Pro 18:17 The one who states his case first seems right, until the other comes and examines him.

Have you ever seriously challenged the basics of the faith you have accepted? In a discussion about beliefs, a Hindu man told me our beliefs are the product of our upbringing. In general, I agreed with him. For example, there are many Lutheran churches in the upper mid west, Baptist churches in the South and Catholic churches almost everywhere. An article in the September 2008 Outreach magazine provided this quote from Jasser Mohamed, an 18 year old college freshman in America, "If I had been born a Christian maybe I'd be one. Being Muslim is who my family is, it's who I am."

I received limited religious indoctrination growing up. I occasionally attended church in at least five different denominations and some informal Bible study groups in college and still was not a Christian.

How do people pick a church? With recent shallow theology in the pews, the old paradigm that over 80% of the people select churches based on relationships more than theology is likely still true. Some go to church where their parents did, but that number is declining even faster than attendance. People are naturally attracted to something new. It is just human nature. We see new stores built less than a mile from struggling established stores and vacant retail property. We should be able to rise above it in the Lord's work - "his mercies never come to an end; [23] they are new every morning; great is your faithfulness." (Lam 3:22-23).

The new church movement is attracting people who choose denominations like many Americans choose clothes, hairdos, and cell phones - they want to have the latest thing. A 2009 Barna study produced the following insights. Overall, 50% of the adults interviewed agreed that Christianity is no longer the faith that Americans automatically accept as their personal faith. By a three to one margin (71% to 26%) adults noted they are personally more likely to develop their own set of religious beliefs than to accept a comprehensive set of beliefs taught by a particular church.[7]

There is an app for that. Several websites determine the best denomination fit for us. Based on 24 questions, both essentials and strongly held traditions, one app tells our percentage fit with about 40 groups. I entered my responses and found the results to be quite accurate.

Loyalty grows from association, like support for a political party, a sports team, or a denomination. Some of our loyalties approach idolatry. The Israelites burned incense to the bronze snake Moses made - 2Ki 18:4. Where we start has a lot to do with where we end up. The Green Bay Packers were the team to beat when I was getting interested in sports. They won the first two Super Bowls. I have remained a Packer fan to this day. With the exception of the fact that they are the only team owned by the town (not some rich family), I am cheering for the jerseys. All the players and coaches on those early teams are long gone. The host of a campground we visited was wearing a Dallas Cowboys jacket. He had already mentioned he was from Arizona before moving to Idaho. I asked him how he became a Cowboys fan. He said, "I blame that on my grandfather. He was from Texas and got me cheering for the Cowboys." He has been cheering for the helmets with the Texas star ever since. Some choose denominations and translations of the Bible by the same influence.

We experience a similar response to songs like the "Star Spangled Banner" or our school fight song. The heritage we grow up with has a great bearing on our emotions and loyalties as adults. Racial bias is another example. It likely begins at home and further cultivated by a variety of external influences. Our foundational beliefs are taught and caught in similar ways.

Why do we have such spite for those closest to us? People dislike (hate) teams in their own conference even more than those from other parts of the country. It is amazing how we are heartbroken when a player on our favorite team is out for the season due to an injury while we are happy when a player gets hurt on a rival team. What a difference a jersey makes! If they had ended up on our team, they would be our hero. We just want our team to win. Is it the same with our denomination? Some Presbyterians contend with other Presbyterian bodies more than other faith groups. At times, we act like theological gangs. I try to keep an open mind when I meet someone new, unless they are a Bears, Vikings or Lions fan (Packer rivals).

At times, we look at someone from a rival denomination with a jaundiced eye, judging them for their affiliation alone. God knows our hearts and may see them to be a more faithful child than we are. God does not care about jerseys nearly as much as He does our faith, displayed by the obedience of our heart. However, He does hold our "coaches" accountable for their leading! Loyalties can generate powerful emotions. Fans have thrown bottles at officials in sporting events. I saw religion and sports intersect as students in the upper deck at my alma mater threw large fish at the Notre Dame football team. At a recent high school basketball game both stands emptied into a brawl on the court. This was raw emotion, no alcohol involved. Some of us are so convinced we are right that all discussions are useless endeavors. They must believe some doctrine is more important than following Scripture. We should not be surprised that some non-believers want no part of what we are.

The Shadow of a Leader

The leaders heavily influence the practice of the Christian faith. Whether sports, government or religion, most of us are submissively willing to follow a charismatic, captivating leader. Throughout recorded time, leaders have come forward to create new approaches to worship and serve our God. Their motives are the same as those in the charts presented earlier in this chapter. Those splits led to factions, bickering, hatred and wars. Some claim that more people died in religious wars than all other wars combined.

3. EVOLUTION OF DENOMINATIONS

The *Handbook of Denominations in the United States* described how 53 of 202 US denominations were started or splintered off through the initiative of one or two leaders - *New Guys*. Some were almost single handed, writing creeds and other denominational documents themselves. The motivation for those 53 new bodies involved all ten categories in the data summary above. Two of those leaders started two new denominations each. Some of their motivation was scriptural, but starting a new body usually is not. We R2B1. The motives described in chapter 7 can lead us to seek our own thing. Ultimately, we have only one leader, the Lord.

This is nothing new. Examples in Scripture illustrate that fascination with leaders has been going on since the beginning. Paul provides examples of strife and rivalries over who has the right leader - 1Co 3:3-5. He makes it clear that Jesus was the answer, yes, the final answer. He did not intend for there to be an ongoing string of prophets bringing new truth to add to the gospel as the Jewish leaders added to the OT with new requirements in the Talmud.

> 1Co 1:10-13 I appeal to you, brothers, by the name of our Lord Jesus Christ, that all of you agree, and that there be no divisions among you, but that you be united in the same mind and the same judgment. [11] For it has been reported to me by Chloe's people that there is quarreling among you, my brothers. [12] What I mean is that each one of you says, "I follow Paul," or "I follow Apollos," or "I follow Cephas," or "I follow Christ." [13] Is Christ divided? Was Paul crucified for you? Or were you baptized in the name of Paul?

Despite Paul's warnings in chapters one and three of 1 Corinthians, leaders have created dozens of new beliefs and denominations, most against God's will for one body. Many denominations quote their *new guy* as much as Scripture. One website had guidance for reading the instructions provided by their prophet. Some of their guidance seems confusing as it dealt with issues of that day. It is important to have a history and basis for our beliefs. However, inspired teaching comes from the Bible. Shouldn't we be quoting Scripture as a rule and the person that enlightened the passage as the exception? It is far better to look at a loved one directly than an image or hologram of them. It is amazing to listen to people refer to their *new guy* with such heartfelt reverence; from Calvin, Spurgeon, and the Wesley brothers to Joseph Smith, John Wimber, and Chuck Smith to name a few. I was speaking to a pastor who mentioned one of his *new guys* from several centuries ago as only John. I jokingly said, "You mean John Calvin?" He promptly provided the last name of his *new guy*. A good friend, that has attended a Presbyterian church for many years, still describes herself as a Wesleyan. Christian is the ultimate and only label we need? Martin Luther, the leader of the Reformation, has been portrayed by his supporters as a hero of the faith and by his enemies as a cancer in the life of the church. The truth is somewhere in between.

Our relationship with God is built on His revelation to man. It began with Adam and progressed through Abraham, Moses, some kings, the Prophets, Jesus, the Apostles and associates, then Paul. Did it stop there? The Jews believe it stopped with the prophets. Most Christians believe the canon stopped with Paul. Others believe God has provided new revelation to their prophet or apostle, their *new guy* or gal. They offer Eph 4:11-14 as the basis for new revelation. Most believe the reference to apostles (one who was sent) is referring to those who founded the Church with Jesus - Eph 2:20. The selection of apostles mentioned in Mar 3:14-15, and Act 1:21-22 limited the candidates to those who witnessed the resurrection. Prophecy can come from many in the church - Rom 12:6, and 1Co 14:26, 29-31. It has several purposes - edification, and exhortation, and comfort. (1Co 14:3), or foretelling the future - Act 11:28, 21:10-11.

They also refer to Act 3:19-23 as the text supporting Jesus providing revelation to their prophet/apostle.

Act 3:19-23 Repent therefore, and turn back, that your sins may be blotted out, [20] that times of refreshing may come from the presence of the Lord, and that he may send the Christ appointed for you, Jesus, [21] whom heaven must receive until the time for restoring all the things about which God spoke by the mouth of his holy prophets long ago. [22] Moses said, 'The Lord God will raise up for you a prophet like me from your brothers. You shall listen to him in whatever he tells you. [23] And it shall be that every soul who does not listen to that prophet shall be destroyed from the people'.

The key to the passage is when this will occur, not "until the time for restoring all things spoken of by the prophets of long ago." A search for the word restore in the OT found the following passages all describing the restoration of the nation of Israel - Isa 1:24-27, 57:14-19, Jer 29:11-16, 30:15-22, 31:20-25, 32:41-44, 33:10-18, 25-26, 50:19-21, Eze 39:26-29, Joe 2:23-32, and Amo 9:13-15. Several spoke of events that have not happened - natural phenomenon; iniquity shall be sought in Israel, and there shall be none; all Israel shall be brought back from foreign lands; and all who devour you (Israel) shall be devoured. These writings from "the mouth of His holy prophets long ago" would indicate that this event has not happened. Act 3:24-25 clearly describes Jesus as the Messiah reflecting the prophets description in about 320 messianic prophesies. Moses described Him as "a prophet like me from among you" - the Jewish people. Is your prophet Jewish?

Deu 18:15 "The LORD your God will raise up for you a prophet like me from among you, from your brothers--it is to him you shall listen.

Jesus is the prophet described in Act 3:22. Mat 23:39 supports this interpretation as Jesus states He will not return until they (Israel) acknowledge Him. A review of six commentaries found a consistent interpretation of this passage as restoration of Israel into divine favor in the future, and Jesus is the prophet. We should be listening to everything He said. If you believe this verse refers to a modern day prophet, or know someone who does, dig into the Holy Bible yourself and see where it leads you. Some will cite 1Jn 2:27 as the basis for new inspiration from the Holy Spirit to form a new denomination.

1Jo 2:27 But the anointing that you received from him abides in you, and you have no need that anyone should teach you. But as his anointing teaches you about everything, and is true, and is no lie--just as it has taught you, abide in him.

Hundreds of passages describe our need to be taught. This passage is obviously speaking to an exception when it says "no need that anyone should teach you." Taken in context, it is talking about false teachers; vs. 25 warns of "those who are trying to deceive you." The anointing referred to is "what you heard from the beginning" in vs. 21; also referred to in vs. 27. Many consider that passage to mean the Holy Spirit will illuminate the Bible to us. Many other passages support that understanding.

Jhn 14:26 But the Helper, the Holy Spirit, whom the Father will send in my name, he will teach you all things and bring to your remembrance all that I have said to you.

1Co 2:13 And we impart this in words not taught by human wisdom but taught by the Spirit, interpreting spiritual truths to those who are spiritual.

Both passages tell of the Spirit teaching us, no mention of a prophet or apostle being an intermediary. We are told the Holy Spirit "will guide you into all the truth" (Jhn 16:13). God does give us understanding of Scripture, "then He opened their minds" (Luk 24:45). It does not say anything about His imparting of new truth; in fact, Scripture describes the opposite. There are several passages in the Bible that state we should not add or take away from Scripture - Deu 4:2, 12:32, Pro 30:5-6, Mat 5:19, Gal 1:8-9, and Rev 22:18. In the last days we will receive guidance from Jesus rather than prophets.

Heb 1:1-2 Long ago, at many times and in many ways, God spoke to our fathers by the prophets, [2] but in these last days he has spoken to us by his Son, whom he appointed the heir of all things, through whom also he created the world.

Scripture describes the Lord's revelation to us through prophets using past tense - 1Co 2:10, and Eph 1:8. There is no mention of future revelation. No prophecy of Scripture comes from someone's own interpretation.

2Pe 1:19-21 And we have the prophetic word more fully confirmed, to which you will do well to pay attention as to a lamp shining in a dark place, until the day dawns and the morning star rises in your hearts, [20] knowing this first of all, that no prophecy of Scripture comes from someone's own interpretation. [21] For no prophecy was ever produced by the will of man, but men spoke from God as they were carried along by the Holy Spirit.

Jesus proved who He was with many miracles that only God can perform. Paul's validation is the Damascus road experience, his temporary blindness, and many miracles - Act 14:9-10, 16:18, 20:10-11. God would validate other prophets in a similar way - 2Co 12:12. God "confirms the word of His servant and fulfills the counsel of His messengers" (Isa 44:26). We have not seen this for the *new guys*.

Why would God withhold revelation that His people needed to hear for over 1,800 years after Jesus? Scripture gives several examples where people claimed to be providing revelation from God, but were not. Miriam and Aaron said, "Has the LORD indeed spoken only through Moses? Has he not spoken through us also?" (Num 12:2). God rebukes their challenge in Num 12:4-15. Ezekiel speaks directly to pastors who preach what is not true because people want to hear it.

Eze 13:3 Thus says the Lord GOD, Woe to the foolish prophets who follow their own spirit, and have seen nothing!

Ezekiel continues describing these prophets in 13:10-16, whitewashing God's pending judgment. Jesus warned us about false prophets - Mar 13:21-22a. Paul provides a stern warning about new revelations.

Gal 1:6-9 I am astonished that you are so quickly deserting him who called you in the grace of Christ and are turning to a different gospel-- [7] not that there is another one, but there are some who trouble you and want to distort the gospel of Christ. [8] But even if we or an angel from heaven should preach to you a gospel contrary to the one we preached to you, let him be accursed. [9] As we have said before, so now I say again: If anyone is preaching to you a gospel contrary to the one you received, let him be accursed.

There are several more warnings about teaching what is not from Scripture.

1Co 4:6-7 I have applied all these things to myself and Apollos for your benefit, brothers, that you may learn by us not to go beyond what is written, that none of you may be puffed up in favor of one against another. [7] For who sees anything different in you? What do you have that you did not receive? If then you received it, why do you boast as if you did not receive it?

Many have challenged the validity of the religious status quo of their day; we should always be discerning. Some claimed new revelation and were just wrong in different ways. Several denominations believe they have received new revelation from God, beyond what the Bible teaches. They cannot all be correct as other groups claim different new revelations. What irony, when someone else has a new revelation we call them a cult; yet we call our *new guy* an apostle, prophet, founder, great teacher, etc. Several denominations have leaders they follow as a prophet or an apostle in the ascendency from the apostles of Jesus. It is unclear how there can be multiple paths of ascendency for the various denominations that claim one. Dozens have claimed new revelation from God since the adoption of the Bible canon. How do we know which to believe? They certainly do not agree. Scripture gives us a test for true prophets - they must be completely accurate, in <u>every</u> prophecy, or they are not from God.

> Deu 18:21-22 And if you say in your heart, 'How may we know the word that the LORD has not spoken?'-- [22] when a prophet speaks in the name of the LORD, <u>if the word does not come to pass or come true, that is a word that the LORD has not spoken</u>; the prophet has spoken it presumptuously. You need not be afraid of him.

We have a similar call to test the message from the prophets in 1Jn 4:1, and Paul instructs in 1Co 14:32 that others are to validate the message from a prophet. True prophets from God will be true all the time - Jer 14:14, 23:16; Eze 13:2, 22:28; Mar 13:22; Acts 17:11.

What does this say about the prophets that were not 100% correct? Some of these modern apostles have had their directives changed by their successors. At least one was not led by God, or maybe both. The Lord may even test us with false teachers.

> Deu 13:1-3 "If a prophet or a dreamer of dreams arises among you and gives you a sign or a wonder, [2] and the sign or wonder that he tells you comes to pass, and if he says, 'Let us go after other gods,' which you have not known, 'and let us serve them,' [3] <u>you shall not listen to the words of that prophet</u> or that dreamer of dreams. For <u>the LORD your God is testing you</u>, to know whether you love the LORD your God with all your heart and with all your soul.

The passages listed above include stern words for those who claim to be prophets of God and are not. If you discount the teachings of Paul, you are not a prophet from God.

1Co 14:36-38 Or was it from you that the word of God came? Or are you the only ones it has reached? [37] If anyone thinks that he is a prophet, or spiritual, he should acknowledge that the things I am writing to you are a command of the Lord. [38] If anyone does not recognize this, he is not recognized.

There are many warnings about strange teachings.

Heb 13:8-9 Jesus Christ is the same yesterday and today and forever. [9] Do not be led away by diverse and strange teachings, for it is good for the heart to be strengthened by grace, not by foods, which have not benefited those devoted to them.

Notice the reference to the immutability of Christ in the same passage. If someone relates a new revelation contrary to Scripture, direct them to Heb 13:8-9 and pray for them. We hear 2Ti 3:16 quoted often about the inspiration of Scripture, do not forget the next verse. It informs us Scripture is all we need.

2Ti 3:16-17 All Scripture is breathed out by God and profitable for teaching, for reproof, for correction, and for training in righteousness, [17] that the man of God may be complete, equipped for every good work.

We are given the purpose of apostles and prophets.

Eph 4:11-14 "he gave the apostles, the prophets, the evangelists, the shepherds and teachers, [12] to equip the saints for the work of ministry, for building up the body of Christ, [13] until we all attain to the unity of the faith and of the knowledge of the Son of God, [14] so that we may no longer be children, tossed to and fro by the waves and carried about by every wind of doctrine, by human cunning, by craftiness in deceitful schemes."

With 33,800 denominations, it seems like many claiming to be apostles and prophets have <u>not</u> been building up the body until we **all** attain unity. We would all agree leadership is an extremely important responsibility in any endeavor. Leaders can do great good and great harm. Scripture warns of the consequences of our teaching.

4. BEGIN WITH THE END IN MIND

So whether we are at home or away, we make it our aim to please him. [10] For we must all appear before the judgment seat of Christ, so that each one may receive what is due for what he has done in the body, whether good or evil.
2Co 5:9-10

Teachers must have great concern about the judgment seat of Christ.

> Jas 3:1 Not many of you should become teachers, my brothers, for you know that we who teach will be judged with greater strictness.

When teaching, sharing, or evangelizing, do we focus on sharing the truth, the whole truth, and nothing but the truth. Or are we trying to convince others to believe as we do? Do we overemphasize issues of lesser importance and neglect or distort some essentials? We teachers will be held accountable. Many churches do not speak much about the judgment of believers in heaven. Later chapters will look at several aspects of teaching; this one focuses on the consequences of not teaching God's truth, which includes seeking unity. This is the shortest chapter in the book. However, when we have been there 10,000 years it may be the most important to our eternity. Knowing what is at stake will make the chapters that follow even more important.

The title of this chapter is taken from the book *7 Habits of Highly Effective People* by Stephen Covey. It applies equally well to business endeavors and our ministry. What are our objectives as teachers? The following passage provides great guidance.

> Rom 15:5-6 May the God of endurance and encouragement grant you to live in such harmony with one another, in accord with Christ Jesus, [6] that

together <u>you may with one voice glorify the God and Father</u> of our Lord Jesus Christ.

First, we are to be in accord with Jesus. If we are teaching or behaving in a manner that is contrary to the truth and example He presented, we need to pray for the Lord to help us get back on track. Second, we are to live in harmony with each other, not just tolerance, but harmony. These steps enable us to bring glory to God and Jesus.

Teachers Will Be Graded

We see many examples where God punished teachers for failing in these responsibilities. God reproved Moses for his disobedience in the provision of water at Meribah; God did not let him go into the Promised Land. He explains it to Moses in Deu 32:51 - "because you broke faith with me in the midst of the people of Israel at the waters of Meribah-kadesh, in the wilderness of Zin, and because you did not treat me as holy in the midst of the people of Israel." This also appears in Psa 106:32-33. This seems harsh until we consider how much instruction God had invested in Moses. If He did this to one as special to Him as Moses, what will He do (or has He done) to the teachers who peddle theology that is twisted or distorted for recognition, pride, or profit? Luk 12:48 supports this concept - "from him to whom they entrusted much, they will demand the more."

Teachers will be held accountable even for what should have been taught, but was not. The prophet Isaiah warned the people about empty worship and their false teachers - Isa 29:12-14.

Isa 44:24-25 "I am the LORD ... [25] who frustrates the signs of liars and makes fools of diviners, who turns wise men back and makes their knowledge foolish."

Scripture directs us to teach the full truth of God's judgment otherwise the teacher will be held accountable for lost unbelievers. Eze 3:18 and 20 gives us two examples where failing to teach the people properly will have the same result - "but his blood I will require at your hand." This is such an important mandate that he repeats the same words in Eze 33:8.

The following passage is a detailed indictment of the leaders of Israel for failure to lead them in their relationship with God. Some pastors today fit one or both of these condemnations. Scripture instructs us not to muzzle the ox, but it does not say to lavish the ox with multimillion-dollar homes, super luxury cars, personal jets, etc. Many will refer to the success of the ministry they led as justification for these rewards. Jesus may have another perspective when they reach His judgment seat.

> Eze 34:1-6 The word of the LORD came to me: [2] "Son of man, prophesy against the shepherds of Israel; prophesy, and say to them, even to the shepherds, Thus says the Lord GOD: Ah, shepherds of Israel <u>who have been feeding yourselves</u>! Should not shepherds feed the sheep? [3] You eat the fat, you clothe yourselves with the wool, you slaughter the fat ones, but you do not feed the sheep. [4] <u>The weak you have not strengthened,</u> the sick you have not healed, the injured you have not bound up, <u>the strayed you have not brought back, the lost you have not sought</u>, and with force and harshness you have ruled them. [5] So they were scattered, because there was no shepherd, and they became food for all the wild beasts. [6] My sheep were scattered; they wandered over all the mountains and on every high hill. My sheep were scattered over all the face of the earth, with none to search or seek for them.

Sounds like the lost sheep of today.

Judgment For Believers

The same concept applies to teachers in the church age, "bringing upon themselves swift destruction" (2Pe 2:1). We will all face the judgment seat of Christ, also known as the Bema seat. He will evaluate everything we have done in life - Jhn 5:21-22, 27. Imagine facing Jesus, who endured crucifixion and God's judgment for our transgressions. Some may say these passages refer to salvific judgment at the Great White throne. The context is clear, this judgment is for believers. The book *Your Eternal Reward*, by Erwin Lutzer;[1] is a great description of our meeting with Jesus in heaven and how we should prepare for that encounter. The Bible has a lot to say about true and false teachers. How does Jesus feel about the latter?

> Rev 22:12 "Behold, I am coming soon, bringing my recompense with me, to repay each one for what he has done.

We should know what makes Jesus mad. He was seldom angry about the sin of common people. He did get angry with those who should have known better. He frequently railed about the legalism and oppression displayed by the Jewish leaders. Jesus spoke about the requirements the blind guides added. Does He feel the same about our distorted doctrine today? - Luk 20:44-47

> Mat 15:9-14 in vain do they worship me, teaching as doctrines the commandments of men."" [10] And he called the people to him and said to them, "Hear and understand: [11] it is not what goes into the mouth that defiles a person, but what comes out of the mouth; this defiles a person." [12] Then the disciples came and said to him, "Do you know that the Pharisees were offended when they heard this saying?" [13] He answered, "Every plant that my heavenly Father has not planted will be rooted up. [14] Let them alone; they are blind guides. And if the blind lead the blind, both will fall into a pit."

He even got impatient with his disciples on occasion.

> Mar 10:13-14 And they were bringing children to him that he might touch them, and the disciples rebuked

them. [14] But when Jesus saw it, he was indignant and said to them, "Let the children come to me; do not hinder them, for to such belongs the kingdom of God.

Our eternity with God begins at belief - guidance, provision, protection, and yes, judgment. They are all elements of His love. He will judge all the deeds of those who call Him Father.

1Pe 1:17-18 And if you call on him as Father who judges impartially according to each one's deeds, conduct yourselves with fear throughout the time of your exile, [18] knowing that you were ransomed from the futile ways inherited from your forefathers,

Luk 12:2-3 Nothing is covered up that will not be revealed, or hidden that will not be known. [3] Therefore whatever you have said in the dark shall be heard in the light, and what you have whispered in private rooms shall be proclaimed on the housetops.

Mat 12:36 I tell you, on the day of judgment people will give account for every careless word they speak.

Paul explains the challenge in evaluating ourselves; it is hard to see our own failings. Notice that judgment will go beyond deeds to the purposes in our hearts. Paul saw nothing against himself (must not have been married).

1Co 4:4-5 For I am not aware of anything against myself, but I am not thereby acquitted. It is the Lord who judges me. [5] Therefore do not pronounce judgment before the time, before the Lord comes, who will bring to light the things now hidden in darkness and will disclose the purposes of the heart. Then each one will receive his commendation from God.

Heb 4:12 For the word of God is living and active, sharper than any two-edged sword, piercing to the division of soul and of spirit, of joints and of marrow, and discerning the thoughts and intentions of the heart.

There are many more passages that speak about the judgment of believers in heaven - Ecc 12:13-14; Jer 17:10; Mat 5:19-20; Jhn 3:21; Rom 2:6, 14:10-12; Rev 20:12-13; and 22:12.

Psa 62:12 and that to you, O Lord, belongs steadfast love. For you will render to a man according to his work.

Varieties of different rewards are linked to obedience. Scripture speaks of the importance of elders providing a good example, by doing so "you will receive the unfading crown of glory" (1Pe 5:1-4) - Mat 6:19-20, Luk 6:22-23, Col 3:23-24, and Heb 10:35-36.

Mat 16:27 For the Son of Man is going to come with his angels in the glory of his Father, and then he will repay each person according to what he has done.

Several authors advise us we can lose our reward.

1Co 9:24-27 Do you not know that in a race all the runners run, but only one receives the prize? So run that you may obtain it. 25 Every athlete exercises self-control in all things. They do it to receive a perishable wreath, but we an imperishable. 26 So I do not run aimlessly; I do not box as one beating the air. 27 But I discipline my body and keep it under control, lest after preaching to others I myself should be disqualified.

2Jo 1:8 Watch yourselves, so that you may not lose what we have worked for, but may win a full reward.

Mat 25:21 His master said to him, 'Well done, good and faithful servant. You have been faithful over a little; I will set you over much. Enter into the joy of your master.

The following are additional passages dealing with rewards in heaven - Luk 6:35; Jhn 4:36; Phl 4:17; Heb 10:35-36; and Jas 1:12. If you still do not believe these passages are speaking to believers, go back and read them in context. "To overdo the sorrow aspect of the judgment seat of Christ is to make heaven into hell. To under do the sorrow aspect is to make faithfulness inconsequential" - Samuel Hoyt.[2]

Some take these passages and make them into a works based salvation, that is clearly not the message. Others take isolated passages in Scripture and establish an elaborate process of earning specific rewards in heaven. All we really need to do is obey what God has taught us in the Bible; then trust Him - the rest will be great.

5. MYSTERIES AND ANTINOMIES

> Have you not known? Have you not heard? The
> LORD is the everlasting God, the Creator of the
> ends of the earth. He does not faint or grow weary;
> his understanding is unsearchable. Isa 40:28

Many of the doctrinal differences within Christiandom are the result of two scriptural challenges - mysteries and antinomies. We are quite familiar with the concept of a mystery. It is something that God has decided not to fully reveal to us yet. The gospel is a good example. It was a mystery even to the people of Israel until fully revealed in the life, death and resurrection of Jesus.

Mysteries

The so-called mystery religions of Paul's day used the Greek word (mysterion) in the sense of something revealed only to the initiated. Paul himself, however, used it to refer to something formerly hidden or obscure but now revealed by God for all to know and understand. Paul referred to our salvation through Jesus as a revealed mystery in at least five different letters - Rom 11:25, 1Co 2:7, Eph 1:9, 3:4, 9, Col 1:27, 2:2, 4:3, and 1Ti 3:16.

> Rom 16:25 Now to him who is able to strengthen you according to my gospel and the preaching of Jesus Christ, according to the revelation of the mystery that was kept secret for long ages.

So why do we feel we need to put God in a systematic theology box with a treatment of every verse in Scripture? God will not fit in any box - Job 11:7. These collections of beliefs are a noble effort to manage apostasy, but sometimes contribute to the problem.

Our natural interest in spiritual matters leads us to read astrology, get our fortune told, and even read fortune cookies. That natural spiritual longing, and a hefty measure of pride, causes believers to seek an answer. We love and hate a mystery. We enjoy seeing one unfold in a TV show, movie or novel. We hate one that is unsolved, like the TV programs that end with "to be continued". From crossword puzzles to interpreting Scripture, we want the answer. God is well aware of our nature; He made us that way.

We need a more specific definition of mystery for this discussion - a passage of Scripture that does not have a broad consensus of interpretation. If Christians are still arguing about it after 1600 years, it is likely a mystery. Some may feel it is crystal clear and still be wrong.

Even with all the information we have amassed, there are still mysteries in God's creation. Scientists cannot fully explain how gravity and magnetic fields work. The more we know, the more we realize we do not know. As much as scientists tell us they have it all figured out, we will not know it all on this side of heaven. The New Horizons space probe traveled close to the body formerly known as the planet Pluto. Astrophysicists gained information that rendered their planetary mechanics theories to be extensively flawed. For example, Pluto has an atmosphere. Think of all our conclusions that were dead wrong, such as the sun orbits the earth. Several OT writers have told us of the complexity of God. Isa 40:12-28 provides a lengthy interrogatory on the great and unsearchable nature of God. God humbled Solomon, the wisest person of his day, with mysteries.

> Ecc 3:11 He has made everything beautiful in its time. Also, he has put eternity into man's heart, yet so that he cannot find out what God has done from the beginning to the end.

> Ecc 8:16-17 When I applied my heart to know wisdom, and to see the business that is done on earth, how

neither day nor night do one's eyes see sleep, [17] then I saw all the work of God, that man cannot find out the work that is done under the sun. However, much man may toil in seeking, he will not find it out. Even though a wise man claims to know, he cannot find it out.

Other Scripture writers support this concept - Job 5:9, 11:7; Psa 139:17; and Isa 55:9

Mic 5:12 But they do not know the thoughts of the LORD; they do not understand his plan, that he has gathered them as sheaves to the threshing floor.

Paul informs us this is still true in the church age.

1Co 2:16 "For who has understood the mind of the Lord so as to instruct him?"

In over 60 places, Scripture reminds us to fear the Lord. In at least a dozen passages, He is described as beyond our comprehension. Why do we continue to formulate concrete beliefs about how He has and will deal with His creation? We cannot tolerate a mystery! Yet, we will never understand the full nature of God - 1Co 1:19-27 and Isa 29:14.

1Co 1:19 For it is written, "I will destroy the wisdom of the wise, and the discernment of the discerning I will thwart."

The phrase "know that I am the Lord" appears 88 times in the ESV all describing God to us. Yet, Scripture still reveals He is beyond our comprehension.

Isa 55:8-9 For my thoughts are not your thoughts, neither are your ways my ways, declares the LORD. [9] For as the heavens are higher than the earth, so are my ways higher than your ways and my thoughts than your thoughts.

Man's urge to put an explanation on every mystery in the Bible is like understanding fire down to the molecular level. We do not need to understand how material is liquefied, then vaporized, followed by rapid oxidation to enjoy the light and warmth that a fire provides. We can simply strike a match to get the flame that meets our needs. Similarly, theologians have postulated many beliefs resulting in differences on issues that have little relevance in advancing the kingdom. Not every Scripture mystery can be solved; attempts to do so can do more harm than good.

> "I am deeply distressed by what I only can call in our Christian culture the idolatry of the Scriptures. For many Christians, the Bible is not a pointer to God but God himself... God cannot be confined within the covers of a leather-bound book. I develop a nasty rash around people who speak as if mere scrutiny of its pages will reveal precisely how God thinks and precisely what God wants." - Brennan Manning.[1]

> Mat 11:25 At that time Jesus declared, "I thank you, Father, Lord of heaven and earth, that you have hidden these things from the wise and understanding and revealed them to little children;

Thus, He intended for there to be mysteries, and not just a few. What does "revealed them to little children" mean? We must accept some things at face value without trying to explain how they came about. God never answered the questions Job asked through the first 37 chapters of that book other than to say, "Who is this that darkens counsel by words without knowledge?"(Job 38:2). His treatment of Job in the end gives a clue that Job was far closer to understanding the mysteries of God than his friends.

> 1Co 13:12 For now we see in a mirror dimly, but then face to face. Now I know in part; then I shall know fully, even as I have been fully known.

We may fully understand Scripture in heaven. As for now, there are mysteries that are not clear. In Jesus' day, Jews differed on OT passages that are now clear. They could not agree on where the Messiah would be born - Jhn 7:27.

Why are there so many issues that have been debated and not answered for almost 2,000 years? God put mysteries in the Bible for many reasons. "He rewards those who seek him" (Heb 11:6). He put them in there to get us to dig, study, and understand the Word. He knew the digging would bring us closer to Him.

> Pro 25:2 <u>It is the glory of God to conceal things</u>, but the glory of kings is to search things out.

Digging is great until we get to one that has not been fully revealed, and we force an answer. With a big enough hammer, (cherry picking verses and using them out of context) we can drive a square mystery into a round interpretation. Good teachers admit these are mysteries; yet we can't resist adding, "this is what I believe..."

A few of the mysteries are answered in the Bible by using Scripture to edify Scripture, reading it in the correct context. Others are still mysteries. We have a huge responsibility to know the difference, effectively explain those revealed, and fully present those that are not.

> 1Co 4:1 This is how one should regard us, as servants of Christ and <u>stewards of the mysteries of God</u>.

Some mysteries are in the form of an analogy, the parables are an example. Scripture uses a familiar experience to give us some insight into a concept of God that is beyond our full understanding. The limited understanding will still direct our steps.

> Eph 5:31-32 "Therefore a man shall leave his father and mother and hold fast to his wife, and the two shall

become one flesh." [32] This mystery is profound, and I am saying that it refers to Christ and the church.

The prophecy of Christ in the OT was extensive but intentionally subtle. God wanted those who would see His hand in creation, and His dealing with the nation of Israel, to seek Him through faith. Reaching people 6,000 years ago was very difficult. A message on social media was not an option. Most did not even have a written language, others the ability to read. God's approach to use a select group of people to demonstrate His love and provision as well as His guidance and correction was pure genius. He is the perfect Daddy. Many people came to faith and salvation through God's chosen people.

Gen 17:13 both he who is born in your house and he who is bought with your money, shall surely be circumcised. So shall my covenant be in your flesh an everlasting covenant.

It makes sense that He nurtures each of His children based on their nature and knowledge. That is how we should deal with our children. Good teachers know there is no one size fits all for reaching young people or unbelievers.

Deu 29:29 "The secret things belong to the Lord our God, but those things which are revealed belong to us and to our children forever...."

He blessed the Israelites with clear revelation and miracles to get them to believe. They became spoiled, demanding more and more, and turned to other gods. In many ways, we have done the same with the revelation of Scripture.

We do not know much about the crowns mentioned in six NT passages - 1Co 9:25-26, 1Th 2:17-20, Phl 3:20-4:1, 2Ti 4:6-8, Jas 1:12, and 1Pe 5:1-5. We may lay them at the feet of the Lord God Almighty - Rev 4:10. There are still many mysteries in Scripture and in life to strengthen our faith - 1Pe 1:8.

> Heb 11:1 Now faith is the assurance of things hoped for, the conviction of things not seen.

This may be the toughest mystery of all. What does a loving, just, benevolent God do with those who have never heard the gospel? This question poses a significant challenge to theologians on radio call in shows. Most mention Jhn 14:6, "No one comes to the Father except through me (Jesus)." Several denominations have come up with some convoluted practices to help those who died unsaved. This is an important issue to those with a loved one in that situation. There are several passages in Scripture that deal with those who die with no knowledge of the law - Luk 12:48; Jhn 9:41, 15:22, 24; Rom 4:15, 5:13, and 2Pe 2:21.

> Rom 2:14 For when Gentiles, who do not have the law, by nature do what the law requires, they are a law to themselves, even though they do not have the law.

There are many theories about the meaning of these passages, none approach God's actual treatment of these people. Perhaps this mystery leaves room for God to be God in these matters. Regardless, we do not want to leave anyone without the knowledge of the gospel.

Scripture speaks of being baptized for the dead - 1Co 15:29. My Study Bible footnote for that passage provides three popular interpretations, finishing with - "it will always be obscure"[2], a.k.a. a mystery. The size of the footnote in my Bible is an indication of the controversy surrounding a contended passage. Another example is 1Co 11 on head coverings. Were this issue an essential, the Holy Spirit would have led Paul to make it clear rather than to leave it for us to ponder the literal or illustrative interpretation. Previous generations adopted specific guidance from this passage. Maybe some of these other contentious issues will fade in favor of the urgency of displaying and sharing the true gospel.

Here are just a few other mysteries with two or more popular answers.

- Jer 12:1 - Righteous are you, O LORD, when I complain to you; yet I would plead my case before you. Why does the way of the wicked prosper? Why do all who are treacherous thrive?
- 2Th 2:6 - Who's holding the lawless one back?
- Who wrote the books of Hebrews, James and Jude?
- 1Pe 3:19 - Who did Jesus preach to?
- 1Jn 5:16 - What is the sin that leads to death?
- Is the tribulation before, after, or during the millennium?

It is far better to leave them a mystery than to join the "ignorant and unstable" who "twist them to their own destruction" (2Pe 3:16). God did not intend for us to twist these mystery passages to fit our other beliefs that are not fully accurate. There are interpretations of this passage that do not fit well with the rest of Scripture.

1Ti 5:11-12 But refuse to enroll younger widows, for when their passions draw them away from Christ, they desire to marry [12] and so incur condemnation for having abandoned their former faith.

Our convoluted beliefs have little kingdom value and can harm the faith of seekers. For example, some say the use of the word replenish in Gen 1:28 and 9:1 (KJV) could indicate there were people here before Adam. God did wipe out almost all of humanity once and was going to wipe out the Israelites again when Moses interceded for them - Psa 106:23. This could explain some of the fossil record people are trying to use to prove evolution. Some tell their atheist friends God wiped out previous human creations, hoping to explain the fossil record and bring them to faith. One problem, that concept conflicts with the Genesis account of creation.

Science can be a major obstacle to someone believing Jesus is their Savior. This is not a good topic to start sharing the gospel. We reach them by sharing the truth of the gospel and showing it is true by the new creature we have become - Pro 11:30. This is not diminishing the value of apologetic work for defending our faith. Apologetic books dealing with atheistic objections may help remove obstacles to considering the gospel.

There is a pioneer spirit in all of us. We want to go where we have not been and see what we have not seen before. There is precious little in theology that has not been explored and postulated but SHOULD be. In other words, do not try to unscrew the inscrutable.[3] It may tickle our adventurist nature, and might even sell a few books; but is it furthering the kingdom? Understanding all Scripture is far more difficult than solving a double-sided white jigsaw puzzle. It is extremely difficult, trimming pieces to fit leads to sure failure.

Sometimes the famous line, "You can't handle the truth," from the movie, A Few Good Men, applies to us. Jesus hid the meaning of what would happen to Him in Jerusalem from the disciples. He may hide things from us for our own good.

> Luk 18:35 But they understood none of these things. This saying was hidden from them, and they did not grasp what was said.

Writing this book has revealed how much I did not know and the impact that has on my teaching. This treatment of mysteries provided great insight into the frequently repeated Donald Rumsfeld quote "But there are also unknown unknowns — the ones we don't know we don't know."[4]

Antinomic Passages

Other difficult passages may be an antinomy - a contradiction between two beliefs or conclusions that are in themselves reasonable, a paradox. It is especially difficult for us to accept these apparent contradictions in Scripture, knowing that they must both be true. We often embrace one side of antinomic passages using them to support denominational differences. We compile references to support our unwavering position and sternly refuse to consider the other side, or rationalize it away. We are like two jaw fish seen on nature videos, piling up barriers around our position wanting nothing to do with those in the hole next door. This is far worse than admitting the passages that appear to contradict each other are a different form of mystery. Four times in the book of Exodus God says He will harden Pharaoh's heart. Many use this to support some contested doctrine. Yet, Scripture also describes Pharaoh hardening his own heart.

1Sa 6:6 Why should you harden your hearts <u>as the Egyptians and Pharaoh hardened their hearts</u>?

They both have to be true; Pharaoh's heart was hardened by God and himself. The mechanics of that is still a mystery of God. If two passages seem to conflict with each other, dig deeper and pray more. God in His flawless wisdom wants us to search these Scripture differences even though a full understanding may not be found in this life. Many passages tell us our prayers receive answers and make a difference - Mar 11:24-25, Jas 5:16, and 1Jn 3:22, 5:15. Other passages say everything follows God's will - Job 42:2, Psa 115:3, Isa 58:8-10, and Mat 19:26. How can both of these be true? Yet, we know they must be. One way for it to be true is for our prayer to match the will of God. Does that make our prayer list useless? Not at all! We should be praying for the Lord to show us His will in every matter. He ultimately decides. There are some passages where it appears God changes His mind. The parable of the persistent widow is an example. There are several more examples presented in chapter 10. Clearly, the results of our prayers are a many faceted mystery.

One possible explanation why Scripture is not prescriptive on a particular issue is to leave God room to exercise His omnipotence, justice, grace, and mercy. We have all said "That's not fair," to our parents, our boss, the TV, even to God. In many ways, God deals with us as individuals; some get significantly different treatment. Thank the Lord we all do not get the justice that Ananias and Sapphira received in Acts 5. If He had provided more specifics, we would likely have turned them into more rules and regulations, similar to those the Pharisees came up with. Then we would spend even more time keeping score than committing to ministry.

Some scriptural antinomies are not mysteries at all. We gain an understanding through careful investigation of all God's Truth. When looked at correctly, they fit like a hand in a glove. For example, many refuse to pray in public based on the guidance in Mat 6:6. Other passages that instruct us to pray in groups - Mat 18:19. The common theme in Matthew 6 is motive not application. Mat 5:16 instructs us to "let your light shine before others so that they may see your good works and give glory to your Father who is in heaven." Mat 6:1 warns us "Beware of practicing your righteousness before other people in order to be seen by them." There is no contradiction; it is all about our motive.

The following appear to be conflicting verses - Heb 11:31 Rahab saved by faith, Jas 2:25 Rahab saved by works. This is a beautiful linking of these biblical concepts. Notice in Heb 11:31 God spared Rahab "because she had given a friendly welcome to the spies." That deed was the product of her faith, which is in full agreement with the James passage.

In Jhn 14:16 Jesus promises "And I will pray to the Father, and he shall give you another Comforter." While in Jhn 16:7 Jesus reiterates "for if I go not away, the Comforter will not come unto you; but if I depart, I will send him unto you." Who sends the Comforter, God or Jesus? The Bible does not contradict itself. The only way for these passages to agree is for the Father, Son and Holy Spirit to be one, as the Bible says in many places.

Paul notes what appears to be a scriptural antinomy from the OT.

Rom 9:26-28 "And in the very place where it was said to them, 'You are not my people,' there they will be called 'sons of the living God.'" [27] And Isaiah cries out concerning Israel: "Though the number of the sons of Israel is as the sand of the sea, only a remnant of them will be saved, [28] for the Lord will carry out his sentence upon the earth fully and without delay."

Rom 11:12 refers to all Israel being saved "how much more will their full inclusion mean!" The solution seems to be in Rom 9:6 "It is not as though God's word had failed. For not all who are descended from Israel are Israel." Some theologians will contend it is not that simple; they might be right.

We often respond to the apparent contradictions unwisely. We should proceed with caution asking the Lord to give us guidance and great discernment to negotiate these mysterious passages like a theological mine field. Other chapters deal with antinomies relevant to the topic.

It should be no surprise that many of our religious differences and debates center around these scriptural mysteries and antinomies, here is a doozy.

Rom 11:25 Lest you be wise in your own sight, I do not want you to be unaware of this mystery, brothers: a partial hardening has come upon Israel, until the fullness of the Gentiles has come in.

Why are so many Jewish people unaware of this mystery? One could say God hardened their hearts as He did Pharaoh's heart. The first part of the passage gives us an insight into the problem. They are wise in their own sight, too smart to accept the teaching of Jesus and His disciples. Reading the NT would be so revealing, as many of them know the OT better than we do. They would see how the OT fits the NT like a hand in a glove. It is still a mystery to them because they will not respond to God's call by studying the NT.

5. MYSTERIES AND ANTINOMIES

When God says let there be a mystery there will be a mystery. That does not affect what God is calling us to do today. Most of the mysteries in the Bible have little bearing on this life. There are dozens of passages that speak to our holiness, use of gifts, fruitfulness, evangelism, doing good, readiness, righteousness, etc. - 2Pe 1:5-7, 3:14. That should be our priority over pondering unsolvable mysteries.

6. FALSE TEACHERS

But you must remember, beloved, the predictions of the apostles of our Lord Jesus Christ. [18] They said to you, "In the last time there will be scoffers, following their own ungodly passions." [19] It is these who cause divisions, worldly people, devoid of the Spirit. Jde 1:17-19

The subtitle passage for this chapter contains some very strong words; it is speaking to false teachers. If two or more have a different interpretation of an essential truth, at least one is wrong and their revelation did NOT come from God. Making a non-essential into an essential is also false teaching.

Rom 1:18-19 For the wrath of God is revealed from heaven against all ungodliness and unrighteousness of men, who by their unrighteousness suppress the truth. [19] For what can be known about God is plain to them, because God has shown it to them.

Warnings

Paul warns us about false teachers in at least five letters - 2Co, Gal, 2Th, 1Ti, and Titus. He devotes multiple chapters to false teachers and distorted beliefs in 2Co and 2Th. They were a problem in his day and he knew they would be in ours. Four other NT authors address this problem in five books - Mat, Mar, 1Pe, 2Pe, Rev. They are causing the name of Jesus to be defamed.

2Pe 2:1-3 But false prophets also arose among the people, just as there will be false teachers among you, who will secretly bring in destructive heresies, even denying the Master who bought them, bringing upon themselves swift destruction. [2] And many will follow their sensuality, and because of them the way of truth will be blasphemed. [3] And in their greed they will exploit you with false words. Their condemnation from long ago is not idle, and their destruction is not asleep.

We must not let the teaching of those with errant human motives lead us astray. Their doctrine mixes some truth with some postulation to create an incorrect interpretation. It is like historical fiction, highly enticing. Most cults began that way; their roots were in biblical truth. They alloy elements from Scripture and new teaching to manipulate beliefs and practices. Some will say, "This doesn't apply to us, we are growing." Growth alone does not indicate God is blessing a ministry.

> Rom 16:17-18 I appeal to you, brothers, to <u>watch out for those who cause divisions</u> and <u>create obstacles contrary to the doctrine that you have been taught; avoid them.</u> [18] For such persons do not serve our Lord Christ, but their own appetites, and by smooth talk and flattery they deceive the hearts of the naive.

Jeremiah informs us that God's people support the false teaching, is that true today.

> Jer 5:30-31 An appalling and horrible thing has happened in the land: [31] <u>the prophets prophesy falsely, and the priests rule at their direction; my people love to have it so,</u> but what will you do when the end comes?

Do people in habitual sin always realize it? If they fully understood the consequences and did a thorough evaluation, they would likely stop. Do those who are teaching false doctrine know they are doing it? Like Eliphaz in Job 15:11, we usually assume our thoughts and words are from the Lord. Often they are not. When they are, we frequently find a way to humanize them. As Casting Crowns points out in one of their many great songs, "It's a Slow Fade" - "led by someone else who was misled, and all wrapped in pride." It is not reasonable to say surely I would know if I were teaching, or hearing, false doctrine.

Dissension arose between the Pharisees and the Sadducees with one or both being wrong. People have beliefs of which they are totally convinced are true and they are totally wrong like the crowd that demanded Jesus be crucified - Mat 27:25. In Act 22:21-22 the Jews wanted to kill Paul for his teaching. We must ensure our zeal is 100% for truth; otherwise, the consequences are severe and certain.

> 2Pe 3:15-17 just as our beloved brother Paul ... does in all his letters when he speaks in them of these matters. There are some things in them that are hard to understand, <u>which the ignorant and unstable twist to their own destruction, as they do the other Scriptures.</u> [17] You therefore, beloved, knowing this beforehand, take care that you are not carried away with the error of lawless people and lose your own stability.

Paul warns Timothy to avoid false teaching. Timothy was probably a bit offended hearing this from his beloved mentor. He needed to hear Paul's wisdom just like we do.

> 1Ti 6:20-21 O Timothy, guard the deposit entrusted to you. <u>Avoid the irreverent babble and contradictions of what is falsely called "knowledge,"</u> [21] for by professing it some have swerved from the faith. Grace be with you.

He gave a similar warning in Col 2:8-10. Paul gives us an example of Judaizers adding extra requirements to salvation. He challenged them, "why are you putting God to the test by placing a yoke on the neck of the disciples that neither our fathers nor we have been able to bear" (Act 15:10). False teachers urged people to adopt a requirement for circumcision - Gal 1:7, 2:3. Consider Jhn 12:40, "He has blinded their eyes and hardened their heart". Will He do the same to those adopting false teaching today? That is an extremely scary thought; am I right or spiritually blind? We must answer this question and change our teaching accordingly.

God hates "a false witness who breathes out lies, and one who sows discord among brothers" (Pro 6:19). We teach controversial doctrine at great risk! Just like the other denominations that need to hear these passages, we must ensure **our** teaching is pure. Jesus usually spoke humbly and lovingly to the people. He reserved the strong authorative words for the errant teachers who should have known better - Mat 15:14, 23:13-16, and 23-24. Paul gave the following guidance for false teaching.

> Gal 5:8-10 This persuasion is not from him who calls you. ⁹ A little leaven leavens the whole lump. ¹⁰ I have confidence in the Lord that you will take no other view, and the one who is troubling you will bear the penalty, whoever he is.

Examples of False Teaching

False teachers have produced many contested issues in the body of Christ. The media has a field day using our disputes to ridicule the whole body. Here are some examples where theologians have taken a grain of Scripture and built a monument out of it.

Some dispensationalists believe Mat 10:5-6 reveals that teaching from Jesus only applies to Jews. They teach that we gentiles need only heed the books in the Bible written by Paul, claiming the rest were only for Jewish converts. WOW! Why would Jesus, the son of God and our Savior, provide new teaching to the Jews alive in His day and then supersede it through His apostle just a few years later? How can a student, Paul, be wiser than His teacher, Jesus? They even go to the extreme of saying there are two gospels, one for Jews and one for gentiles. Paul does say in a number of places he was the apostle to the gentiles. He explains the Spirit led him to preach in certain areas and not preach in others. It makes sense that he would focus on a people group with common issues and challenges; missionaries do that today. However, Scripture records several places where Paul preached to the

Jewish people - Act 13:14-15, 14:1, 17:1-4, 17:10-12, 17:17, and 18:4. There were probably Jewish people present during many of his messages, as he often preached in Synagogues.

One group espouses three levels of heaven attained by specific works. There are many theories of what the three levels of heaven refer to in 2Co 12:2; they cannot be conclusively supported. Theories are fun to contemplate. Do not teach them as fact and add requirements on the believers based on them.

Some consider the phrase kingdom of God (used 66 times from Mat through 2Th) and the kingdom of heaven (used 31 times in Mat only) as two different periods in the life of God's church. While others feel they are two descriptions of the same thing. Matthew refers to the people of Israel using the word heaven instead of the word God to avoid any chance of misusing His name - Exo 20:7. That makes sense, as Matthew's primary audience was Jewish. Matthew and Luke use the respective phrases for the same quote of Jesus in Mat 11:11 and Luk 7:28.

Some believe demonic possession ended with Christ's death. Why take such an absolute position on a topic that is not clear in Scripture? Many contemporary behaviors could be manifestations of demonic possession. Pushing doctrine that is not in accord with the whole Bible will harm the fellowship of believers.

> Gal 2:13 And the rest of the Jews acted hypocritically along with him, so that even Barnabas was led astray by their hypocrisy.

We can sometimes see things in Scripture that probably are not there. For example, the author of a daily devotion claimed Num 24:17b was a prophecy for the star of Bethlehem. The note in my study Bible[1] seems to be much more consistent with the text and the rest of Scripture - it is referring to David or Jesus. Another example is Jhn 20:7. A pastor interpreted this as the cloths maintaining the shape of Jesus' head and face

95

even after He had gone, like the abandoned shell of a cicada. This is novel, but there is no basis. Some of these artistic interpretations do not pose a problem with the essentials of theology. However, when we start to apply this creativity to Scripture, it can spread to non-essential differences that cause divisions. Even worse, they spawn new requirements for salvation; that is apostasy. This intellectual approach often emphasizes wayward beliefs over the priorities God has for us. A. W. Tozer put a good perspective on these great theologians - "The devil is a better theologian than any of us and is a devil still."[2] Thomas Merton also sums up the situation insightfully - "Our idea of God says more about ourselves than about Him."[3] Many of us are play dough theists; we make God who we want Him to be. Sometimes we resemble those who fashioned gods from a piece of wood - Hos 4:12. "If you believe what you like in the gospels, and reject what you don't like, it is not the gospel you believe, but yourself" - Saint Augustine.[4]

In the OT, the false gods were asherah poles and graven images. Today they are paper and ink, and electronic media describing God the way we choose to see Him. Theological beliefs are extremely important. They form our understanding of God's revelation and the basis for our response to Him. These beliefs affect what we share with others about our faith. They must be based on properly interpreted Scripture. This means we cannot take anything out of context, and we cannot ignore passages that appear to conflict with our position. We cannot support a requirement for salvation with an isolated text, or extra biblical material. The consequences of false teaching are great - Col 2:4-8.

> Act 20:29-30 I know that after my departure fierce wolves will come in among you, not sparing the flock; [30] and from among your own selves will arise men speaking twisted things, to draw away the disciples after them.

God considers false teaching to be an especially serious offense. The OT told the Israelites to put false teachers to death.

Deu 13:5 But that prophet or that dreamer of dreams shall be put to death, because he has taught rebellion against the LORD your God,

There is judgment of false teaching in Jer 14:13-16; and Eze 13:1-15, and 22:28-31; and a warning from Jesus in Mat 5:19.

Mat 23 is all about what not to do as a teacher. Jesus provides seven woes for specific errant teaching, calling the teachers hypocrites in each woe. The Greek word translated to hypocrite in English means an actor under an assumed character (stage-player).

The following are their offenses in addition to hypocrisy:

- add burdens on the people (vs. 4)
- boastful and self aggrandizing (vs. 5-12)
- obstruct people from entering the kingdom of God (vs13)
- make people proselytes in sin (vs. 15)
- creating false oaths (vs. 16-22)
- neglected justice, mercy, and faithfulness (vs. 23-24)
- pious show, but full of sin inside (vs. 25-28)
- condemn, punish and kill the true prophets (vs. 29-34)

They had "neglected the weightier matters of the law" (Mat 23:23).

Does the following judgment fall on those who are interpreting or revising Scripture incorrectly today?

Luk 11:50, 52 so that the blood of all the prophets, shed from the foundation of the world, may be charged against this generation, ...[52] Woe to you lawyers! For you have taken away the key of knowledge. You did not enter yourselves, and you hindered those who were entering."

Our family does a lot of hiking. One of the first things we do when we get home is check for ticks. We use repellant because the consequences can be extreme. Similarly, none of us wants to find we are teaching other than truth. False teaching is happening, and the consequences are extreme. Paul advises us to test our faith, which should find any error within us.

> 2Co 13:5 <u>Examine yourselves, to see whether you are in the faith</u>. <u>Test yourselves</u>. Or do you not realize this about yourselves, that Jesus Christ is in you?--unless indeed you fail to meet the test!

Earnestly pray these Psalms from David and then look for indication of any wayward beliefs. "Search me, O God, and know my heart! Try me and know my thoughts" (Psa 139:23), "Through your precepts I get understanding; therefore I hate every false way" (Psa 119:104). We should hate even the possibility of false teaching. We are to "have nothing to do with irreverent, silly myths. Rather train yourself for godliness" (1Ti 4:7).

Published interpretations of selected verses do not make them true. If two commentaries differ on a point of essential doctrine, one or more of the following are true:

- one or both interpretations are wrong
- it is not an essential issue, as it does not impact salvation
- the interpretation is contextual to the situation, both can be true based on circumstances

We Must Respond

We must verify we hear the truth as the Berean Jews did in Act 17:11. What do we do if someone is teaching false doctrine in <u>our house of God</u>? AFTER we are sure there are no specs in our eye, we can see clearly to examine the teaching of others. God will deal with the false teachers - Act 23:3, but He expects us to challenge them.

Jesus warned his disciples - "Beware of the leaven of the Pharisees and Sadducees" (Mat 16:12). Paul stresses the importance of dealing with false teaching and provides the consequences of letting it continue.

> 1Ti 1:3-7 As I urged you when I was going to Macedonia, remain at Ephesus so that you may charge certain persons not to teach any different doctrine, [4] nor to devote themselves to myths and endless genealogies, which promote speculations rather than the stewardship from God that is by faith. [5] The aim of our charge is love that issues from a pure heart and a good conscience and a sincere faith. [6] Certain persons, by swerving from these, have wandered away into vain discussion, [7] desiring to be teachers of the law, without understanding either what they are saying or the things about which they make confident assertions.

We see similar guidance in at least 17 NT passages - 2Pe 3:17, and Rev 2:2. Scripture is conclusive; we are not to affiliate with these false teachers. Jesus made it clear when He spoke to the church of Thyatira we cannot "tolerate that woman Jezebel, who calls herself a prophetess and is teaching and seducing my servants" (Rev 2:20). Four of the seven churches addressed in the book of Revelation had a problem with false teachers. Jesus found great fault with those who did not deal with false teachers and other theological compromises - Rev 2:14-15, 20. God dealt with those who allowed false teaching to continue - Mic 3:9-12. Jesus commended the churches that tested to identify false prophets - Rev 2:2-6. We must ensure without doubt that false teaching is occurring BEFORE we take action. Matthew informs us we can recognize false teachers by their fruit.

> Mat 7:15-17 "Beware of false prophets, who come to you in sheep's clothing but inwardly are ravenous wolves. [16] You will recognize them by their fruits. Are grapes gathered from thorn bushes, or figs from thistles? [17] So, every healthy tree bears good fruit, but the diseased tree bears bad fruit.

Paul directs us to "test everything; hold fast what is good. Abstain from every form of evil." (1Th 5:21-22).

> 1Jo 4:1-3 Beloved, do not believe every spirit, but <u>test the spirits to see whether they are from God</u>, for many false prophets have gone out into the world. ² By this you know the Spirit of God: every spirit that confesses that Jesus Christ has come in the flesh is from God, ³ and every spirit that does not confess Jesus is not from God. This is the spirit of the antichrist, which you heard was coming and now is in the world already.

In addition to managing ourselves, Jeremiah said do not listen to them.

> Jer 23:16, 26 Thus says the LORD of hosts: "Do not listen to the words of the prophets who prophesy to you, filling you with vain hopes. <u>They speak visions of their own minds, not from the mouth of the LORD</u>. ²⁶ How long shall there be lies in the heart of the prophets who prophesy lies, and who prophesy the deceit of their own heart,

How should we respond when being taught what appears to be false doctrine? Davy Crockett would say, "Be always sure you are right, then go ahead."[5] We have three options to avoid those teaching false doctrine. Challenge them and get them to stop - Mat 18:15, get the false teacher out of your church - Tit 1:11 and 2Jn 1:10, or leave that church - 2Jn 1:11.

Read a broadly accepted study Bible, most will provide alternative interpretations on disputed passages. That is usually a clue that it is a contested non-essential. Most reputable study Bibles do not offer alternative interpretations for passages dealing with essential doctrine. Read commentaries to gain additional perspectives on a particular passage. This should include some that do not agree with your perspective. That is the only way we can be sure enough to raise the issue. Ask other teachers in your church how they interpret the passage, not mentioning your concerns with the other teacher - Mat 18:15. Then approach the suspect teacher with your question, not accusation, one-on-one. Ask them to explain what the subject passage means. Give them a chance to explain what they were teaching, and then express concerns about the apparent interpretation. If that does not work, involve other leaders. If they agree with the concern, proceed with the steps in Mat 18:16-17. Paul instructs us to rebuke deceptive teachers to make them sound in faith.

> Tit 1:10 -14 For there are many who are insubordinate, empty talkers and deceivers, especially those of the circumcision party. [11] They must be silenced, since they are upsetting whole families by teaching for shameful gain what they ought not to teach. [12] One of the Cretans, a prophet of their own, said, "Cretans are always liars, evil beasts, lazy gluttons." [13] This testimony is true. Therefore rebuke them sharply, that they may be sound in the faith, [14] not devoting themselves to Jewish myths and the commands of people who turn away from the truth.

> Tit 3:10 -11 As for a person who stirs up division, after warning him once and then twice, have nothing more to do with him, [11] knowing that such a person is warped and sinful; he is self-condemned.

We are doing real well with the "have nothing more to do with him" guidance, as there are over 33,800 Christian bodies worldwide. We are not doing so well with the "together you may with one voice glorify the God and Father of our Lord Jesus Christ" (Rom 15:6). We need to reverse the trend of division in God's family and reap the benefits described in chapter 12 of this book. Look at the giants of the Christian faith. Do they spend more time drawing the lost to Christ and uniting the body, or putting down those they do not agree with? Most overwhelmingly focus on sharing and living the gospel and making disciples.

It is very difficult to question broadly accepted essential teaching in our denomination when other members accept it. That leaves two main options. If possible, follow the Mat 18 process here as well. Take opportunities in group study situations to challenge incorrect doctrine taught as an essential. Refer to Scripture that clearly contradicts their position. If we are correct, the Lord will bless our efforts. The other option is to investigate carefully and move to a denomination that is more faithful to Scripture. Both options have their challenges.

What impact do the errors in our non-essential doctrine have in the lives of believers? Does the benefit of driving the points in conflict outweigh the harm done by the battle and the damaging witness we give to the unsaved world? Scripture is clear, we can be right in a very wrong way. Ensure you are correct, some areas of difference in our non-essential teaching may be correct. The following passage involves a belief about food. The concept of hurting a weaker brother could apply to some non-essential beliefs.

> 1Co 8:9, 12 <u>But take care that this right of yours does not somehow become a stumbling block to the weak....</u> [12] Thus, sinning against your brothers and wounding their conscience when it is weak, <u>you sin against Christ</u>.

If we are driving a person to accept our beliefs on a matter that is not an essential, we may be causing them to sin even if we are right - Rom 14:15, 23. It is far more effective to let our walk show who has the better understanding of God's revelation, earning their respect for our views? There are suggestions for reaching out to those in other denominations in chapter 12.

7. MOTIVES FOR FALSE TEACHING

"Seek not to grow in knowledge chiefly for the sake of applause, and to enable you to dispute with others; but seek it for the benefit of your souls." — Jonathan Edwards

Why is there so much false teaching today? The absence of advanced degrees after my name is indication that I probably do not have great revelations on why people cling to and teach false doctrine. I turned to Scripture and found enough to write a full chapter. You're thinking, "I've read the Bible, I can skip this part." Please read on. Topical studies provide a unique opportunity for self-examination - "Create in me a clean heart, O God; and renew a right spirit within me" (Psa 51:10). You would also miss all the charming anecdotes and commentary.

If we rationalize around some passages of Scripture to support our beliefs, there is a good chance our doctrine is wrong! Why do we cling to beliefs we struggle to defend?

Scripture gives us a variety of motives; the first is itchy ears. Paul's prediction has become fact. The temptation for teachers will continue until the Lord returns.

> 2Ti 4:3-4 For the time is coming when people will not endure sound teaching, but having itching ears they will accumulate for themselves teachers to suit their own passions, 4 and will turn away from listening to the truth and wander off into myths.

Itchy ears lead teachers to feel they are doing well when telling people what they want to hear. Eventually we will experience the result that Aaron did when he succumbed to the pressure from the Israelites to craft a golden idol. The Bible is clear;

expressing our faith for recognition is a sin - Mat 6:2, 5, 7, and 16. Popularity does not mean we are teaching truth.

> Luk 6:26 "Woe to you, when all people speak well of you, for so their fathers did to the false prophets.

I asked a Muslim friend why the Sunnis and Shiites battle each other. He responded with a question, why do Protestants and Catholics fight each other? I answered, "For power and influence." He replied, "Same reason." John Bunyan, a great 16th century preacher and author of *Pilgrims Progress* experienced prison four different times as a Church of England King/Queen took power. He was released when one that favored the Protestants took over. Queen "Bloody" Mary (1553-1558) had people burned at the stake for their beliefs. She had hundreds of Protestants executed; including her own cousin.[1] True religion is not shared through manipulation. Arguing and debating our theological differences is not very effective, and can do more harm than good. Even if you are correct, contrived concurrence may not put the truth in a wayward heart. One who mistakenly believes they are a Christian could become more resolved in their beliefs through resentment.

> Tit 1:16 They (unbelieving) profess to know God, but they deny him by their works. They are detestable, disobedient, unfit for any good work.

The Protestants and Catholics have been at odds since the Protestant Reformation began in the 16th century. It continues today. The motives for that confrontation are similar to the motives listed in this chapter with power and influence being the most prominent over the years. We should not look down our nose at others. I have heard many people say getting a job in that area or that state is tough unless you are in the right religious body. We have made progress; the numbers burned at the stake by fellow Christians are a lot less.

Teachers like positions of prestige - Mar 12:38-39. Scripture indicates false teaching often accompanies pride.

1Ti 6:3-6 If anyone teaches a different doctrine and does not agree with the sound words of our Lord Jesus Christ and the teaching that accords with godliness, [4] he is puffed up with conceit and understands nothing. He has an unhealthy craving for controversy and for quarrels about words, which produce envy, dissension, slander, evil suspicions, [5] and constant friction among people who are depraved in mind and deprived of the truth, imagining that godliness is a means of gain. [6] But godliness with contentment is great gain,

Pride and prestige were big problems for the Pharisees and Sadducees and other religious leaders - Mat 23:5-7, 12. It is no different today.

Jas 3:14-16 But if you have bitter jealousy and selfish ambition in your hearts, do not boast and be false to the truth. [15] This is not the wisdom that comes down from above, but is earthly, unspiritual, demonic. [16] For where jealousy and selfish ambition exist, there will be disorder and every vile practice.

Pride is such a powerful influence in our lives. The following verses are amazing. Jesus knew the hearts of Zebedee's sons James and John; He addressed their pride before they mentioned their ambition. A short time later, driven by pride, they asked for the seats of honor anyway.

Mar 9:34-35 But they kept silent, for on the way they had argued with one another about who was the greatest. [35] And he sat down and called the twelve. And he said to them, "If anyone would be first, he must be last of all and servant of all."

Mar 10:37 And they said to him, "Grant us to sit, one at your right hand and one at your left, in your glory."

Pride stirs up strife - Pro 28:25-26, we frequently see this displayed in denominational battles and church splits. God wants unity and scripturally correct beliefs. Unity will enable us to influence each other toward true doctrine.

Pro 11:2 When pride comes, then comes disgrace, but with the humble is wisdom.

Be careful with pride, "God opposes the proud, but gives grace to the humble"(Jas 4:5-6, also Psa 18:27, Luk 1:51).

Isa 66:2 All these things my hand has made, and so all these things came to be, declares the LORD. But this is the one to whom I will look: he who is humble and contrite in spirit and trembles at my word.

A subset of pride is the collection and display of knowledge - religious elitism. Gene Veith described it this way – "When obsessing over theology becomes a way to avoid obedience."[2] "Do you see a man who is wise in his own eyes? There is more hope for a fool than for him" - Psa 26:12. At least the fool has an idea of his condition.

1Co 8:1-3 Now concerning food offered to idols: we know that "all of us possess knowledge." This <u>"knowledge" puffs up, but love builds up</u>. [2] If anyone imagines that he knows something, he does not yet know as he ought to know. [3] But if anyone loves God, he is known by God.

Another motive for abusing the truth in Scripture is our position and financial security. In 1Ki 12:25-33 Jeroboam set up a whole system of counterfeit religion to preserve his position and keep the people from going back to Jerusalem and the true God. The people willingly followed. The NT describes many Jewish leaders that were jealous of those following Jesus and, later, those following Paul - Act 13:45. Their desire to preserve their positions drove them to do many ungodly things: killing prophets - Luk 11:47, Act 7:52 and promoting the crucifixion of our Lord.

Jhn 11:48 If we let him go on like this, everyone will believe in him, and the Romans will come and take away both our place and our nation."

They even had their followers afraid to challenge them.

Jhn 9:22 His parents said these things because they feared the Jews, for the Jews had already agreed that if anyone should confess Jesus to be Christ, he was to be put out of the synagogue.

It is very easy to condemn the Pharisees and Sadducees for allowing their fear of losing their position to bring them to the desperation of killing Jesus, even as they watched Him do miracles - Luk 6:11, 22:1. We have that same prideful, selfish, lack of faith, and blindness. We doggedly stick to doctrine that is widely challenged, and criticize and condemn other denominations. We can trust the Guy that owns the cattle on a thousand hills to take care of us if we faithfully seek unity.

I have read several books for men that speak of our yearning for competition, conquest, and fighting. We see it everywhere in our society today - military battles, gangs, gambling, sports, and barbaric fighting on TV. Perhaps this is another motive for theological debate. Good Christian men cannot allay their need for battle in most of the aforementioned ways, so they vent it through theological disputes over non-essentials. I wonder which of these outlets disappoints God most.

In 2002, an ossuary was found with the inscription "James son of Joseph brother of Jesus." The government of Israel attacked the relic dealer as a fraud. The trial lasted for four years with many experts lining up on both sides of the issue. The court convicted him of illegal trafficking of antiquities but not for fraudulent relics. They did not conclusively prove it was the tomb of our Lord's brother, nor did they prove it was not. They have made a lot of money showing it in museums.

Opposition to the claim of the archeologist was likely from the impact it had on Jewish beliefs. Interesting how the alliances form on theological issues. Others joined the Jews to challenge this claim, as they do not believe Jesus had a brother. The following is an excerpt from an article addressing the trial decision. "The particulars of science matter little to zealots defending a creed.... Attacking scientists is increasingly common as religious and ideological zealots flatly reject data that offend their creeds and beliefs."[3] It's interesting that people hold more tightly to their doctrine than the scientific investigation, and a <u>potential</u> proof of truth.

My childhood home did not have any wallpaper, never gave it much thought as a child. My grandmother had wallpaper in her house. My favorite was the fish and shells in the bathroom. Wallpaper was out of style for a while. The first house Peg and I lived in had wallpaper in several rooms, unfortunately none with fish and shells. Now the styles have evolved back to no paper again. The trendsetters change styles periodically so they can sell paint and wallpaper to those who want to spend time and money to stay current. Some people are obsessed with matching the latest thing while others strive to be different. There is a similar evolving trend in neckties. I have saved many old ties hoping to avoid the purchase of new ones the next time the style swung from wide to narrow. The style police are innovative; they also vary the material, patterns, etc. so I almost never succeed in getting past Peggy to the door with one of my old ties on. Body art and piercings are other expressions of difference that have swept the world and become the norm. Many people do not want to be different alone so they follow along with almost anything. Errant Christian beliefs are not a good place to express our childhood love of the game follow the leader.

Some organizations seem to place a priority on doctrine that is unique from others, even though Scripture support is limited. It is interesting that many of these involve new revelations. They seem to look for differences to make them unique, and then focus on them. Let's call these opponents of unity *dividers*. The following is a test to identify dividers using the approach of a popular comedian.

- If you have ever taught a class on other denominations and never mentioned any of your body's contested beliefs - you might be a divider.
- If you spend more time arguing about religion with other Christians than you do living and sharing the gospel - you might be a divider.
- If you refer to your denominational literature more than you do the Bible - you might be a divider.
- If you read the Bible savoring the passages that support your beliefs and skip over those that do not - you might be a divider.
- If you quote the founders of your denomination more than you do Jesus - you might be a divider.
- If you criticize other denominations on non-essential issues - you might be a divider.
- If you have never read any material challenging your denominational tenets - you might be a divider.
- If you are more concerned about the greatest differences than you are about the Greatest Commandments - you might be a divider.

Rather than a motive, the cause of the distorted teaching may be their hardness of heart.

> Eph 4:18 They are darkened in their understanding, alienated from the life of God because of the ignorance that is in them, due to their hardness of heart.

Some motives deal with the person, me. We should not be "seeking my own advantage, but that of many, that they may be saved" (1Co 10:24, and 33). Hopefully the following passage does not apply to anyone reading this book. However, it does apply to some who promote a distorted gospel and create a norm that lures others to modify their positions away from truth. It is a tough reality. If we are not teaching biblical truth, we are NOT being Spirit led. The devil is delighted when we cause confusion and divisions. Do not fall into that trap. It is a slippery slope, with many casualties and dire consequences.

> 2Co 11:12-15 And what I am doing I will continue to do, in order to undermine the claim of those who would like to claim that in their boasted mission they work on the same terms as we do. [13] <u>For such men are false apostles, deceitful workmen, disguising themselves as apostles of Christ.</u> [14] And no wonder, for even satan disguises himself as an angel of light. [15] <u>So it is no surprise if his servants</u>, also, disguise themselves as servants of righteousness. Their end will correspond to their deeds.

If we even suspect these motives are affecting our teaching, we must change our motivation and beliefs. They are not from God.

> 1Jo 2:16 For all that is in the world--the desires of the flesh and the desires of the eyes and pride of life--is not from the Father but is from the world.

These motives for false teaching are evident in the conduct of some pastors and other religious professionals. Some spend millions on themselves. Others, caught in various scandals, besmirch themselves, their peers, and the body of Christ. TV programs, movies and music portray these charade pastors with an all too familiar behavior. Their conduct and teaching do not reflect biblical guidance. Paul provides a warning for extreme false teaching.

> 2Ti 2:12 if we endure, we will also reign with him; if we deny him, he also will deny us;

I am not sure what it means for Him to deny us, and I do not want to find out.

8. TEACHING BIBLICAL TRUTH

For since, in the wisdom of God, the world did not know
God through wisdom, it pleased God through the folly
of what we preach to save those who believe. 1Co 1:21

We are the voice for Jesus today, an immense responsibility
with great potential for good and harm.

> Luk 10:16 "The one who hears you hears me, and the
> one who rejects you rejects me, and the one who rejects
> me rejects him who sent me."

Teaching is the core of this book, from cover to cover. We
examined what it should not be; now let's investigate what it
should be. Our motives in teaching (including writing) must
be to please God. Paul was not out to please followers with
what he taught "but just as we have been approved by God to
be entrusted with the gospel, so we speak, not to please man,
but to please God who tests our hearts" (1Th 2:4). The spread
of the gospel and the salvation of the lost must be the priority
above our personal agendas and the theological battles we
pursue. Paul DOES seek to please people with the gospel.

> 1Co 10:32-33 Give no offense to Jews or to Greeks or
> to the church of God, ³³just as I try to please everyone
> in everything I do, not seeking my own advantage, but
> that of many, that they may be saved.

We are not only teaching people the gospel for their salvation,
we are showing them how to live by our example and how to
share the gospel effectively.

> 2Ti 2:2 and what you have heard from me in the
> presence of many witnesses entrust to faithful men
> who will be able to teach others also.

111

We are influencing the beliefs and actions of those we teach. Most important is the next generation of Christians, especially our children. Jesus said, "Whoever causes one of these little ones who believe in me to sin, it would be better for him if a great millstone were hung around his neck and he were thrown into the sea" (Mat 9:42). Some say "these little ones" is referring to children, others say new Christians; to be safe we should take it to mean both. It is amazing how easy it is to volunteer to teach children or youth at church, most folks do not want to deal with the challenges. Many churches have screening criteria and training required to teach; this is tough but very worthwhile. Children are impressionable blank canvases. Thank goodness we can usually paint over canvas once we know what we are doing.

Paul provides a great summary of the vital elements of teaching in chapters two and three of First Corinthians. The concepts appear throughout the NT.

Clearly Teaching Truth

1Co 2:2 For I decided to know nothing among you except Jesus Christ and him crucified.

Paul repeats this highly important guidance again in his second letter to the Corinthians.

2Co 2:17 For we are not, like so many, peddlers of God's word, but as men of sincerity, as commissioned by God, in the sight of God we speak in Christ.

Not even Jesus taught His own ideas, "I do nothing on my own authority, but speak just as the Father taught me" (Jhn 7:16, 8:28). The Holy Spirit only speaks what He hears, He is sent by God but "will not speak on His own authority" (Jhn 16:13). We should change "not an iota, not a dot" in our teaching of Scripture (Mat 5:18). Even Paul realized he was to preach the message Jesus gave him personally with no additions - 1Co 2:2.

> 1Co 1:17 For Christ did not send me to baptize but
> to preach the gospel, <u>and not with words of eloquent
> wisdom</u>, lest the cross of Christ be emptied of its power.

We must ensure we have learned the truth from Scripture
before we pass it on. To all who teach, Paul instructs - we
"must hold firm to the trustworthy word as taught, so that he
may be able to give instruction in sound doctrine" (Tit 1:9).

> 1Ti 4:6-7 If you put these things before the brothers,
> you will be a good servant of Christ Jesus, <u>being trained
> in the words of the faith and of the good doctrine that
> you have followed.</u> [7] <u>Have nothing to do with irreverent,
> silly myths.</u> Rather train yourself for godliness;

Over the years, my belief system has resembled a Rubik's
cube. I have proudly gotten one side all the same color only to
find other Scripture that contradicts my treasured concept -
the other five sides were a mess. We must be careful not to
look at Scripture through preconceived ideas. Those who do
not believe the Bible apply filters to scientific data to support
their worldview. Many of us accept errant concepts and do not
remember why. That is like cutting the end off a ham before
putting it in the pan to cook and discarding a perfectly good
piece of meat because Grandma did it that way. If you have
not heard this timeless illustration, ask someone over 50.
Before passing something on as truth, we must ensure it is
well supported by <u>all</u> of Scripture.

A naïve acceptance of suspect theology can lead to a faulty
attitude about salvation as John described to the brood of
vipers - Luk 3:7. Other Christian bodies usually contest these
questionable beliefs. To take an unbending position on a
passage in the Bible that God has not made clear is arrogant,
especially when theologians have debated it for hundreds of
years. Holding distorted beliefs can be similar to telling a lie;
we have to adopt other distorted beliefs to support the first.
Know the Bible well, as teaching truth perpetuates itself.
False teaching will abound in the absence of teaching truth.

Most people turn away from theological debates and the preachers that dwell on them. If you feel you must promote divisive beliefs that have not been settled in almost 2,000 years, do it among clergy or in separate meetings with those who want to contest a particular position. Do not teach it to the flock in general. If you cannot convince other clergy, why involve the flock in controversy and potential errant teaching? The following passage should be a commitment for those authorized to teach.

> 2Co 4:1-2 Therefore, having this ministry by the mercy of God, we do not lose heart. ² But we have renounced disgraceful, underhanded ways. We refuse to practice cunning or to tamper with God's word, but by the open statement of the truth we would commend ourselves to everyone's conscience in the sight of God.

Even if we are teaching a class of believers, there is nothing more important than the gospel. First, we must instill a compassionate urgency for the lost. Second, we need to equip them to communicate the gospel in an effective manner to their audience. The audience can be as varied as humanity itself. The majority of Paul's letters to Timothy were directly or indirectly about teaching, including a focus on preserving biblical truth.

> 2Ti 2:15-18 Do your best to present yourself to God as one approved, a worker who has no need to be ashamed, rightly handling the word of truth. ¹⁶ But avoid irreverent babble, for it will lead people into more and more ungodliness, ¹⁷ and their talk will spread like gangrene. Among them are Hymenaeus and Philetus, ¹⁸ who have swerved from the truth, saying that the resurrection has already happened.

What we want to believe does not change truth. Having an unbelieving son leads me to hope he may respond to my sharing the truth with him until he understands. Prolonged attempts yielding nothing may lead me to believe there is nothing I can do. My circumstance does not change truth. My opinion on who shot President Kennedy does not change the truth of who actually did. This passage describes many teachers of the Word, including me: "A prudent man conceals knowledge, but the heart of fools proclaims folly" (Pro 12:23). I have heard more than once - he is not always right, but he is never in doubt.

Shortly after becoming a Christian, I offered this oft-heard statement by Ben Franklin in a Bible study - "God helps those who help themselves." When asked for a reference, I said I thought it came from the Bible. The leader asked me to bring the reference to the next meeting; I brought a confession instead. "In everything the prudent acts with knowledge, but a fool flaunts his folly" (Pro 13:16). Important points in Scripture show up several times. We must take the effort needed to ensure we are teaching truth. Most of us read the Bible like the newspaper, selecting specific articles. We hear sermons, read devotions and attend studies dealing with selected passages. We seldom read the Bible searching for a particular topic. We should not be promoting a controversial doctrine until we have read the Bible cover to cover focused on that contested topic alone, objectively looking at <u>both</u> sides as best we can.

Qualification to Teach

It is vital that we are ready to teach in knowledge, maturity, and preparation. Some are asked to teach before they are ready or do a poor job preparing - 1Ti 1:7-8. "Can a blind man lead a blind man? Will they not both fall into a pit?" (Luk 6:39). Does that mean we should not teach until we are perfect? No, if those responsible for education in your fellowship feel you are qualified in knowledge and example, go for it. The ultimate cue to share our faith is when people ask why they see a difference in our life compared to our past or to those around us - 1Pe 3:15.

> 1Ti 4:16 Keep a close watch on yourself and on the teaching. Persist in this, for <u>by so doing you will save both yourself and your hearers</u>.

We spent several years of my childhood on a farm. During a few winters, the ponds froze over enough for us to ice skate. We would decide if the ice was thick enough by trial and error. When we fell, we would hear the ice crack and pop. Then we got up and continued skating. We did not think much about the potentially fatal consequences if the ice gave way. It was hard to determine the thickness of the ice from observation alone. We can be on theological thin ice in our teaching and not realize it; or worse we may be all wet.

"The Word of God is like a lion. You do not have to defend a lion. All you have to do is let the lion loose, and the lion will defend itself." - Charles Spurgeon.[1] God created our unbelievable world of complexity, beauty, functionality, resiliency... it was designed for us. I believe He also provided the perfect guidance in Scripture. We should follow what we understand - 2Ti 3:14, and pray for clear wisdom and discernment of what we do not. To be sure about an interpretation of a passage, try an approach similar to the ancient mariners test of aligning with three lanterns for guidance entering a harbor.[2] The following three tests must all be yes for that interpretation to likely be correct. If these three do not line up, we may be generating controversy where God did not intend; or worse, we are wrong!

1. There must be no Scripture passages that seem to contradict our position - Mat 5:19, 22:29; 1Ti 4:7, 6:3-4; 2Ti 3:15-16; 2Pe 3:16
2. Your interpretation is consistent with a consensus of broadly accepted Christian commentaries - Pro 30:6, 2Co 4:2.
3. The Holy Spirit has given a full peace about this interpretation - Neh 9:20, Jhn 14:26, and 16:13.

Speaking of clear Bible understanding, I came across a story about a candidate for church membership who appeared before a church council for examination.[3]

One of the council members asked him, "What's your favorite book in the Bible?" The man said, "The Book of Parables."

The book of Parables? They scratched their heads a bit and then said, "Can you tell us about it?"

So the young man boldly proclaimed, "Once upon a time a man went down from Jerusalem to Jericho and fell upon thieves. And thorns grew and choked the man. He went on, and he didn't have any money. And then he met the Queen of Sheba and she gave the man a thousand talents of gold and silver and 100 changes of raiments. And when he was driving along, under a fig tree his hair got caught in a limb. And it left him hanging there. And he hung there for many days and many nights, and ravens came and brought him food and water. And one night, while he was hanging there, his wife Delilah came along and cut his hair. He dropped and fell on a stony ground and it rained for 40 days and 40 nights so he hid himself in a cave. He went on and he came to Jerusalem and he saw Queen Jezebel sitting up on a window, and when she saw him, she laughed. So he said, 'Throw her down from there.' So they threw her down. And then he said 'Throw her down again.' And they threw her down again, 70 times 7. And the fragments they picked up were 12 baskets full." And then he turned to the council and he said to them, "Now whose wife will she be in the days of judgment?"

None of the council members were qualified to question him, so the candidate became a member.

Before we denounce this guy, do you have any confused and fuzzy understandings of the Word of God? Unfortunately, some take bits and pieces of Scripture and put them together to make incorrect beliefs.

For many years, I wondered why seminary students are required to take Hebrew and Greek languages. We have all these highly refined translations so why spend the time on the original language. English cannot always provide a word with the same meaning as the Greek. In many cases, several Greek words have one translated English counterpart. For example, Greek has four words translated as love in English (Agápe, Éros, Philia, and Storge). Some of the rich meaning is lost in English. Look at the use of love in Jhn 21:15-17 and compare it to the associated Greek word and meaning. There are many interlinear Bibles available on the internet. The Blue Letter Bible website has a good one.

The Bible is like a large, intricate puzzle; we cannot put 7 pieces of a 1,000-piece puzzle together and have any hope of seeing the full scene. We have to put them all together to see the full picture and specific details. Taking things out of context is especially dangerous. The following aspects of biblical context came from the GotQuestions.org website.[4]

- literal meaning - what it says
- historical setting - the events of the story, to whom is it addressed, and how it was understood at that time
- grammar - the immediate sentence and paragraph within which a word or phrase is found
- synthesis - comparing it with other parts of Scripture for a fuller meaning
- outline and structure of the book, then the chapter, then the paragraph

I would add one more element of context – the perspective or intent of the reader. We must stay objective. Considering all aspects of context is crucial to biblical exegesis (interpretation and understanding).

Translation is a daunting task. We encounter different meanings for words in any language based on the context. This leaves room for distortion. For example, the word hot in American English can mean - high temperature, attractive, stolen, latest thing, energized, high energy, or angry; there are probably more. They change over time; saying cool is no longer cool. A comparison of the last phrase in Isa 49:7 from 12 popular translations finds three different verb forms. There are eight in past tense, two in present tense and two in future tense. Some original language translations are that tough, while others reflect a theological bias. We need to keep translations as pure as possible, not making them another doctrinal battlefield.

> Isa 49:7b "Kings shall see and arise; princes, and they shall prostrate themselves; because of the LORD, who is faithful, the Holy One of Israel, who <u>has chosen</u> you."

I asked an elder friend which translation he thought was correct. He answered, "Yes." God knows it all past, present and future so all are correct for Him - interesting perspective. If a verse has significant differences in various English versions of the Bible, be cautious and very thorough. Responding to a question with "It's all Greek to me" is not effective teaching.

As discussed in chapter 3, errant prophecy can be a source of false teaching in the body. A prophet from God will be correct all the time. If we are going to put it out, we had better be right. Thomas Jefferson made his own bible. He felt Jesus was only a great teacher and moral example. He left out all the miracles and the resurrection. Writing it down does not make it truth. His butchering of the Bible and his grossly misinterpreted letter to the Danbury Baptist association in the state of Connecticut regarding the separation of church and state make him a favorite of anti-Christians.[5] Worthy of repeating a previous caution, "no prophecy was ever produced by the will of man." (2Pe 1:20-21).

Be an Example of What We Teach

> 1Co 2:3-6 And I was with you in weakness and in fear and much trembling, [4] and my speech and my message were not in plausible words of wisdom, <u>but in demonstration of the Spirit and of power</u>, [5] so that

your faith might not rest in the wisdom of men but in the power of God. [6] Yet among the mature we do impart wisdom, although it is not a wisdom of this age or of the rulers of this age, who are doomed to pass away.

Years ago, Charles Barkley (Hall of Fame basketball player), appeared in a TV commercial saying he was not a role model. To the kids that obsessively admired him; he was providing an example of how to act regardless of any disclaimer he presented. It is incredibly discouraging to see news outlets tell of a fanatic, claiming to be Christian, has done or said something heinous. I heard the imperial kludd of the KKK speak on a news program. In addition to interrupting the broadcaster repeatedly, he quoted many Bible passages, out of intent and context, to support their radical values, behavior, and agenda. We are called to be ambassadors for Christ in everything we say and do - 2Co 5:11-20.

It is hard to argue with the following quote: "The greatest single cause of atheism in the world today is Christians who acknowledge Jesus with their lips and walk out the door and deny Him by their lifestyle. That is what an unbelieving world simply finds unbelievable"[6] - Brennan Manning. People are watching us for an example to follow.

> Heb 13:7 Remember your leaders, those who spoke to you the word of God. <u>Consider the outcome of their way of life, and imitate their faith.</u>

Scripture emphasizes following Godly examples in several places - 1Th 1:6, 2Th 3:7-9. Paul's letters to Timothy and Titus are referred to as the Pastoral Letters. They contain extensive guidance for those tending a flock and provide the qualifications for elders (overseers) and deacons. I would contend they contain the qualifications for teachers also. We must put an equal priority on our modeling Jesus and our teaching. If we master the former, we will leave opponents of the gospel "having nothing evil to say about us" (Tit 2:7-8). "A good example is far better than a good precept" - D. L. Moody.[7]

"Preach the gospel, and if necessary, use words," frequently attributed to St. Francis Assisi.[8] Our walk speaks far louder than our words. That old saying "it is easier for faith to be caught than taught" is as true today as ever before. Relaying the perfect truth of Scripture without a consistent walk, may cause people to disregard our teaching. In Mat 23:2-4, Jesus told His disciples to listen to the Jewish leader but not to follow their example. Many preachers and teachers have caused more harm to the spread of the gospel with their actions than they ever helped it with their words. Scripture gives us guidance for assessing our example of faith.

> 1Jo 3:9-10 <u>No one born of God makes a practice of sinning</u>, for God's seed abides in him, and he cannot keep on sinning because he has been born of God. [10] By this it is evident who are the children of God, and who are the children of the devil: whoever does not practice righteousness is not of God, <u>nor is the one who does not love his brother</u>.

If your life as a teacher does not do well with these tests, then you are likely not providing a good example, not credible as a teacher, and worst case, you may not be one born of God. Ensure you do not "become a stumbling block to the weak" (1Co 8:9).

> Jas 3:17 But the <u>wisdom from above is first pure, then peaceable, gentle, open to reason, full of mercy and good fruits, impartial and sincere</u>.

We must ensure our teaching exhibits these characteristics. Being a good role model is echoed in other passages of Scripture - 1Co 13:2-3, 8; 1Ti 4:12; Tit 2:7; 1Pe 5:3; Jas 3:13. We must not tarnish the name of Jesus by instructing others in matters of faith who know we are not walking with the Lord.

Unfortunately, in far too many cases we provide the enemy with ammunition to shoot at us. Pride can harm our example by leading to harmful and hurtful debates; from our "insolence comes nothing but strife" (Pro 13:10). We are to "avoid foolish controversies, genealogies, dissensions, and quarrels about the law" (Tit 3:9). Many issues are not worth arguing about. Stop it before it starts.

> Pro 17:14 The beginning of strife is like letting out water, so quit before the quarrel breaks out. Pro 20:3 It is an honor for a man to keep aloof from strife, but every fool will be quarreling.

Our public image is critical to the viability of our teaching, both in and outside the church.

> 1Pe 2:12 Keep your conduct among the Gentiles honorable, so that when they speak against you as evildoers, they may see your good deeds and glorify God on the day of visitation.

If we do not have a tight rein on our tongue, our religion is worthless. Ouch!

> Jas 1:26 If anyone thinks he is religious and does not bridle his tongue but deceives his heart, this person's religion is worthless. The religion that God loves is unstained from the world.

> Pro 21:23 Whoever keeps his mouth and his tongue keeps himself out of trouble.

PLEASE verify everything that is not from the Bible before passing it on. Social media is another place we can destroy our credibility. We can harm our Christian witness with any topic - family, church, politics, gossip, humor, etc. It is easy to verify information; there are websites that make a living fact checking.

Our arrogance is one reason atheists attack Christianity. We are prideful in our salvation, in our self-perceived righteousness, and in our condemnation of sinners. Did you like teachers who used that approach in school? They imply you are stupid and they know everything, so sit there be quiet and hang on their every word.

We can come across as know-it-alls <u>even when we are right</u>. Paul gives the sailors a good old-fashioned I told you so during a Mediterranean cruise. "Men, you should have listened to me and not have set sail from Crete and incurred this injury and loss" (Act 27:21). Later when they ran aground on Malta, the guards wanted to kill all the prisoners. God probably had to work some of His magic to save Paul from the sailors he gave the tongue-lashing. "It is easier to preach ten sermons than it is to live one" - unknown.

There Will Be Mysteries

1Co 2:7-8 <u>But we impart a secret and hidden wisdom of God</u>, which God decreed before the ages for our glory. [8] None of the rulers of this age understood this, for if they had, they would not have crucified the Lord of glory.

As discussed in chapter 4, there are mysteries in the NT, too. During my career as an engineer and manager, we often dealt with the Nuclear Regulatory Commission (NRC). We received repeated training on how to respond. If the NRC asked a question and we were not sure of the answer - "I don't know, but I'll find out" was the only acceptable response. Postulation, extrapolation, assumption, etc. were a sure path to trouble. That is true in our Bible teaching also. We cannot have an answer for everything. There are still many mysteries, and only God knows all - Rom 11:33-36. Teach that which you have complete assurance is true and pray for the Holy Spirit's guidance in the rest. Teach both sides of a contested passage or concept. Let the Holy Spirit lead them into an understanding or to accept that it is still a mystery.

Be Open to the Spirit's Leading

1Co 2:9-14 But, as it is written, "What no eye has seen, nor ear heard, nor the heart of man imagined, what God has prepared for those who love him"-- [10] these things God has revealed to us through the Spirit. For the Spirit searches everything, even the depths of God. [11] For who knows a person's thoughts except the spirit of that person, which is in him? So also no one comprehends the thoughts of God except the Spirit of God. [12] Now we have received not the spirit of the world, but the Spirit who is from God, that we might understand the things freely given us by God. [13] And we impart this in words not taught by human wisdom but taught by the Spirit, interpreting spiritual truths to those who are spiritual. [14] The natural person does not accept the things of the Spirit of God, for they are folly to him, and he is not able to understand them because they are spiritually discerned.

This is the toughest guidance to follow. It is often difficult to know when we are being Spirit led (vs10) or when are we being a "natural person" (vs. 14). Do not assume the Holy Spirit is leading our understanding and everyone who disagrees is wrong. It could be me. This is especially important when feeling an uneasiness about something that has or is about to be shared. The Spirit also leads us in what NOT to teach. The more controversial the topic, the more we need to apply the "lantern test" described earlier and carefully listen for His still small voice - Isa 30:21.

Teach What They Need

1Co 3:1-3 But I, brothers, could not address you as spiritual people, but as people of the flesh, as infants in Christ. [2] I fed you with milk, not solid food, for you were not ready for it. And even now you are not yet ready, [3] for you are still of the flesh. For while there is jealousy and strife among you, are you not of the flesh and behaving only in a human way?

Paul spoke to people where they were spiritually, taking the needed approach for the spread of the gospel - he became all things to all people.

1Co 9:19-22 For though I am free from all, I have made myself a servant to all, that I might win more of them. [20] To the Jews I became as a Jew, in order to win Jews. To those under the law I became as one under the law (though not being myself under the law) that I might win those under the law. [21] To those outside the law I became as one outside the law (not being outside the law of God but under the law of Christ) that I might win those outside the law. [22] To the weak I became weak, that I might win the weak. I have become all things to all people, that by all means I might save some.

We are to teach people based on their age and spiritual maturity maintaining a good balance between theology and application, including both the Old and New Testaments. Extremes in these areas are unhealthy. Some say we are under a new covenant and do not need to study the OT at all. We would be missing a rich history that provides the basis for the NT. The authors of the NT must have believed the OT was important. Including direct or indirect citations, the OT is referenced approximately 800 times in the NT.[9] Jesus clearly supported the validity of the entire OT in Mat 5:17-19.

"The Word of God well understood and religiously obeyed is the shortest route to spiritual perfection. And we must not select a few favorite passages to the exclusion of others. Nothing less than a whole Bible can make a whole Christian." - A. W. Tozer.[10]

We must ensure our teaching emphasis is consistent with the emphasis in Scripture. Concepts mentioned once do not warrant much of our time. An extensive example is "the love of money is a root of all kinds of evils" (1Ti 6:10); Jesus taught more on money than almost any other topic. Throw in greed, covetous, and envy; it is surely near the top.

I have heard many times the contemporary *river of Christianity* described as spiritually a hundred miles wide but only a few inches deep. I read several publications from a group that claims Jesus as their Savior, though some consider them a cult. The author said people are frequently attracted to their in-depth study of the Bible. He suggested the way to respond to them is to have structured comprehensive Bible studies. They are one of the few Christian bodies growing in America today. All Christian churches should offer this ministry.

Jesus has asked me thousands of times, "do you love me," when He asks me to "feed my sheep" (Jhn 21). I take that to mean - encourage, forgive, serve, love, judge not, share, show the way, etc. Many times, I realize I had not. Are you sensitive to those teachable moments? Paul had great concern for the Colossian people ensuring their "hearts may be encouraged, being knit together in love, to reach all the riches of full assurance of understanding and the knowledge of God's mystery, which is Christ" (Col 2:2). We are to "consider how to stir up one another to love and good works" (Heb 10:23-25). Jesus provides a charge to His disciples in Mat 28:19-20; most believe He is speaking to all future Christians as well. His words in vs. 20 are just as important - "teaching them to observe all that I have commanded you."

Avoid Leader Worship

1Co 3:4-9 For when one says, "I follow Paul," and another, "I follow Apollos," are you not being merely human? [5] What then is Apollos? What is Paul? Servants through whom you believed, as the Lord assigned to each. [6] I planted, Apollos watered, but God gave the growth. [7] So neither he who plants nor he who waters is anything, but only God who gives the growth. [8] He who plants and he who waters are one, and each will receive his wages according to his labor. [9] For we are God's fellow workers. You are God's field, God's building.

Chapter 3 discussed the impact of a leader. Teachers are to direct those we disciple to Jesus not ourselves.

We Will Be Judged

1Co 3:10-15 According to the grace of God given to me, like a skilled master builder I laid a foundation, and someone else is building upon it. Let each one take care how he builds upon it. [11] For no one can lay a foundation other than that which is laid, which is Jesus Christ. [12] Now if anyone builds on the foundation with gold, silver, precious stones, wood, hay, straw-- [13] each one's work will become manifest, for the Day will disclose it, because it will be revealed by fire, and the fire will test what sort of work each one has done. [14] If the work that anyone has built on the foundation survives, he will receive a reward. [15] If anyone's work is burned up, he will suffer loss, though he himself will be saved, but only as through fire.

Recall the discussion in chapter 4 regarding the judgment of teachers. We will be held to a higher standard. Of those who have been given the knowledge and gifts to teach, much will be demanded - Luk 12:47-48, Rom 3:12-16.

Be Humble

1Co 3:18-20 Let no one deceive himself. If anyone among you thinks that he is wise in this age, let him become a fool that he may become wise. [19] For the wisdom of this world is folly with God. For it is written, "He catches the wise in their craftiness," [20] and again, "The Lord knows the thoughts of the wise, that they are futile."

Our motives for teaching should be the opposite of those promoting false teaching. We see many passages urging us to avoid pride. It is a very common improper motive. "Whoever humbles himself before God is the greatest in the kingdom of heaven" (Mat 18:3-4, and Luk 9:48).

> Phl 2:3 <u>Do nothing from selfish ambition or conceit,</u> but in humility count others more significant than yourselves.

We should approach teaching with humility as these examples from Scripture did. Abraham said, "I who am but dust and ashes" (Gen 18:27). Isaiah wrote, "Woe is me! For I am lost; for I am a man of unclean lips, and I dwell in the midst of a people of unclean lips" (Isa 6:5). Peter said to Jesus after a miracle, "Depart from me, for I am a sinful man, O Lord" (Luk 5:8). The Lord has promised He will bless our humility.

> 2Co 12:9 But he said to me, "My grace is sufficient for you, <u>for my power is made perfect in weakness.</u>" Therefore I will boast all the more gladly of my weaknesses, so that the power of Christ may rest upon me.

This is obvious, but why do we see so much boasting and haughtiness at all levels of instruction? We must bathe our teaching endeavors in prayer. <u>Always</u> pray that the Spirit leads in your preparation and delivery - Mat 7:7, Luk 11:9-10, Act 4:31, Pro 15:28. Ask others to pray for your teaching as Paul did.

> Eph 6:18-19 praying at all times in the Spirit, with all prayer and supplication. To that end keep alert with all perseverance, making supplication for all the saints, [19] <u>and also for me, that words may be given to me in opening my mouth boldly to proclaim the mystery of the gospel,</u>

Counseling is Another Form of Teaching

Counseling others on their behavior is as volatile as nitro-glycerin. A sure cue to offer help is a request for assistance. When you feel the need to initiate correction, talk to your pastor. Pray together and seek an approach and content that will likely bring benefit. This is another area we have earned our hypocrite label. Pastors feeling led to correct should seek wisdom also, consider asking a trusted confidant to pray with them about it and provide feedback on the same areas of approach, content, and likelihood of benefit. Many cliché sayings come and go but "two heads are better than one" has lasted for a very good reason; it is supported by Scripture - Mat 18:16.

Again, the most important decision in sharing biblical truth is to ensure we are NOT adding or taking away from the message of Scripture.

> Pro 30:5-6 <u>Every word of God proves true</u>; he is a shield to those who take refuge in him. [6] <u>Do not add to his words,</u> <u>lest he rebuke you and you be found a liar.</u>

9. CLERGY INTERVIEWS

> "One of the best ways to persuade is with
> your ears - by listening to them." -
> US Secretary of State Dean Rusk

Well aware of my literary skills, our pastor suggested I read a book on writing to help this engineer write in a foreign language, English. The book, *On Writing Well*, by William Zinsser, provided some excellent guidance. Please do not think less of his book based on the quality of this one; it is tough to teach this old dog new tricks. One of his best suggestions was to consult the experts on our writing topic. I set out to interview at least one leader (pastor, priest, minister, bishop, etc.) from each faith group listed in Appendix A. The table below is a list of the denominations represented by the pastors who agreed to an interview. Where possible I approached local churches both for accessibility and to rekindle ministerial associations in the area.

Anglican	Mennonite
Calvary Chapel	Nazarene
Church of Christ	Non-denominational
Church of God	Presbyterian Church in America - PCA
Evangelical Lutheran Church in America - ELCA	Presbyterian Church USA - PCUSA
Evangelical Presbyterian Church - EPC	Roman Catholic Church
Greek Orthodox	Seventh Day Adventist - SDA
Independent Baptist	Southern Baptist Convention
Jehovah's Witness - JW	United Methodist - UMC
Latter Day Saints - LDS	

Representatives from the Friends (Quaker) as well as the Brethren and Pietist Churches declined interviews. There were limited options for these groups in our area.

Recruiting clergy for interviews was not easy; most church pastors are extremely busy. They probably thought I was coming to argue and challenge their beliefs. Imagine that! Cold calls were a great challenge, similar to approaching strangers with the gospel. Several friends arranged interviews with the leaders of their church. There were several who declined to meet even for an hour. Did the topic prompt their reluctance? Perhaps they did not see a relevant work coming from a layman. I have spoken with these and many other pastors regarding the topics of this book, their input influenced every chapter.

Objectives

My primary objective was to listen. I heard a Palestinian man speak on Moody radio about a ministry he started after gaining insights and compassion for the people of Israel just by listening to their viewpoint. His project guides people to listen to their enemies with empathy to better understand their plight.

Most would say other Christian organizations are not our enemies. I would whole-heartedly agree; but we treat them that way sometimes.

> "An enemy is one whose story we have not heard." – Gene Knudsen Hoffman, compassionate listening pioneer and international peacemaker.

> "Compassionate Listening is a process rather than a product. It is healing precisely because it does not pretend to have the answers. Rather, it engages the participants in processes that have each side seeing the humanity of the other, even when they disagree." - *Rabbi David Zaslow, Ashland Oregon*

If this compassionate listening can address and mitigate the hatred between the people of Israel and Palestine, then it should really work well for the theological rift between Christian denominations.

I sought to understand the specific differences between various groups. I wanted to get a perspective from a representative of the denomination, not just read their literature and assaults from critics. The following are the general areas examined.

- how they accomplish biblical mandates for the body of Christ
- views on Scripture
- views on denominationalism and ecumenism
- what separates the denominations within a faith group (Baptist, Methodist, Catholic, etc.)
- what they see as distinctive about their denomination, are they essentials or preferences
- understand the basis for some of their differences

These interviews represent a glimpse of the variations in the Christian Faith. That was especially apparent for those groups with many splintered bodies. Most of the clergy interviewed seemed to be putting their best ecumenical foot forward. Their unique tenets usually did not come up unless I brought them up. It was interesting that some quoted from other than their usual Bible translation to support a contested doctrine of their group. These interviews provided great insight into the hearts and minds of these bodies. They also gave a perspective for how people have arrived at their position on various beliefs and expressions in their relationship with God.

Findings

The interview documentation was limited to practices with value for growing back together. Uniquely good practices were mentioned with the group name to give credit where due. The denominations associated with the other end of the spectrum are not included. Comments on those practices can speak to those who need to hear them.

Pastors responded to 19 standard questions, including a few added after the initial interviews. The following is a summary of the results.

1. Do denominations harm people coming to faith?

Everyone said yes. They provided the following basis for their response:

- The differences and debating are confusing to those in and out of the church.
- There is a lot of robbing saints from each other.
- I do not see the value in open arguing; in many cases we would be better off taking the middle ground.
- Our behavior fuels the media's criticism of Christianity.
- It is sad so much is made of the less significant areas of disagreement when there is good agreement on most essentials.
- Battles and bad press cause people to become dechurched.
- Discord in teaching causes confusion and impacts credibility.
- It is not clear who the true Christians are; Jhn 13:35 says they will know we are Christians by our love for each other. That love often is not apparent.
- There is only one faith, and one baptism (Eph 4:5). I noticed most groups claimed they had the correct one faith and one baptism. If their faith is in Jesus and the baptism is into Him through the Holy Spirit they could all be correct.
- Several participants saw value in the variety of expressions so people can find a good church fit.
- The decline of Christianity in America and squabbling over saints has made it a bigger problem now than in the 20th century. The theological compromise of many denominations has weakened the perception of Christians in the eyes of the lost.

2. How did you come to be in your denomination?

The table below summarized the paths leading to their affiliation. Interesting to note two were not a Christian until they were an adult. The total is greater than the number of interviews as two interviews involved two people.

Born into it	11
Family changed to it	1
Moved due to outreach from others	1
Changed to church of spouse	3
Personal search	5

The next four questions were to be answered with how their denomination meets these four biblical mandates in a manner that is unique to their faith group. Everyone wanted to share all the good things their church was doing; there were many. Replies were included if they were given by no more than two responders and are beneficial to unity. Some ministries included as unique are probably more widely practiced than I am aware of; they are still good ideas.

3. Great Commandment 1 - "You shall love the Lord your God with all your heart, soul, mind and strength" (Mar 12:30).

There were many great practices shared; their examples were not unique to two or fewer groups.

4. Great Commandment 2 - "You shall love your neighbor as yourself" (Mar 12:31).

All respondents defined their neighbor as anyone. The ELCA pastor said it was the closest person who needed his help. The PCA pastor provided a great reminder, "My spouse is my first neighbor." The Nazarene pastor said their congregation knocks on doors in needy neighborhoods asking for prayer requests and other needs.

5. Great Commission - repentance and forgiveness of sins should be proclaimed in his name to all nations (Luk 24:47).

They described many great ministries both home and abroad. There was only one reported that is unique to me. This UMC church baptizes people into the body of Christ, their joining the UMC and local church are separate optional decisions. That sounds like what we read in the Bible. Several other bodies recognize a baptism performed in another Christian body.

6. Religion that is pure and undefiled before God, the Father, is this: to visit orphans and widows in their affliction, and to keep oneself unstained from the world (Jas 1:27).

Again, many described amazing ministries, only a couple of them were unique. The PCUSA has a Self Development of People program that helps people start small businesses in the USA and abroad. I have not heard of this in America. The Mennonite people have principles of separation from worldly living that bring them closer to God.

I was amazed at the similarity in how the denominations accomplished these four biblical mandates for the primary responsibilities of being a follower of Jesus.

7. Do you have a denominational document of theology?

The diversity of these documents was astounding. They ranged from none to several books. One stated their only book was the Bible; their association has a brief statement of beliefs held in common among most Christian churches, similar to Appendix H. Another association said that each individual congregation adopts its own document (a few pages) using the association document as a guide. As with other denominational documents, the longer they have been around, the larger their document.

8. Do you participate in a cross denominational meeting of pastors on a regular basis (Yes = at least quarterly)? Many of those who said "No" felt there were no suitable options available.

| Yes - 3 | Occasionally - 3 | No - 13 |

9. Would you be willing to participate in one if it were available?

| Yes - 15 | No - 3 | Unsure - 1 |

10. Is there any recognized Christian denomination you would not meet with? (added later)

| Yes - 4 | No - 7 | Not asked - 8 |

Those responding yes would not participate with denominations that have adopted policies that clearly defy Scripture.

11. Is the Rose Publishing Denominations Comparison accurate for your denomination?

Appendix G provides a sample summary from this brochure. The response to this question was surprisingly brief for most clergy. Four identified no exceptions at all. This is likely due to several factors. First, the document is extremely well done. Second, most responders wanted to reply in the spirit of ecumenism, not picking at nits. Third, the level of detail in the summary did not address recent policy changes adopted in some denominations (both added and dropped). I only interviewed one denomination from each group, with some containing over 40 denominations.

Many of the responses were either personal or editorial. The following are the exceptions provided.

Denomination	Topic	Exception to information in the publication
Methodist	Scripture	Scripture is infallible but tempered by reason & experience.
Anglican	Scripture	Add "and the Holy Spirit" after "but must be interpreted by tradition and reason." Anglicans would not say Solo Scriptura; things must be viewed through a lens of tradition. "We have always done it this way."
Lutheran	Sacraments	ELCA does not see Baptism as required for salvation. There are times this cannot happen. God decides, it is not for us to judge.
Mennonite	Scripture	Original writings were inerrant; they consider the KJV to be fairly accurate. Our church places emphasis on doctrine as well as obedience, how else do you know what to follow?
Mennonite	Salvation	Salvation is the product of faith and repentance.
PCA	The Church	Add "and baptized children" after "the body of Christ"

JW and LDS are not presented in the Rose Publishing Denominations Comparison. They are included in the Christianity, Cults and Religions brochure, which uses similar categories to summarize beliefs. The following were their exceptions.

Denomination	Topic	Exception to information in the publication
LDS	Founder	* Jesus was original founder * Joseph Smith was the prophet of restoration
LDS	Writings	Bible is not seen as less reliable than the LDS writings, as far as the Bible is translated correctly.
LDS	Jesus	* We do not teach that Jesus was the product of a sexual union. * We do not teach that Jesus was married. * The atonement from Jesus satisfies the requirements for all sin.
LDS	Salvation	Do not have to be LDS for eternal life; we do baptism for the dead.
LDS	death	* Everyone has a chance to accept the gospel either in life or in death. * Depending on the circumstances, murderers can serve their civil penalties, repent, and be forgiven and gain eternal life, to the extent possible as determined by the Savior Jesus Christ.
LDS	Other Beliefs	* The temple endowment is sacred more than secret although only LDS members may attend. * Not all caffeine drinks are prohibited, only tea and coffee.
JW	Death	All do not believe the 144,000 spirits that will live in heaven has been reached.

12. What are the main differences that separate your denomination from others in your faith group (Appendix A)? Please provide the biblical basis for your positions.

There were surprisingly few doctrinal differences given. Their responses to this question fell into these general reasons.

- none - if someone were to take the initiative, several denominations could be brought together
- rejection of the authority or inerrancy of Scripture
- ordination of women
- marriage and ordination of homosexuals
- pride - if we all remained faithful, available, and teachable; we could come back together
- socio economic - some denominations primarily contain the same economic status
- race and ethnicity - the members of some denominations are predominately the same race or ethnicity, and appear to like it that way
- funding of missionaries - some want to choose specific teams to support rather than an agency

It was surprising there were so few exceptions taken to the Rose Publishing Summary of Beliefs, while there are many obstacles to denominations in the same faith group coming back together. In many groups there were bodies that have adopted doctrine that differ from what others in the same group consider consistent with Scripture.

13. Is your denomination growing in America? To what do you attribute that?

Growing - 7	Stable - 1	Not Growing - 8	Don't know - 2

Several said they are growing worldwide, and several said they are growing in America in number of members, but maybe not in percent of population. The Pew Research Center data presented in chapter 1 showed a plateau or decline in every Christian category in America. We are losing out to *Unaffiliated*; that is almost as bad as losing an unopposed election. The non-Christian percentage of the population is growing. Some of this is the result of non-Christian immigrants. That should be a blessing; the Lord is bringing the lost to us. However, some immigrants come with a strong Christian faith. What is all this telling us? The reasons the pastors gave for their growth and decline were quite diverse.

Growing

• new approach to church
• diverse ministries to the community
• focus on Christian living
• church planting

Declining

• people drifting away from church - no further cause was offered
• death of members exceeds new members
• evolving cultural expectations
• Milllennials not attracted to denominations
• Milllennials reject some biblical teaching (rules)
• weak evangelism
• decline in past sources - large families, and believing immigrants
• controversies over the beliefs that are moving away from Scripture
• our denomination is more interested in consensus building through politics and religious experience than following and sharing Jesus

All twenty-one of the people interviewed said that denominations harm the spread of the gospel. Only one mentioned denominations as a cause for the decline of Christianity in America, and that one limited it to Milllennials. We seem to be ambivalent to the impact of our divisions.

Reducing the dysfunction between denominations could really help start revival in America and across the world.

14. Why do you think newer denominations grow so fast?

This question was a real window to core perceptions on how to do church. The answers are compiled below. The positive responses are obvious, but not so easy to accomplish. The negatives provide sound wisdom for new bodies and perhaps an attitude of sour grapes. Two churches were formed in the last 10 years. The cautions in the negative perspectives below were not a problem in either church. They are both faithful to Scripture, had many vital ministries to their communities, and are both growing, one quite rapidly.

Positive responses

• God is doing things that are not valued by existing churches
• People identify with current issues, more relative to culture, "check out the new movement."
• People are naturally attracted to new ideas.
• Most new movements have innovative leaders - great communicators, some have written books.
• Barna surveys indicate people are attracted to positive leadership.
• Most have open minded and progressive leadership.
• They have comprehensive children's programs.
• Established denominations rely a lot on generational replacement while new bodies have a stronger emphasis on evangelism. Many of the newer bodies have a strong focus on their relationship with the Holy Spirit's leading. People find that focus appealing.
• Many new movements are charismatic, young folks are attracted to this.
• Some new groups are more tolerant in their beliefs about the guidance in Scripture.

Negative responses

- People today are attracted to new things rather than real value.
- Some are more tolerant of liberal ideas, and much less accountable for behavior.
- Natural vitality of a new movement carries them for a while, then the predictable organizational dynamics come into play and the growth frequently stagnates.
- Churches follow a natural life cycle: vitality, complacency, and then decline.
- As most of them advertise, people are attracted to churches that claim to be non-denominational, Spirit-filled, non-traditional, and accentuate self-help over doctrine.
- Most are feel good churches; ministry expectations of their membership are limited.
- Willow Creek discovered in a recent congregational survey that they were not making disciples. When the going gets tough these shallow Christians will all fall away.
- They have lightened the cross inappropriately making it easier for the flesh.

Interesting to note the Hillsong Church was mentioned both as an example of a good new movement and a bad one. Like most denominations, they are seeking the proper response to the world's evolving standards for human sexuality while being faithful to God's standards. History has proven repeatedly His guidance protects us from ourselves.

Again, only one mentioned non-denominational, and that in the vein of weak doctrine. Ecumenism is not the only answer. It should be seriously considered. Can we take the elements of the new churches that help them to succeed and apply them in our established churches without the focus on preferential denominational differences? I looked into the claim of failings at Willow Creek (WCA), and it was accurate. The rest of the story is they did the following to address the weaknesses in their association.

- funded a survey to be conducted at all WCA churches world wide
- published the survey results in a report titled "Reveal" and set up a website for others to benefit from their experience
- developed a process for church members to establish their own spiritual development plan

We should be addressing weaknesses at all of our churches.

15. What are your beliefs about the inspiration and inerrancy of Scripture?

All interviewed agreed Scripture is inspired. The inerrant camp was quite diverse.

12 - inerrant, see note	2 - inerrant but must be interpreted	5 - NOT inerrant

Note - two said inerrant for teaching but not history, three said inerrant for essentials but translation errors exist.

Without getting specific, there was a strong correlation between declining denominations and their position that the Bible is errant.

16. What translation of the Bible do you use?

Seven mentioned using multiple translations, including some published specifically for their denomination.

KJV - 6	NIV - 3	NASB - 2	NLT - 2
NRSV - 2	Greek -1	ESV - 1	Not Asked - 2

17. Do you have an opinion on Act 8:37 being in the Bible? It is not in some reputable translations.

This question assessed their position on the debates about the best manuscripts to use for translations. The majority were not aware of the controversy. One added that he avoids contested verses.

- 3 - Not in earliest manuscripts
- 10 - It's in my translation
- 2 - Not in my translation
- 4 - Yes - include and note as contested verse

18. Why do you believe ecumenical movements have failed to unite the body theologically?

The following are their responses.

- sin - pride, greed, desire to control
- They have different emphasis based on their backing. For example, the OT writers give us two different perspectives. Prophets were not generous to Kings; their emphasis was the responsibility of God's people. While clergy, usually employed by the King, were more favorable to the hierarchy and sovereignty of God. In addition, some socio-economic aspects influence theology.
- Each organization has a different focus and priority. Resolving theological differences is not a priority for most.
- Some people consider everything in Scripture to have the same importance.
- Pride, urge to be right. There is some truth and good in all denominational traditions.
- Stubbornness, refusal to deal with pride and arrogance. They do not realize they do not understand what Scripture is saying, an example of Jesus' statement in Luk 8:18.
- pride and lack of purity in purpose
- There has been some success in the past, like Full Communion Agreements. There is too much focus on differences instead of celebrating agreements. Many have a motive to justify existence, and fear of being wrong.

- Human nature, people hold strongly to their opinions.
- They were not inclusive enough, appealing mostly to main line churches. Some denominations chose not to participate and others did not feel welcome. They failed to avoid the pitfall of letting social positions divide us.
- No one can agree on the fullness of this one truth.
- Man created the differences but man will not fix them, they must be revealed from God.
- I am not familiar with specifics of the ecumenical movements.
- Competition for believers causes some pastors to avoid participation in joint activities within their own denomination for fear of losing sheep.

The most common response was pride, which was also the primary motive for false teaching in chapter 7.

19. Are there any other distinctions you would like to share about your denomination?

- The ELCA has Full Communion Agreements with many Protestant bodies. They are working toward one with the Roman Catholic Church. The Evangelical Presbyterian Church, the Church of God, and the independent church provide Communion celebration to any believing Christian. Open communion is not a unique concept; several other pastors mentioned shared communion with specific limitations. A few of the bodies interviewed limit communion to members only.
- The independent church was ranked the seventh fastest growing congregation in America by Outreach magazine.
- The Chattanooga District of the Nazarene Church initiated a Good Friday joint service and invited others in the Holiness Faith Group. They also have done joint publishing with some of those denominations.
- The ELCA has a practice of designating contested non-essentials as Adiaphora. It is a Greek word used by stoics to refer to that which was neither moral nor immoral. They feel it helps reduce debates over non-essentials. The Anglicans

145

use a phrase with a similar purpose - Via Media, a Latin phrase meaning the middle road. They compromise or agree to disagree and move on to more important matters.

- The Catholic Church families frequently assign godparents to their children. In this day of parenting challenges and deficiencies, religious divergences and abandonment, the assignment of mature, functional godparents for a child of faith is a great idea.
- The Anglican Priest said, "We don't need all these denominations, everybody can be an Anglican." That is a great attitude on unity. All respondents would likely have said the same thing about theirs.
- By following the Levitical dietary guidance, SDA followers live about 10 years longer than the average of the population.
- The Mennonite people care for their elderly in the homes of their family. They do not use conventional insurance; they are self-insured as a group. The State of Tennessee accepted this practice to meet the requirement for automobile liability insurance.

Fourteen of the 19 interviewed provided literature, loaned books, or invited me to church activities to further illustrate their ministry and present their beliefs. There was a general correlation - the more they felt challenged in their beliefs, the more information they gave me.

Each interview also involved from three to 22 questions specific to their denomination. The questions were usually about areas of doctrinal contention with other groups. The longer they have been around, the more controversy there is. Most provided scriptural basis for their positions, others did not. They rarely discussed passages that favored other positions. The answers to the specific questions are not included; most did not provide any information that is not available in a detailed treatment of their body.

I asked most for their position on abortion. The answers ranged from strongly opposed, to allowed for certain circumstances, to tolerated, and one had no position. The Nazarene pastor added a great follow-up statement - "We must make way for grace and redemption. Too many times we are known for what we are against and not what we promote."

Conclusions

The intent and presentation of these interviews was to foster understanding, seek areas of agreement, and not to offend anyone. The interviews gave great insight into the diverse practice of Christianity. Several spoke off the record on sensitive issues; their request was honored. I learned a great deal about their love for the Lord, their history and the basis of their beliefs. Many of our differences are style, approach, perspective and emphasis. Yet, some strongly defended what may be biblically incorrect or sometimes harmful concepts. Several defended doctrines and practices with tradition and denominational literature instead of the Bible.

Over the centuries, there have been innumerable theological debates yielding little progress. If change is to come, it will likely have to come from within each body. That change can occur intentionally or by the slow process of time. The latter has yielded progress with several denominations shedding some extreme positions. This slow process is inadequate, as new deviations form faster than we outlive the ones we have. The following quote is not from a theologian, but it profoundly fits our situation. "Surely there comes a time when counting the cost and paying the price aren't things to think about any more. All that matters is value - the ultimate value of what one does" - James Hilton, novelist.

Some may not agree that denominationalism is a significant obstacle to the spread of the gospel and people finding true faith in Jesus. Has the diversity of beliefs benefited the kingdom of God? Have the splits brought about resolution of the problems with the parent denomination or church? In some cases changes occurred, in most they did not. We need to commit to the essentials of the Christian faith and turn away from the urge to do our own thing.

10. EXAMINATION OF CONTESTED DOCTRINE

And he said to me, "It is done! I am the Alpha and the Omega, the beginning and the end. To the thirsty I will give from the spring of the water of life without payment. The one who conquers will have this heritage, and I will be his God and he will be my son. But as for the cowardly, the faithless, the detestable, as for murderers, the sexually immoral, sorcerers, idolaters, and all liars, their portion will be in the lake that burns with fire and sulfur, which is the second death." Rev 21:6-8

The Arminianism verses Calvinism (A&C) debate has raged for centuries from seminaries to Christian Ed classrooms. There is compelling Scripture supporting both sides of these five contested points regarding our salvation. I am certainly not going to solve it. My intent is to provide an example of a thorough and objective review of these contested doctrines. The result of an evaluation should be a position on that doctrine that is as Scripture based as possible and a perspective on its importance for the time and resources used to ponder, teach or question that doctrine.

This debate is a product of the Protestant Reformation beginning in the 16th century. The Calvinist perspective emerged in the Belgic Confession dating back to 1561 or before. Jacobus Arminius was a Calvinist, even defending this doctrine in debates. His research into these issues resulted in changing his beliefs; his new teaching drew a group of followers. In 1610, one year after his death, they published five articles regarding salvation known as the *Remonstrance* (an expression of opposition). The summarized version below lists them in order to match the acrostic *TULIP* sequence for the five points of Calvinism. The {} contain the original order.

1) {3} On their own, humans can do nothing good. Jhn 15:5

2) {1} Before the foundation of the world, God chose to save everyone who shall believe on this His Son Jesus. Jhn 3:36

3) {2} Jesus died for everyone, but His death only redeems believers. 1Jo 2:2

4) {4} People can choose to reject God's attempts to save them. Act 7:51

5) {5} Scripture doesn't clearly state whether Christians can forfeit their salvation. 1Ti 1:19; Heb 3:6, 14, 11:13; and 2Pe 1:10

Responding to this teaching, the Calvinists assembled the Synod of Dort and published a revised version of the Belgic Confession known as The Canons of Dort containing a response to each of the five Arminian articles; many refer to them as the Five points of Calvinism (summarized below).

1) Human beings are by nature spiritually dead. Mar 7:21-23, Rom 6:20, 1Co 2:14, and Eph. 2:12-16. No one naturally desires to seek Christ. Rom 3:10-12 and Eph 2:1-3

2) If someone trusts Christ, it is because God chose to regenerate that person. God's choice is unconditional; it is not based on any human decision. Jhn 6:44, Rom 9:10-16, 21, and Eph 1:4-8

3) Christ's death atoned only for those who would believe in him. Isa 53:12, Mat 25:32-33, 26:28, Jhn 17:9, Act 20:28, and Eph 5:25-27

4) When God regenerates someone, that person will neither resist nor reject God's grace. Jhn 6:37, 44, Act 13:48, Rom 9:16, and Phl 2:12-13

5) Every Christian will persevere in faith until the end. Jhn 6:47, 10:27-28; Rom 8:1, 29-39, 1Co 10:13, and Phl 1:6

The pastors supporting the Remonstrant position were invited to the Synod of Dort. They protested the lack of accurate representation of the voting members of the Dutch Reformed Church that supported the Arminian position. Consequently, they withdrew from the assembly. They were ejected from the Synod of Dort and later directed to abstain from ministerial activities such as preaching, exhorting, administering the sacraments, and visiting the sick. It is clear these folks did not jointly work to achieve a consensus biblical interpretation, and the battle lines were drawn.

Pure logic gives the following options for each side of each point.

- completely correct in all circumstances
- conditionally correct - supported by Scripture under specific conditions or circumstances
- not true at all

Georg Wilhelm Friedrich Hegel would support the second option - "Truth is found neither in the thesis nor the antithesis, but in an <u>emergent synthesis which reconciles the two</u>."[1] Hundreds of books have been written promoting and challenging the concepts of A&C. There have been thousands of blogs and articles written on this dispute.

It appears elements of both perspectives are open to misinterpretation or perhaps wrong. How can we ask others to deal with the specks of wood in their eye if we have some in ours - Mat 7:3? It is an example of doctrine that is causing the problems mentioned earlier - it is divisive, confusing to believers as well as non-believers. We should divert the resources from this battle to help spread the gospel. My goal is to follow 1Ti 4:16 thoroughly testing them against Scripture.

There is a continuum of beliefs from the Free Will (also called open theism) to the hyper-Calvinist beliefs on the other extreme. The points on the continuum are attempts to describe God's complexity and autonomy with human intellect. Many identify with how many points of Calvinism they support. It is unlikely that there is one discrete point on the continuum that is completely correct. It is more likely that God's eternal judgment of humanity is too complex for us to comprehend completely.

The preceding chapters have built a case to test our long contested doctrine and belief statements against **all** of Scripture. Scripture must be the overarching basis for conclusions. The passages cited to support the A&C positions are not as conclusive as some would contend. Both sides claim the Scripture passages that support their beliefs outnumber those that do not. The other side would argue the opposite. When we are defending our theology, we read with a bias that can blind us to the full council of Scripture. I hope to learn in heaven why God did not make it clear when He inspired the writers of His Word. Perhaps it was to get us to read it carefully and repeatedly; it has done that for me.

Point 1 - Total Depravity vs. Free Will or Human Ability

The Scriptures enlisted to support the Calvinist point make a conclusive case that in our original state we are totally depraved. Based on that condition they conclude, "Therefore God must predestine."

> 1Co 2:14 The natural person does not accept the things of the Spirit of God, for they are folly to him, and he is not able to understand them because they are spiritually discerned.

The full Arminian statement agrees on the depraved condition of humans. To support the remainder of the Arminian first point, they reference Jhn 15:5, which states we must be born again and Spirit led to affect anything truly good. However, they disagree on man's ability to respond. This is the key element for both perspectives going forward into the other four points. The role of man's choice, or response to God, will be examined with the other four points.

Point 2 - Unconditional Election vs. Conditional Election

The doctrine of election is a concept usually associated with reformed denominations. Baptist groups also debate this doctrine. The American, National, and Free Will Baptists generally support Arminian concepts, while a majority of the Southern Baptists favors Calvinist election. The following is the opening to an AP article in June 2013.

> "Is God's saving grace free to anyone who accepts Jesus, or did God predestine certain people for heaven and hell before the beginning of the world? That's a 500-year-old question, but it is creating real divisions in 2013 in the nation's largest Protestant denomination."

A Barna Study, published in November 2010, determined that 31% of Protestant pastors identified their church as Calvinist or Reformed.[2] Based on the self-reported membership in the 2011 *Yearbook of American & Canadian Churches*[3] the percentage would drop below 20% if Catholic and Orthodox Christians were included. The percentage of the 3+ billion Christians worldwide that are not reformed is likely even larger. We all know that numbers do not make a theology true, but it should give one pause to ponder.

This Calvinist tenet states that God chose who would be saved "without any consideration of merit within the individual." The Calvinist Scripture references support the fact that God could choose whom He wanted to save without consideration of their decisions, but not much proof that is what He always does. Consistent with their perspective on our depravity, the Arminians state that God elects those who believed "through Christ, those who, through the grace of the Holy Ghost, shall believe on this His son Jesus." They provide no insight into why God chooses those who would receive "the grace of the Holy Ghost in order to believe."

Although not stated in the second point of Calvinism, they both agree that God did the election of those to salvation "before the foundation of the world" - Jhn 17:24, Eph 1:4, 2Th 2:13, 2Ti 1:9, 1Pe 1:20, and Rev 13:8. However, there are several passages that use the present tense for God choosing believers, - Mat 11:27, Luk 10:22, Jhn 6:35-37, Eph 1:13, Num 16:5,7, Deu 14:24. There are even a few that use future tenses - Jhn 17:20-21, 1Ti 1:16 and 2Ti 2:25.

All of the Scripture references linked to election are true, so how do we reconcile the present and future actions? The passages written about eternity past are from God's perspective. God can see every occurrence from eternity past to eternity future - Isa 46:9-10. The passages dealing with the future are from man's perspective. "We all believe in predestination," said the clay to the Potter; "we just can't agree on the basis of His election."

The Calvinism second point states "Nor does God look into the future to see who would pick Him". This does not seem to be consistent with all Scripture, which reveals that He does consider foreknowledge - Rom 8:29, and 11:2-6, and 1Pe 1:1-2.

Some say they believe in single sided election - God elects those who go to Heaven, and passes over the rest allowing them to die in their sins and go to hell. They refer to the first as His declarative will and the latter His permissive will. This concept appears to avoid the issue of God condemning His creations to Hell. His grace saves some and He allows the others the destiny they have earned. It is similar to an effort to save as many starving and threatened refugees as possible. That is a good thing; otherwise, they would all have perished. The analogy breaks down at that point. God has the power to save all. We all deserve to go to hell. There must be a difference in these two groups or God would appear to defy His nature described in the rest of Scripture. What is God's motive in saving some and condemning others? The following passage provides two reasons.

Eph 1:5-6 In love [5] he predestined us for adoption to himself as sons through Jesus Christ, <u>according to the</u>

> purpose of his will, [6] to the praise of his glorious grace, with which he has blessed us in the Beloved.

God brilliantly displays his glory in His saving of the elect. Eph 1:12 also mentions our salvation "might be to the praise of his glory." However, that does not provide any insight into why He chooses. He created the wicked knowing they would be condemned - Pro 16:4. There is no mention of praising His glory in the condemnation side of election. Several reputable translations include "good pleasure" related to His purpose set forth in Christ in Eph 1:9. Some would say "for His good pleasure" refers to His being pleased to do what is just and right. Sounds good, but why is it just and right for God to condemn some who deserve it and not others "for all have sinned and fall short of the glory of God" (Rom 3:23)?

Scripture describes some things that bring pleasure to God. In Jhn 8:29 Jesus always does the things that please God. Enoch was "one who pleased God"; The Lord took him up without experiencing death - Heb 11:5. Heb 13:6 instructs us to "share with others, for with such sacrifices God is pleased." In addition, 1Th 4:1 reminds us "that as you received from us how you ought to walk and to please God." These passages show God is pleased with our loving obedience. Saving the elect provides God good pleasure.

> Luk 12:32 "Fear not, little flock, for it is your Father's good pleasure to give you the kingdom.

Does it make sense that God, described in the following passages, would elect people to go to everlasting death for His glory or pleasure "without any consideration of merit."

- His Grace - Psa 84:11, Eph 1:7, Jas 4:5-6
- Merciful - Psa 86:15
- Justice - Psa 103:6, Pro 16:11, Isa 45:21
- Equity - Psa 98:9, 99:4, Isa 11:4
- Impartial - Job 34:18-19; Mat 5:45; Act 10:34-35, 15:9; Rom 2:9,11, 10:11-13; Col 3:25; 1Pe 1:17; Jas 3:17

- Loving - Psa 108:4, Hos 11:4, Jhn 3:16, Eph 2:4-5
- Forbearance - Psa 103:8; Act 17:30; Rom 2:5, 3:35, 10:21
- Long suffering - Isa 48:9, Eze 20:17, 2Pe 3:9
- Compassion - Isa, 55:7, Lam 3:22, Hos 11:8, Joel 2:13, Mic 7:19
- Forgiving - Psa 103:3; Isa 43:25, 44:22; Jer 3:12, Mat 6:14; 1Jo 1:9

Why would God choose some over others without cause? We all deserve condemnation is not the full answer. Many would assert it is His grace, which is true; but grace alone does not explain the basis for His decision. My search of the Bible did not find any reference to God having a capricious element to His being. How could He? He is flawless love; He exhibits perfect mercy and grace. His choosing those to be condemned based on the purpose and good pleasure of His will must always be consistent with His unchanging nature described in Scripture - Jas 1:17.

There are many beliefs about salvation, some even claiming they chose God. Scripture is crystal clear; God does the choosing or electing.

> Col 1:26-27 the mystery hidden for ages and generations but now revealed to his saints. [27] To them God chose to make known how great among the Gentiles are the riches of the glory of this mystery, which is Christ in you, the hope of glory.

These passages also state God does the choosing - Gen 18:19; Exo 33:19; Deu 7:6-7, 10:15; 1Ch 16:13; Neh 9:7-8; Psa 3:8, 33:12, 65:4, 86:13, 89:3,20,24, 106:5; Jer 1:4-5; Hag 2:23; Mat 12:18, 22:14, 24:31; Mar 13:20; Jhn 5:21, 10:25-30, 15:16,19, 17:9; Act 2:39, 10:41, 13:17,48; Rom 8:29-30,33, 9:6-26, 11:5, 7; 2Co 5:18-20; Eph 1:4-5,16-19, 4:1; Col 3:12; 1Th 1:4, 2:12; 2Th 2:13; 2 Ti 1:8-9; Tit 1:1; Heb 3:1; Jas 1:18, 2:5; 1Pe 1:3, 2:8-9, 5:10; 2Pe 1:10; and Rev 13:8.

However, none of these passages state that God decided who would go to heaven or everlasting death "without any

155

consideration of merit within the individual." Some, however, do mention the basis for His decision. We are saved by faith. As subtle as the mystery of the Messiah is in the OT, claiming salvation through His provision in the NT is very simple - believe. Believing is clearly NOT a work - Eph 2:8-9. Believe, or a synonym, is used over 100 times in the NT as a condition for salvation.

It is also clear where our faith comes from. God puts the knowledge in our hearts through His Holy Spirit - Act 16:14, Gal 1:15-16, Tit 3:5, and Eph 2:8. The disciples understood this; they asked God to increase their faith - Luk 8:8, and 17:5. The following passages are examples of God's revelation to us. Again, we do not see the basis for His choice - Mat 11:27 and Gal 1:15-16.

> Jhn 6:63, 65 It is the Spirit who gives life; the flesh is no help at all. The words that I have spoken to you are spirit and life...[65] And he said, "This is why I told you that <u>no one can come to me unless it is granted him by the Father</u>."

How does He give us this saving faith? Numerous passages state our belief came from experiential influences.

> Jhn 4:39 Many Samaritans from that town <u>believed in him because of</u> the woman's testimony,...

The first miracle Jesus performed in Cana, recorded in Jhn 2:11, led the disciples to believe. Jesus told the disciples he let Lazarus die so they would believe - Jhn 11:15. The miracle of Lazarus led many Jews to believe - Jhn 12:11 and 18. Jesus and his disciples did many miracles with a stated purpose that people would see and believe - Mat 11:4; Jhn 2:11, 3:2, 4:53, 6:14, 7:31 10:25, 38, 11:42, 20:29-31; and Act 8:6, 9:35, 42, 13:12. There are numerous passages giving other experiential reasons people came to believe: hearing Jesus teach - Jhn 5:25, 13:19, 14:11, 14:29, 16:30, and 20:31; listen, understand, and accept - Pro 8:33-35; Mar 4:16; Luk 8:15;

Jhn 5:24, 6:40, 6:45, 17:8; Act 17:11-12; Rom 10:17; Gal 3:2-5; 1Th 2:13; and Rev 22:17; and the testimony of others - Jhn 4:39. It appears we have a role to listen and accept. Act 26:17-18 describes how God used Paul to open the eyes of Jews and Gentiles; his writing is still doing that today. Salvation is the most important objective of humanity. Why would Scripture give so many other reasons to believe if the real reason is unconditional election?

Humans do not always respond to this allocation of faith. Why was Jesus amazed at the faith of the centurion - Mat 8:10? Conversely, in Nazareth "He marveled because of their unbelief" (Mar 6:6). Why did Jesus reward so many people for seeking Him in faith if that faith was given to them - Mar 10:52, Luk 7:50, 8:48, 17:19, and 18:42?

Most of the ill and afflicted described in Scripture either go to Jesus or were taken to Him - Mat 4:24, 6:5-6, 8:2-4, 8:28-34, 9:18, 12:15, and 14:35, 36. There are numerous passages where Jesus tells people their faith healed them - Mat 9:2-8, 20, 29, 15:28, Act 14:9. We have a responsibility to act on the faith He gives us.

Why does the Lord rebuke people for their lack of faith if it all came from Him?

> Luk 8:25 He said to them, "Where is your faith?" And they were afraid, and they marveled, saying to one another, "Who then is this, that he commands even winds and water, and they obey him?"

> Mar 3:5 And he looked around at them with anger, grieved at their hardness of heart, and said to the man, "Stretch out your hand." He stretched it out, and his hand was restored.

Why was Jesus grieved about their hard hearts if He gave it to them? There are similar challenges in other passages - Mat 17:17, Mar 16:14, Luk 11:32, 12:28b, 24:25. He was especially hard on the chief priests and the elders who should have known better and were misleading others - Mat 21:32.

If God takes complete control of our faith, why does Jesus say, "Blessed are those who have not seen and yet have believed" (Jhn 20:29)? Why does Jesus plead with Phillip to believe in the passage below? He makes a similar request to Jairus in Mar 5:36.

> Jhn 14:11 <u>Believe me</u> that I am in the Father and the Father is in me, <u>or else believe on account of the works themselves</u>.

God's choice is not based on any right or entitled treatment, nor is it based on His lack of power. In Jer 18:5-7 God tells Israel He is the potter who can do what He wants with them. However, vs. 8-10 clearly state His response is based on their action, not unconditional judgment. God goes to great lengths to get people to believe - Exo 4:1-17, and 30-31. Why did God give us signs to believe unless our response was somehow involved? He could have used the Holy Spirit to put the gospel in their hearts, and the elect would just step forward. It appears we have a responsibility. Why does the writer of Hebrews warn us not to neglect a great salvation - Heb 2:3, 12:25? In the OT there are several passages that speak of making a choice between God and evil - Exo 32:26, Deu 26:17, 30:19, Jos 24:15, and 1Ki 18:21. Likewise, the NT references our role in election.

> 1Th 2:13 And we also thank God constantly for this, that when <u>you received the word of God</u>, which you <u>heard</u> from us, you <u>accepted it</u> not as the word of men but as what it really is, the word of God, which is at work in you believers.

The Bible speaks about those who did not receive the gospel - Mar 10:15; and Jhn 1:11-12, 3:11, 5:43. Other passages that speak of our refusing to believe are included in the Point 4 discussion later. God provides the water, He makes us thirsty, but Scripture appears to tell us we must "take the water of life."

> Rev 22:17 The Spirit and the Bride say, "Come." And let the one who hears say, "Come." And let the one who is thirsty come; let the one who desires take the water of life without price.

Scripture speaks of man's role (accepting, receiving, believing,) and God's decision, in that order. We know God decided in eternity past; but from our perspective, it is as we experience Him John 1:12-13, Rom 10:11-13.

Paul provides a salvation summary in Philippians chapter 3 - "that by any means possible I may attain the resurrection from the dead" (Phl 3:11) and "I press on toward the goal for the prize of the upward call of God in Christ Jesus" (Phl 3:14). It sounds as though Paul feels he has a part to play in his salvation.

Rom 3:11 states, "no one understands; no one seeks for God"; Paul changed this passage he pulled from Psa 14:2; which is NOT as exclusive - "The LORD looks down from heaven on the children of man, to see if there are any who understand, who seek after God." That difference should lead us to search further. There are many passages in Scripture that encourage believers to seek God - Ezr 8:22; Psa 119:2, 145:8; Deu 4:29; 1Ch15:13, 28:9; 2Ch 15:2, 26:5, 30:18-19; Isa 45:22, 55:6-7; Psa 25:14; Luk 11:9-10; and Heb 11:6. Rom 3:11 must not describe believers. In Acts, the same Paul is speaking in a synagogue about people seeking and finding God.

> Act 17:26-27 And he made from one man every nation of mankind to live on all the face of the earth, having determined allotted periods and the boundaries of their dwelling place, [27] that they should seek God, and perhaps feel their way toward him and find him.

Other passages indicate we will be rewarded for seeking Him - "if you seek him you will find him" (2Ch 15:15). Why would He reward us for the faith He gave us if we have no role in it?

> Jhn 5:44 How can you believe, when you receive glory from one another and do not <u>seek the glory</u> that comes from the only God?

In the passage from Paul below, there are limitations on the mind that is set on the flesh; maybe the limitation on seeking referenced in Rom 3:11 is based on the heart of each person.

> Rom 8:7 For the mind that is <u>set on the flesh is hostile to God</u>, for it does not submit to God's law; indeed, it cannot.

A Syrophoenician woman whose little daughter had an unclean spirit <u>heard</u> of Jesus, came, and fell down at his feet - Mar 7:25-29. Jesus said, "For it is not right to take the children's bread and throw it to the dogs." She answered Him, "Yes, Lord; yet even the dogs under the table eat the children's crumbs." He said to her, "<u>For this statement</u> you may go your way; the demon has left your daughter."

We have a responsibility to find the gate to heaven - Mat 7:14. Paul echoes Isaiah 65 in Rom 10:20-21, reiterating God wants to be found. The following passage teaches us that some who seek will not be successful, yet we are told to strive to enter.

> Luk 13:23-24 And someone said to him, "Lord, will those who are saved be few?" And He said to them, [24] "<u>Strive to enter through the narrow door</u>. For many, I tell you, will seek to enter and will not be able.

A good insight into why God saves is to look at why He condemns. Every related passage in my chain reference Bible showed God's judgment was based on a failing of the person or people. This Scripture reveals the cause of His condemnation and judgment.

> Psa 9:16 The LORD has made himself known; he has executed judgment; the <u>wicked are snared in the work of their own hands</u>.

Rom 1:25-27 **because** you have ignored all my counsel and would have none of my reproof, ²⁶ I also will laugh at your calamity; I will mock when terror strikes you, ²⁷ when terror strikes you like a storm and your calamity comes like a whirlwind, when distress and anguish come upon you.

In 1Ki 19:18 God kept for Himself seven thousand who had not bowed to Baal. Why would it be for His pleasure to keep only seven thousand of His chosen people - "For the simple are killed by their turning away" (Pro 1:32)? "Walk in the ways of your heart and the sight of your eyes. But know that for all these things God will bring you into judgment" (Ecc 11:9). God also had reasons to judge the other nations related to their heart and conduct - Ezekiel 25. Jesus denounces cities that did not respond to His message - Mat 11:20 and Jhn 10:25, 38, 15:24. If He caused them not to believe, why is God angry at the Israelites in the passage below? He ratchets the consequences up to death of the vile and exile of the others to get them to believe. There are similar condemnations in Psa 79-82.

Psa 78:21-22, 32, 62 Therefore, when the LORD heard, he was full of wrath; a fire was kindled against Jacob; his anger rose against Israel, ²² **because** they did not believe in God and did not trust his saving power...... ³² In spite of all this, they still sinned; despite his wonders, they did not believe.... ⁶² He gave his people over to the sword and vented his wrath on his heritage.

Scripture teaches that God does NOT change His mind - Num 23:19, Mal 3:6, and Jas 1:17; though many passages appear to describe just that - Exo 32:12-14, Num 14:11-12, 20, and 2Ki 20:1-6. God appears to change His mind about removing His Spirit from His people because Moses talks Him out of it - Psa 106:23. In Jonah 3:10 God changed His mind from the destruction of Nineveh due to their response. Yet, later, in the book of Naham, He destroyed them when they turned away. There are several other examples of God changing His mind

<u>in human time</u> - Neh 1:8-9; 2Ch 15:2b; Psa 95:8-11; Jer 18:5-10; Joe 2:12-13; Zec 1:3; Mal 2:1-2, 8-9, 3:7; Eph 6:1-3; and Jas 4:8. What is the message in the parable of the persistent widow - Luk 18:1-8? Human action and prayer affect God's decisions.

Jews were broken off for their unbelief - Rom 11:20, but "**if** they do not continue in their unbelief, will be grafted in, for God has the power to graft them in again" (Rom 11:23). There are also future decisions in other passages - Luk 8:12; Jhn 5:24, 11:25, 20:31; Act 16:31; Rom 10:9. There have been names removed from the Lamb's book - Exo 32:33; Psa 69:28; Rev 3:5, and 22:19, it is likely this continues today. I heard a popular radio pastor and acclaimed author postulate that all people were initially included in the Lamb's Book, but some were removed for specific reasons.

In 1Sa 10:7, 21-24 God chose Saul to be King of Israel. Scripture gives us clear basis for His turning away from Saul.

> 1Sa 15:10 -11 The word of the LORD came to Samuel: [11] "<u>I regret that I have made Saul king</u>, for <u>he has turned back from following me and has not performed my commandments</u>." And Samuel was angry, and he cried to the LORD all night.

We are told in 1Sa 12:13-15 and 1Sa 13:13-14 what could have been. God had great plans for Saul and specific reasons for rejecting him. Saul was replaced because he was unfaithful - 1Ch 10:13. In our time, it looks like God changed His mind; but He knew how it would all turn out before any of it happened. We know all these passages are true. We should look for an understanding supported by all of them. God appears to change His mind in our time, based on interactions with humanity. Using His future knowledge, He has made unchangeable decisions in His timeless control of everything. From His eternal omniscient position, it is unchangeable. From our place in time, it is yet to be decided.

In some cases, the Scriptures that support both A&C perspectives are in the same passage, making the apparent contradiction even more mysterious.

> Jhn 6:40, 44-45 For this is the will of my Father, <u>that everyone who looks on the Son and believes in him should have eternal life</u>, and I will raise him up on the last day."

> [44] <u>No one can come to me unless the Father who sent me draws him</u>. And I will raise him up on the last day.

> [45] It is written in the Prophets, 'And they will all be taught by God.' <u>Everyone who has heard and learned from the Father comes to me</u>-

John's gospel records a discussion about purification between some of John the Baptist's disciples and a Jew. In Jhn 3:27 John answered, "A person cannot receive even one thing unless it is given him from heaven." A few verses later, talking about accepting the teaching from Jesus, John states, "Whoever receives his testimony sets his seal to this, that God is true" (Jhn 3:33). By man's logic, it seems like a software do loop. By God's infinite wisdom and justice, He chose those who should be there before we were created.

Ezekiel gives us a cardio antinomy. In chapter 11 and 36, he speaks of God giving us a new heart, while chapter 18 instructs them to make their own new heart.

> Eze 11:19 And <u>I will give</u> them one heart, and a new spirit I will put within them. I will remove the heart of stone from their flesh and give them a heart of flesh,

> Eze 18:31 Cast away from you all the transgressions that you have committed, and <u>make yourselves a new heart</u> and a new spirit! Why will you die, O house of Israel?

> Eze 36:26 And <u>I will give</u> you a new heart, and a new spirit I will put within you. And I will remove the heart of stone from your flesh and give you a heart of flesh.

In chapter 11, the Israelites are returning from exile. In 11:18, God tells them to remove the idols, and then He will give them a new heart. Chapter 18 provides almost the same message. The whole chapter speaks to the Lord's judgment on the disobedient and finishes in vs. 31 telling them to get a new heart (from God) by obeying. The verse from chapter 36 is the Calvinist perspective. He is going to wash them clean for the sake of His name, then give them a new heart <u>so they will obey</u>. A footnote in my Bible asserts that these verses have the same tension that we find in Phl 2:12-13. God could harden our hearts, but does He? Why are we warned in the OT and NT - when we hear God's voice, "do not harden your hearts" (Heb 4:7 quoted from Psa 95:7-8)? Jesus chastises His disciples for hardening their hearts in Mk 8:17-19. There are other election antinomies in neighboring passages - Jhn 15:10 to 16; Act 10:41 to 43; and 1Pe 1:1-2 to 2:6-8.

Calvinists embrace Rom 9:10-14, and 9:22-23 to support their position on the second point. God made his decision when "they were not yet born." We established that He chose the elect in eternity past. Scripture is clear, our works do not save us; beyond that, no specific criteria is given for His choice. These passages must be considered in light of all Scripture.

It is quite presumptuous for humans to say that God ALWAYS does almost anything. We have exceptions to general truths in the Bible. There are several exceptions to Heb 9:27 "And just as it is appointed for man to die once." Two skipped death all together - Enoch - Heb 11:5 and Elijah - 2Ki 2:11, and several others died twice - 1Ki 17:22; 2Ki 4:35, 13:21; Mat 9:25; Luk 7:15; Jhn 11:43; Act 9:40, 20:9. There are many examples in Scripture where God deals with each of us as individuals. Why are there qualifications for elder (overseer) in 1 Timothy that are not in the Titus criteria? They are from the same author inspired by the same Holy Spirit.

In the OT, the Holy Spirit came upon certain people at specific times to enable them to do God's will (Num 11: 24-25). In the NT some are filled with Holy Spirit as in the OT - John the Baptist - Luk 1:15, 41, Elizabeth - Luk 1:42, Zechariah - Luk 1:67, and Simeon - Luk 2:25. The disciples did not receive the Holy Spirit until after Jesus ascended - Mar 13:11 and Jhn 16:7. All believers in attendance at Pentecost received the Holy Spirit. Following Pentecost, some received the HS before baptism - Act 10:47; for some others it was the reverse - Mat 3:16, Mar 1:8, and Act 1:4-5. Scripture indicates that future believers would receive the Holy Spirit at baptism - Act 10:44, Rom 8:9, and Eph 1:13. However, it does NOT say this is always the case.

God's response to our doubt is another diverse example. The following saints got very different treatment for their doubt: Abraham and Sarah - Gen 18; Gideon - Jud 6:20, 38-40, 7:10; Zechariah - Luk 1:21-22; Mary - Luk 1:42; the doubting father in Mar 9:24; and doubting Thomas - Jhn 20:24. God deals with us where we are. Is it reasonable that God hating a person from the womb in Rom 9:13 is a statement of His foreknowledge rather than His choice "without any consideration of merit within the individual?"

Scripture relates in many places Esau was NOT a man of faith; he is the poster boy for the description of the lost - Phl 3:18-19. Scripture gives us specific reasons why a timeless God would have hated him before birth.

> Heb 12:15-16 See to it that no one fails to obtain the grace of God; that no "root of bitterness" springs up and causes trouble, and by it many become defiled; [16] that no one is sexually immoral or unholy like Esau, who sold his birthright for a single meal.

In Gen 28:6-9, God did not want His people to have Canaanite wives; He knew they would be led into false religions. Even though Esau gave up his birthright - Gen 25:32, and married Canaanite wives - Gen 36:2, God displaced the Horites and gave Esau the hill country of Seir - Deu 2:22. God protected

Esau - Deu 2:5. However, Obadiah informs us the nation descended from Esau (also called Edom) came to destruction - Oba 1:10.

In 2Ki 8:20 the nation of Edom revolted against the Israelites. They were destroyed for their behavior. We are given no other reason than was given in Obadiah. Nowhere in Scripture does it say God hated Esau "without any consideration of merit within the individual."

What then is Rom 9:22-23 saying? Taken in the context of all of Scripture, this is a clear statement of God's power, His complete control, His total sovereignty, and our complete dependence on His mercy. His mercy is clearly not a product of our works; that is repeated throughout the NT. Some interpret Rom 9:22-29 as hypothetical - God could do this if He wanted, as opposed to the interpretation that this is definitely what God does with every human. Rom 9:28 supports this, which indicates the product of God's decision is in the future to us, "for the Lord will carry out his sentence upon the earth fully and without delay." Paul concludes this chapter giving us the why of God's choosing.

> Rom 9:32-33 Why? Because they did not pursue it by faith, but as if it were based on works. They have stumbled over the stumbling stone, [33] as it is written, "Behold, I am laying in Zion a stone of stumbling, and a rock of offense; and whoever believes in him will not be put to shame."

Some passages seem to support the Calvinist's position. that belief only comes to those elected by God - Mat 24:31, Luk 18:7, Rom 8:28-30, Eph 1:4-6, and 2Ti 2:10. Another passage used by Calvinists is Jhn 10:26 - "but you do not believe because you are not among my sheep." Jhn 17:2, 6, 9 state God gives eternal life to those given to Jesus. God gave the ones He chose to Jesus. John supports this with "A person cannot receive even one thing unless it is given him from heaven" (Jhn 6:37). We see a similar statement in Jhn 13:18.

Several passages describe God preventing people from believing - Jhn 8:45-47, 10:26, and 12:37-40. "It is veiled to those who are perishing" (2Co 4:3). The following passage states God decides who will be veiled from the truth.

> Rom 11:7-8 What then? Israel failed to obtain what it was seeking. The elect obtained it, but the rest were hardened, [8] as it is written, "God gave them a spirit of stupor, eyes that would not see and ears that would not hear, down to this very day."

There are examples where understanding was hidden to facilitate His ministry. Even the disciples had their understanding impeded - Luk 18:34. Those who support Calvinism would agree we must hear and accept, but they would contend the message is hidden from all except those who were elected. They reference the following passage:

> Luk 8:9-10 And when his disciples asked him what this parable meant, [10] he said, "To you it has been given to know the secrets of the kingdom of God, but for others they are in parables, so that 'seeing they may not see, and hearing they may not understand.

Many pastors teach this passage reveals their punishment for not believing, as opposed to keeping the non-elect from understanding. If we look at God's decisions from His concept of time, these two explanations become the same. Later in Luke's gospel there is a passage supporting that interpretation.

> Luk 19:41-42 And when he drew near and saw the city, he wept over it, [42] saying, "Would that you, even you, had known on this day the things that make for peace! But now they are hidden from your eyes.

God also enables our spiritual vision.

> 2Co 3:16 But when one turns to the Lord, the veil is removed.

If God was doing it all, it seems the order would be reversed, veil removed then we turn to the Lord. Paul gives us another example of the sequence and reason for the Lord's blinding.

> 2Th 2:9-12 The coming of the lawless one is by the activity of satan with all power and false signs and wonders, [10] and with all wicked deception for those who are perishing, <u>because they refused to love the truth and so be saved</u>. [11] Therefore God sends them a strong delusion, so that they may believe what is false, [12] in order that all may be condemned <u>who did not believe the truth</u> but had pleasure in unrighteousness.

Parables were also used to convey knowledge - "<u>I will open my mouth in parables; I will utter what has been hidden since the foundation of the world</u>" (Mat 13:35). Nothing is hidden except to be revealed - Mar 4:22 -25. Jesus includes this statement at the end of the parable of the soils, indicating the ultimate purpose of the parables is to enlighten and reveal. The last verse again supports the perspective that understanding is taken away for a reason - "and from the one who has not, even what he has will be taken away."

If God chose who will be in heaven "without any consideration of merit within the individual", there are several other passages of Scripture that raise questions. Why did God give Adam and Eve the choice to sin or be faithful - Gen 2:16-17, but elect the rest of humanity independent of our decisions? Satan was cast out for His pride and aspiration to be God - Isa 14:12-15. If God condemned satan for his decisions, why would He condemn some humans independent of their decisions? How did Absalom steal the hearts of people if God condemned them before creation - 2Sa 15:6?

Why do we see the dramatic historical swings in the number of Christians in various areas of the world presented in chapter 1? If God were making these elections "without any consideration of merit within the individual," it would seem we would see a more even distribution across the world and across time. Is God turning His grace in election on and off? Why are there so many Christians in South Korea and so few in North Korea? Why do people born in Muslim countries usually end up being Muslim? Similarly, why is the rate that offspring adopt the faith of their parents much higher in some Christian groups than in others? Does God base His election on where we are born or who our parents are?

It is hard for the rich to get into heaven - Mar 10:23-26, Jas 2:5; does God's election have bias favoring the poor or is it just harder for the rich to believe? His seeking Zacchaeus would indicate He loves the rich also - Luk 19.

From Genesis to maps, Scripture teaches us God usually deals with us based on our choices. Most of these passages contain conditional statements *"If - then"*, "because of", "according to" and "so that" to link man's choices to God's response. Searching the Bible looking for them, I compiled a list of over 400. Try it for yourself; you will be astounded. The most familiar if-then passage is:

2Ch 7:14 **if** my people who are called by my name humble themselves, and pray and seek my face and turn from their wicked ways, **then** I will hear from heaven and will forgive their sin and heal their land.

God usually withholds His blessings (provision, protection, guidance, etc.) when people turn away from Him - 2Ki 22:13, Rom 2:8, and Eph 5:6. In AD 70, the Romans sacked Jerusalem because they did not recognize Jesus - Luk 19:43-44. Some Israelites were killed for rejecting knowledge - Hos 4:6.

The following passage provides three big *ifs* and a *then* leading to God's blessing of understanding.

Pro 2:1-6 My son, **if** you receive my words and treasure up my commandments with you, ² making your ear attentive to wisdom and inclining your heart to understanding; ³ yes, **if** you call out for insight and raise your voice for understanding, [4] **if** you seek it like silver and search for it as for hidden treasures, [5] **then** you will understand the fear of the LORD and find the knowledge of God. [6] For the LORD gives wisdom; from his mouth come knowledge and understanding;

The rest of that chapter describes how God will give us wisdom and direct our paths, **if** we meet those three criteria.

There are many more conditional blessing passages - Lev 26:14-34; Deu 11:13-14, 13:18; 2Ch 30:9, 36:15-16; Psa 18:24-27, 91:9-10, 14-16; Jer 42:10-18; Rom 1:22-32, 2:2-9, 11:22; and Rev 3:3. Does it make sense God decides what to do with us in life based on our decisions and response to Him; but makes His choice about our eternity "without any consideration of merit within the individual"? I have not read an author on this topic that does not agree all people are 100% accountable for our decisions. How can that be true if God makes His election about our eternity without consideration of our decisions?

My investigation of point 2 provided many great insights, but left several questions. The pastor who led me to faith answered my initial questions about Calvinism with a perspective from seminary. The archway over the entrance to heaven will have a sign, "Whosoever will come after me" on the other side is a sign that reads "chosen before creation." This simple illustration satisfied an excited new believer overwhelmed with the enormity of what Scripture reveals. Once having explored the rest of Scripture, his simplification falls short of explaining the differences between A&C beliefs. Nonetheless, both messages in his illustration appear to be very true.

Before starting a free will celebration, remember the passages used to support Calvinism reinforce that God is in complete control, He chooses those to be saved, He gives us faith, and He keeps some from understanding. However, support for the statement that He does it "without any consideration of merit within the individual" is hard to see.

It is possible God chooses some as understood by Calvin, and others that believe based on the understanding of Arminius. That would be consistent with what He did in the OT. He chose the Israelites as a nation. Others, like Rahab and Uriah, were brought in through faith in the God they had heard about. Ruth is another example "Your people shall be my people, and your God my God." (Rth 1:16).

Point 3 - Limited Atonement vs. Universal Redemption or General Atonement

Atonement is limited in that God does appoint who will be in heaven. He limits His selections based on His perfect will.

> Act 13:48 And when the Gentiles heard this, they began rejoicing and glorifying the word of the Lord, and as many as were appointed to eternal life believed.

The Holy Spirit inspired eight writers to pin at least 40 passages stating salvation is available to all. Proponents of hyper-Calvinism contend that God's election is only available to those He chose "without any consideration of merit"; therefore, point 2 and 3 are mutually dependant for both A&C positions. Calvinists claim these passages using *all* are referring to all nations, all types of people (race, ethnicity, religious background, location, etc.), all those receiving an epistle, all people in a certain area, or anything other than all people who have ever lived. Scripture refers to all nations where applicable - Rom 16:26, and Mat 28:19. This passage uses every nation and anyone in the same text.

> Act 10:34-35 So Peter opened his mouth and said: "Truly I understand that God shows no partiality, 35 but in every nation anyone who fears him and does what is right is acceptable to him.

The following passages indicate God desires that all be saved. God does not fail; this too is an example of His declarative and permissive wills. Appendix B provides the Hebrew and

Greek words translated to *all* or a similar word in English. The interlinear cross reference is included in the following text.

> 1Ti 2:3-4 This is good, and it is pleasing in the sight of God our Savior, ⁴ who desires all (G3956) people to be saved and to come to the knowledge of the truth.

> 2Pe 3:9 The Lord is not slow to fulfill his promise as some count slowness, but is patient toward you, not wishing that any (G5100) should perish, but that all (G3956) should reach repentance.

> Eze 18:32 For I have no pleasure in the death of anyone (H 4191), declares the Lord GOD; so turn, and live." (also Eze 33:11)

God gave all the Israelites a remedy for the poisonous snakebites. It was not by works of their own; they had to choose to accept it and look at the snake on the pole - Num 21:8-9. Jesus compares that provision to His dying on the cross.

> Jhn 3:14-15 And as Moses lifted up the serpent in the wilderness, so must the Son of Man be lifted up, ¹⁵ that whoever (G3956) believes in him may have eternal life.

Does *everyone* mean all in - Luk 11:10, 12:8, Jhn 6:45, Act 10:43, Rom 10:4, 11, 13, Heb 2:9, and 1Jo 5:1? What about *whoever* in Jhn 5:24, 17:8; Rom 9:33; and Rev 22:17?

> Jhn 4:14 but whoever (G3739) drinks of the water that I will give him will never be thirsty again. The water that I will give him will become in him a spring of water welling up to eternal life."

Jesus came to call sinners and no limitation is mentioned - Luk 5:32, and Mar 2:17. People were saved in the OT by faith as in the NT, all those who would submit.

Joe 2:32 And it shall come to pass that **everyone** (H3605) who calls on the name of the LORD shall be saved. For in Mount Zion and in Jerusalem there shall be those who escape, as the LORD has said, and among the survivors shall be those whom the LORD calls.

God cares for all in the OT also.

Psa 145:9 The LORD is good to all (H3605), and his mercy is over all (H3605) that he has made.

God's great concern for the lost is displayed in Jhn 4:9-14, and Jonah 4:11; He even sought non-Israelites. People brought into the nation of Israel were to "be as a native of the land" (Exo 12:48), aliens become as native-born Israelites - Eze 47:22.

Scripture reveals that Jesus died for the lost, too - Luk 19:10, and Rom 5:18, 11:32. The following are the balance of the 40 passages that refer to salvation being for all (or a similar term) - Isa 28:16, 40:3-5, 55:1; Mat 22:9; Luk 2:10, 3:6; Jhn 3:14-16, 36, Jhn 8:12; Act 2:21; Rom 15:11; 1Ti 2:3-4; Tit 2:11-12; and Rev 3:20.

These 40 verses make it hard to accept the hyper-Calvinist view of limited atonement. However, it is clear from Scripture God does limit those He saves.

<u>Point 4 Irresistible Grace vs. The Holy Spirit Can be Effectually Resisted</u>

"Our God is in the heavens; he does all that he pleases" (Psa 115:3). He could certainly bring people to believe if He wanted. Paul is but one example of the many brought to belief by miracles. God could make His grace irresistible. Did He do it for every person who believes? This point is also interdependent with some others. If God elects "without any consideration of merit"; then His calling is irresistible. However, we see many passages where people refused to believe. Scripture describes how the Jews would not receive Jesus - Mat 22:3, Jhn 1:11-12, Act 7:51, and Heb 4:6-7.

We also see examples where people chose to turn away from God - Pro 1:29-33, Is 65:2, and 66:3. The first three soil types in the parable of the soils immediately or ultimately reject the gospel. Only those represented by the good soil accept it - Mar 4:20.

Scripture gives us three other reasons for not understanding: (1) being wise (in their own minds) - Luk 10:21, (2) being ignorant (lack of study) - Eph 4:18, and (3) hating our brother - 1Jo 2:11. Jesus condemns people for rejecting Him - Mat 25:41-46, Jhn 3:18, 3:36, 5:38-44, and 8:24. Similarly, others are condemned for their rejection of the gospel - Luk 7:30; Jhn 1:11, 16:8-11; Rom 2:5-8; 1Th 4:8; and Pro 28:14, 29:1.

> Jhn 12:48 <u>The one who rejects me</u> and does not receive my words has a judge; the word that I have spoken will judge him on the last day.

> Rom 11:20 That is true. <u>They were broken off because of their unbelief</u>, but you stand fast through faith.

These passages appear to say the gospel was sent but not caught, like the parable of the soils. This passage provides a straightforward cause and effect for condemnation.

> Act 28:27 For this <u>people's heart has grown dull</u>, and with their ears they can barely hear, and <u>their eyes they have closed</u>; **lest** they should see with their eyes and hear with their ears and <u>understand with their heart and turn, and I would heal them.</u>

In Act 7:51-52 Jews were condemned for resisting the Holy Spirit. God certainly has the power to make salvation irresistible, but Scripture does not seem to say He always does.

Point 5 - Perseverance of the Saints vs. Falling from Grace

This is likely the most debated of the five points, many proof texts on both sides. In addition to those mentioned below, the following passages speak of falling away - Eze 18:24-26, Mat 24:10, Luk 9:62, Col 2:8, 1Ti 1:6, 2Ti 4:4, Heb 2:1, and 2Pe 3:17.

There is a lot packed into the following verses. It is describing people who have fully experienced the gospel. It does not mention their having saving faith. It does mention sharing in the Holy Spirit, which could indicate faith, or just the calling of the Lord. Note that verses 7 and 8 link our fruit to our heart condition.

> Heb 6:4-8 For it is impossible, in the case of those who have once been enlightened, who have tasted the heavenly gift, and have shared in the Holy Spirit, [5] and have tasted the goodness of the word of God and the powers of the age to come, [6] and then have fallen away, to restore them again to repentance, since they are crucifying once again the Son of God to their own harm and holding him up to contempt. [7] For land that has drunk the rain that often falls on it, and produces a crop useful to those for whose sake it is cultivated, receives a blessing from God. [8] But if it bears thorns and thistles, it is worthless and near to being cursed, and its end is to be burned.

On the other side of the divide we see several passages that indicate believers will not fall away - Jhn 6:37-39, 10:27-30; Rom 8:28-30; 1Co 1:8-9; 1Pe 1:5, 9; and 1Jn 3:9, 5:18. Those who say salvation cannot be lost would note that 2Pe 2:20-22 describes those who fell away as dogs and pigs - clearly not believers. Verse 20 states they had knowledge, it does not mention faith.

Many pastors explain it in a way that all the references fit. The intellectual knowledge of the gospel alone does not result in salvation; we must have faith. We can fall away from the knowledge of the gospel. There is a dramatic illustration of this in Mat 7:19-22 and Luk 13:24-28, when Jesus tells those who called "Lord, Lord" to depart from Him in heaven for He never knew them. They had knowledge of God, but not saving faith. There are people who call on the name of God that do not have committed faith in Jesus as their Savior. It is like driving on a trip 100% sure we are on the right road and be 100% wrong; they are lost.

There are other passages that support the concept that true faith will continue to the end - Mat 10:22, Mar 13:13, Jhn 8:51, Rom 2:6-7, Gal 6:9, Jas 1:12, 2Pe 1:10, and Rev 3. Paul tells us Jesus sustains us to the end.

> 1Co 1:7-9 as you wait for the revealing of our Lord Jesus Christ, ⁸ who will sustain you to the end, guiltless in the day of our Lord Jesus Christ. ⁹ God is faithful, by whom you were called into the fellowship of his Son, Jesus Christ our Lord.

Paul gives us a hint about this knowledge without true faith. He states that they are being saved "unless you believed in vain." He may be saying they had head knowledge not heart belief.

> 1Co 15:1-2 Now I would remind you, brothers, of the gospel I preached to you, which you received, in which you stand, ² and by which you are being saved, if you hold fast to the word I preached to you--unless you believed in vain.

Hebrews directly links the unbelieving heart of people in the fellowship (brothers) that would lead us to fall away. This is a clear caution to those who think they believe, but may not.

> Heb 3:12 Take care, brothers, lest there be in any of you an evil, unbelieving heart, leading you to fall away from the living God.

Matthew 24 seems to support both positions - "many will fall away and betray one another" (Mat 24:10), "the one who endures to the end will be saved" (Mat 24:13). We can fall away from the gospel, but if we endure to the end, we had saving faith. The perseverance crowd would claim that those who fell away never had saving faith.

Some passages seem to challenge the thesis that only those with head knowledge and no faith will fall away.

- "some have made shipwreck of their faith" (1Ti 1:19)
- "Spirit expressly says that in later times some will depart from the faith" (1Ti 4:1)
- "They are upsetting the faith of some" (2Ti 2:18)

Both sides claim Paul's teaching in Col 1:23 - "if indeed you continue in the faith, stable and steadfast, not to shifting from the hope of the gospel that you heard" (also Heb 3:14). Some will claim that it is possible not to continue in faith. While others contend the proof of the faith is to continue to the end - "If you abide in my word, you are truly my disciples, and you will know the truth, and the truth will set you free." (Jhn 8:31-32).

Matthew fuels the mystery. "For false christs and false prophets will arise and perform great signs and wonders, so as to lead astray, <u>if possible, even the elect.</u>" (Mat 24:24).

Consider this example - two families have 12-year-old sons who were baptized and made public professions of faith. One family is Arminian and the other Calvinist. The boys drift away from the Lord through high school and the years that follow. At their deathbed, they both denounce faith in God. One family would say he had fallen away, the other would say he never truly believed. The real issue is that they did not go to heaven, how we describe the condition pales in comparison.

We should keep our opinion on this issue to ourselves. Since we do not know the condition of a person's heart - 1Co 4:5, we should not tell them that they cannot lose the faith that they may not even have. We must assume they may only have an intellectual knowledge of the gospel and tell them the same thing so many authors tell us in the NT - "be all the more diligent to confirm your calling and election" (2Pe 1:10).

Do We Need an Answer?

This passage addresses the election and perseverance questions - obey and leave nothing to an assumption.

> Mat 3:8-10 Bear fruit in keeping with repentance. [9] And do not presume to say to yourselves, 'We have Abraham as our father,' for I tell you, God is able from these stones to raise up children for Abraham. [10] Even now the axe is laid to the root of the trees. Every tree therefore that does not bear good fruit is cut down and thrown into the fire.

Do we even need to know the answer to this mystery? Regardless of whether we can lose our faith or not, we should live our life the same way. Read the Bible cover to cover with the question "do I match the descriptions of those who are saved?" Our role to respond is of no value if we do not respond in faith. Our knowledge will not save us - Jas 2:19.

Scholar's Perspective

A review like this must be thorough and objective. I read six books and two booklets on the topic of election and free will. Four of the books and both booklets supported Calvinism, one presented a balanced perspective, and the other was an essay and critique format on free will and predestination. These books referred to others dating back to the 5th century. One author condemned those who say this issue is too complex for us to understand. He should consider 1Co 1:27 "God chose what is foolish in the world to shame the wise." The following is the reference information for each book and some key points.

Whosoever Will - Let Him Take The Water Of Life Freely, 1945, Wm B Eerdmans Publishing Co.; Scripture from KJV; by Homer Hoeksema, Calvin Seminary, was one of the founders of the Protestant Reformed Churches, pastor and theology school professor and editor of the *Standard Bearer* magazine.

Hoeksema wrote this book to respond to the hymn "Whosoever Will" based on Rev 22:17. He admits that there are Scripture passages that support both positions.

Chosen By God - Know God's Perfect Plan For His Glory And His Children, 1986, Tyndale House Publishing; Scripture from the NKJV; By R. C Sproul, Pittsburgh Theological Seminary, professor at Reformed Theological Seminary, Chairman of the board of Ligonier Ministries.

Dr. Sproul recognized the importance of this issue as he states the following early in his book: "If my understanding of predestination is not correct, then my sin is compounded; since I would be slandering the saints who by opposing my view are fighting for the angels. So the stakes are high for me in this matter." He recognizes that evil is a problem for the sovereignty of God, concluding that He foreordained it. He concludes God has the power to save all; but he states he has no idea why God saves some but not all. God's sovereignty and man's freedom are not contradictory. God does not create unbelief in the hearts of the lost.

Predestination & Free Will - Four Views of Divine Sovereignty & Human Freedom, 1986, Inter Varsity Christian Fellowship of the USA, edited by David and Randall Basinger.

This book evaluates how God deals with His creation. Each author presents an essay on the issue of free will vs. predestination, followed by a critique by the other three. The authors range from extremely deterministic (Calvinism) to extremely indeterministic (Arminian). Here are the authors and essay titles.

John Feinberg - *God Ordains All Things*
Norman Geisler - *God Knows All Things*
Bruce Reichenbach - *God Limits His Power*
Clark Pinnock - *God Limits His Knowledge*

The introduction of the book states, "There are few issues which cause more confusion than the relationship between God's sovereignty and human freedom." The two extreme positions had limited supporting Scripture, with 20 and 7 references respectively. The middle two positions used 93 and 55 Scripture references respectively.

One possibility not developed is a combination of determinism and indeterminism. God can do anything He wants. While, as several made clear, He chose to make us with a free will.

Chosen But Free - A Balanced View of Divine Election - 2nd Edition, 2001, Bethany House Publishers; most references are from the NIV with some from NKJV, KJV, and NASB; By Norman L. Geisler - ThD from William Tyndale College, PhD from Loyola University; President of Southern Evangelical Seminary. The second edition contains a rebuttal to James White's book described next.

Geisler states the following regarding election:

- God is fully sovereign.
- We have the choice to obey commands in Scripture.
- Fallen man has the power of free choice.
- Humans cannot choose God nor do any spiritual good without His grace.
- The Bible has apparent contradictions that are both fully true.
- Regarding man's salvation, God exercised predetermination and foreknowledge at the same time.
- Not once does Scripture say Christ died only for the elect, Christ died for all humanity.
- God's nature does not change.

Geisler cites Charles Spurgeon, an ardent Calvinist.

> "I cannot imagine a more ready instrument in the hands of satan for the ruin of souls than a minister who tells sinners it is not their duty to repent of their sins or to believe in Christ, and who has the arrogance to call himself a gospel minister, while he teaches God hates some men infinitely and unchangeably for no reason whatever but simply because he chooses to do so. O my brethren! May the Lord save you from the charmer, and keep you ever deaf to the voice of error."

The Potter's Freedom A Defense of the Reformation and a Rebuttal of Norman Geisler's Chosen But Free, 2000 Calvary Press Publishing; Most Scripture is from NASB, with some from KJV, NKJV, and NIV; By James R. White - ThD Columbia Evangelical Seminary, author, debater, and teacher at Golden Gate Baptist Theological Seminary, and others.

This book focuses on challenging the previous book by Geisler on a point-by-point basis.

God Chose To Save, Why Man Cannot And Will Not Be Saved Apart From Election, 2001, Evangelical Press and Calvary Press, most Scripture is from NASB, by Joseph M. Bianchi, journalist, businessman.

Bianchi reduced the issue to a choice of conditional election or absolute election. He confirms we are dealing with a mystery of duality.

A Southern Baptist looks at the Biblical Doctrine of Election, 2000, Founders Press, most Scripture from NKJV, by Ernest C. Reisinger, retired pastor in Cape Coral, Fl., on the board of directors for Founders Ministries, and a trustee for the Banner of Truth Trust.

Reisinger states - God is sovereign in creation, redemption and providence. While, just as clearly, we see the Bible teaches that humans are also 100% responsible. They are both in the Bible. Both are true. However, humanly we cannot reconcile them.

What Are Election and Predestination?, 2006, P&R Publishing, most Scripture from the NIV, by Richard Phillips, Senior Minister of Second Presbyterian Church of Greenville, South Carolina.

Phillips concludes the best way to begin to deal with this issue is to realize that the Bible teaches both doctrines. There is always mystery where the divine and the human meet. We do not have to reconcile them but we must accept that God asserts them both.

Scholar's Consensus

A solution to the debate over A&C doctrine was not found in these eight publications. They provided some points of general agreement.

- God is fully sovereign.
- There are mysteries involved in how God chooses the elect.
- Humans are 100% responsible for their choices.
- People have freedom of choice; at least perceived as such when we experience it. This has to be for us to be accountable for sin.
- Saving faith is a gift from God.
- God draws people to Jesus.

Conclusion

Books totaling thousands of pages have been written with careful interpretation of the relevant Scriptures, and still we have polarized differences. One must ask what difference these doctrines make. They do not change the clear call in Scripture to evangelize the world. They do not change the Scripture mandates to obey. Our beliefs about election have no bearing on God's decision of who will be in heaven. So why bother debating them at all? Is there any value in putting them in our confession statements?

My study Bible has the following note on Act 13:48 - "Possession of eternal life involves both human faith and divine appointment."[4] Only the infinite intellect of God can fully understand how and why He does it. The book *Bringing the Gospel Home* by Randy Newman[5] provides excellent guidance for the difficult process of evangelizing our family. It contained relevant insight into election.

> The rest of my conversation with Randall centered on Paul's words at the end of Romans 11. After three whole chapters of pondering the intersection of God's sovereignty and people's responsibility, Paul concluded, "Oh, the depth of the riches and wisdom and knowledge of God! How unsearchable are his judgment and how inscrutable his ways!" (Rom 11:33) If Paul couldn't totally figure it out, what makes us think we will? If certain things are *unsearchable* and *inscrutable*, shouldn't we be suspicious of explanations that seem totally understandable?

A Barna study in 2010 showed that the percentage of people attending church that describe themselves as Arminian or Calvinist was declining for both groups.[6]

What should we do with the 5 points of Calvinism and Remonstrance? We should avoid divisive interpretations not fully supported by all of Scripture - 1Th 5:21-22. Our teaching should emphasize the Scripture describing our responsibilities and leave the mysteries of election to God.

Years ago, I discussed concerns about unconditional election with Dr. Ben Haden, long time pastor of First Presbyterian Chattanooga and radio pastor on the "Changed Lives" broadcast. He attributed the following statement to Manford George Gutzke - "Calvin worked one side of the street and Wesley worked the other, but it was the same street."

Can we rejoice that we are on the same street and work together rather than wasting time, energy and resources arguing which is the best lane? This mystery has not been solved in four centuries of debate. Does it make sense to waste our time, talent and treasures continuing this argument? Shouldn't we set this aside and focus on the commandments that God has given us in Scripture?

God desires all people to be saved - 1Ti 2:4. Typical of contested passages, the footnote in my study Bible provided several interpretations and ended with this perspective for the passages that speak of God wanting all to be saved, yet aware that He sends people to hell.[7]

> "Other interpreters hold that, though human reasoning cannot resolve the seeming inconsistency, the Bible teaches both truths and thus there can be no actual contradiction. Certainly there is none in the mind of God."

That says it all.

11. DIVISIVE DOCTRINE

Have nothing to do with foolish, ignorant controversies; you know that they breed quarrels. ²⁴ And the Lord's servant must not be quarrelsome but kind to everyone, able to teach, patiently enduring evil, ²⁵ correcting his opponents with gentleness. God may perhaps grant them repentance leading to a knowledge of the truth, ²⁶ and they may come to their senses and escape from the snare of the devil, after being captured by him to do his will. 2Ti 2:23-26

Read that passage again. Other than no direct reference to unity, it sums up the message of this book. Teach known truth, avoid quarrels about mysteries, correct gently, and pursue those in doctrinal error regarding essentials as if they are lost - they may be. Pray that the Lord "may perhaps grant them repentance leading to a knowledge of the truth."

As I sat in church one day, not being as attentive as I should have been, I noticed the pastor was only visible with my left eye. As I focused on him, I saw a clear image. When I focused on the person's head that was obstructing the view of my other eye, I clearly saw his head with the pastor being an obscure item in the background. By focusing in the distance, it looked as though the pastor was in the person's head. This seems silly, but it is a simple illustration of how we look at specific passages in Scripture. If we strain hard enough on what we want to see, we can extrapolate a meaning from a passage that is not there. It must have been a captivating sermon that day (not our current pastor).

On a visit to the Tower of London Museum, we saw a large very old bound ledger sized book that was about 12 inches thick. It would not hold all the doctrinal statements and rules developed by various denominations. Many of these doctrinal statements conflict with those from other bodies including some required for salvation. This chapter will deal with a few disputed issues. We often are not careful to limit our arguments when there are young folks or new believers around. The debates over these issues harm the unity in the body of Christ, the spread of the gospel, and, in many cases, our time.

We have friends and family in the denominations represented by these examples. Please read this with a Spirit led open mind. The intent is to promote an objective look at the beliefs and essentials held by our churches then seek to ensure they are in line with all of God's Word. I apologize in advance if this chapter offends anyone.

Anytime we use the phrase "I believe" in the context of theology we are at risk of misleading and confusing. The far better opening is "this passage of Scripture says...." Thank the Lord, many bodies have moved past some errant beliefs and required practices. We have charged a pew tax to sit in our churches, required people to pay money for their sins and those of loved ones, even the deceased. I am confident if we are open to the Spirit's leading, we can get past some others and grow back together as the body of Christ. Take this as input for prayer and Scripture reading, and see where the Spirit leads.

I responded to a friend's greeting "how you doing" with my favorite Dave Ramsey quote, "Better than I deserve." He replied, "Only you can say that." I took it to mean he did not feel similarly blessed. After further discussion, I realized he meant no one else could tell me that I was doing better than I deserved. He was right and I realized we can interpret Scripture very differently from what God intended. Our interpretation is at the core of the doctrinal differences that impede the unity of the body of Christ.

Reading the Bible can be like visiting the zoo. We each have a different response to the animals based on our background and frame of reference, and nothing to do with the animals. Some of us look at the animals and appreciate them all. Others avoid some animals they do not like and spend a disproportionate time viewing their favorites. I have two friends that are extremes. One has an aversion to anything with feathers, he cannot even eat chicken. Another is a committed bird watcher and takes trips specifically to see new and different birds. We do the same with passages of Scripture, focusing on some and neglecting others. The message in Scripture is not the product of our perspective or interpretation.

The writers of Scripture had different messages related to the people and circumstances. Many denominational distinctions are a specific interpretation of a few isolated passages. Some passages have multiple meanings; they appropriately speak to us in different situations or different times in life. Leave the Holy Spirit room to guide without inappropriately judging the interpretation of another. For example, my study Bible offers three different interpretations of the following passage.

> 1Ti 2:15 Yet she will be saved through childbearing--if they continue in faith and love and holiness, with self-control.

All three interpretations appear to be consistent with the rest of Scripture. If they are all correct, and we support one and condemn the others, we are sinning. Other passages have multiple interpretations, with only one of them likely to be accurate. A radio pastor recommended that we pray for the guidance of the Holy Spirit every time we read the Bible. We have to search the Scriptures carefully and openly listen to the Spirit's leading to discern which are correct and which are circumstantially best. Then, make an objective, Spirit led decision on how to apply them to our lives. "When the plain sense of Scripture makes common sense, seek no other sense, lest it result in nonsense" - Dr. David L. Cooper.[1]

There have been many ill-conceived church rules. In his book *Fresh Wind Fresh Fire* Jim Cymbala relates some directives followed by the church he attended as a youth. When seamless hosiery came out, they said it was inappropriate for women to wear them. They were too sensual; women should wear hose with seams. Offenders risked church discipline. A number of years later, as seamless hosiery became the national norm, they decided that hosiery with seams should not be worn; they were just too alluring. That church was off base on their priorities and standards. The following perspectives on divisive issues should help us look at them from a full view of Scripture. Even if our understanding approaches perfection, we need to look for information to help gently bring others to that point.

Bible Translations

The Bible itself is a divisive issue among denominations in several ways. Some forbid the use of other than a selected translation. Others have developed their own translations to support their doctrine. Theological agendas have found their way into translations for centuries; now we see social agendas doing the same.

I am a bit OCD, I like things set and dependable; we all have an amount of that characteristic. I came to faith under a pastor who used the NIV. For years, I used an NIV translation with great exclusivity. Later I learned that none are perfect. The best approach to confirm the intent of a passage is by consulting multiple translations and an interlinear Bible to gain insight from the original language. It is understandable for people to want to stick to one translation for memorizing passages, key word searches, etc. However, if the translation is not based on the information from the best manuscripts and translated into the reader's language, God's message may not be understood.

Translations have caused battles between believers, churches, and other organizations. Many people grew up reading the KJV and memorizing passages from it. That makes it a fond, familiar, and favorite Bible. The KJV used some helpful conventions. For example, "you" can be singular or plural in English. The KJV used "thee" for singular you and "thou" for the plural you. Sounds old, but can be helpful. However, that does not make it the only translation we should use. Refusal to use any translation other than the KJV is somewhat similar to those who killed William Tyndale for translating the Bible into English. They were more concerned with hanging on to what they had than they were about others hearing and understanding the gospel. They were also concerned about errant interpretations. That is similar to refusing to use a computer or the internet because they transmit pornography. Certainly some modern translations, and especially paraphrases, have some misplaced emphasis or possibly worse. That is no reason to ignore them all and condemn anyone who uses them. A former coworker believes the KJV is the only accurate Bible to read. He told his son he was apostate for using the NIV. He could not identify an example passage where his son's version of the NIV was wrong.

The translation battle appears all too often in the body of Christ. In 2008, the Board of Elders of Life Bible Presbyterian Church sued the Far Eastern Bible College over "deviant Bible teachings, demanding they vacate their shared premises." The FEBC supports the concept of Verbal Plenary Preservation (VPP). FEBC teaches that the Textus Receptus, used to derive the KJV, is an exact replica of the original manuscript.[2]

I read a book proclaiming that Jesus would definitely use the KJV were He here today. The book raised all the imperfections with the other modern translations and postulated conspiracies to discredit the KJV and the Textus Receptus. The author's first example of the problems with other translations is four different options for the animal hide used in the tabernacle. It was not his most compelling example but involved the most conflicting versions. He did not mention a single weakness related to the KJV. He contends the KJV is perfect.

There are a few discrepancies in the reputable modern translations of the Bible. However, several very good contemporary translations communicate God's truth to a 21st century unchurched reader better than the KJV language. For example, compare Job 36:33 in the King James to a reputable modern translation. Here are a few examples of the outdated language used in the KJV compared to the ESV. They do make Bible reading more challenging than it should be.

- Exo 13:12 matrix vs. womb
- Job 26:12 divideth vs. stilled
- Mat 20:26 minister vs. servant
- Gal 1:13 conversation in time past vs. former life
- Gal 1:16 heathen vs. gentiles

The NKJV is a very good translation. Criticizing good translations is a distraction from the kingdom. Promoting versions not translated faithfully is even worse. Scripture reveals how God inspired the authors of the Bible- Isa 28:13; Jhn 14:26, 17:17; Gal 1:11-12; 2Ti 3:16-17; 1Th 2:13; Heb 4:12; 1Pe 1:23-25; and 2Pe 1:3-4, 21. That is especially reassuring.

> Psa 12:6 The words of the LORD are pure words, like silver refined in a furnace on the ground, purified seven times.

God certainly could have miraculously preserved the original NT text, as He did the Dead Sea Scrolls. He could have provided a much larger Rosetta stone than He did. He could have preserved the whole Bible if He chose to. He knows our nature. By giving us clues and a trail to follow, He has gotten us to study the Scripture in extreme detail. Something we may not have done if the signed original books of the Bible were available. Setting aside the sentimental aspect, we usually appreciate things we have had to work for more than the articles given to us. The praying, searching, analyzing, and debating have resulted in a far better understanding of God's holy Word.

The dead sea scrolls (dated 50 to over 400 years BC[3]) are almost identical to the previous oldest manuscripts dated in the ninth and tenth century AD.[4] The content of our Bible canon was compiled and debated over several hundred years and received consensus approval in the late fourth century. The chapter names and numbers appeared in the 13th century. The verse numbering used in modern Bibles was adopted in the 16th century. Through the influence of Martin Luther and others, several books of the Catholic Bible were removed from the Protestant Bible in the 16th century.[5] The extracted books are referred to as the Apocrypha. Portions of the Apocrypha were found among the Dead Sea Scrolls.[6]

Appendix C illustrates the evolution of the English Bible. Notice most of the changes have occurred in the last couple of centuries, and continues to escalate to the present. Discoveries of older copies of the NT and other period writings are bringing us closer and closer to what the original authors said. Some will say the reputable modern translations have 98% agreement.[7] That is based on about 600 verses out of the total, ranging from 31,100 to 31,173, being challenged based on manuscripts, historical evidence, etc. Most would agree the essentials of salvation and guidance for Christian life are correct in all reputable translations. The key elements of Jesus' teaching are abundantly clear.

> 2Pe 1:3 "His divine power has granted to us all things that pertain to life and godliness."

It seems to be the Lord's hand at work. Wouldn't God guide the translators as He did the authors? He probably did; at least those who would listen. As in all aspects of life, we sometimes choose to take the bit on the bridle of the Holy Spirit in our mouth and go where we want to go - Psa 32:9. Many theologians try to spin everything to support their beliefs; others have pushed their social agendas. These winds of change have found their way into some translations. This has been the case all the way back to King James, who commissioned the preparation of a new English translation because he didn't want the controversial marginal notes (proclaiming the Pope an Anti-Christ, etc.) contained in the Geneva Bible.[8] He wanted to conform to the ecclesiology and reflect the Episcopal structure of the Church of England and its belief in an ordained clergy.[9] There are other theories regarding his motivation. Textural criticism should be a science, confirming the theology. Bible translators have taken different approaches to translation. Some translations are word for word; others are thought for thought (dynamic equivalent). Some maintain traditional English, while others strive to present a textually correct Bible in contemporary American English. Another key decision is which manuscripts are the best for translation. These influences have resulted in about eight reputable translations, and many others with apparent motives in their content.[10] The latter is the tick on the end of the tail trying to wag the whole dog.

There are many examples of translation disputes born out of theology. A controversy with the RSV translation of the Hebrew word עַלְמָה (*'almāh*) in Isa 7:14 as "young woman" rather than the traditional Christian translation of "virgin." Of the seven appearances of *'almāh*, the Septuagint translates only two of them as *parthenos*, "virgin" (including Isa 7:14). By contrast, the word בְּתוּלָה (*batūlāh*) appears some 50 times. The Septuagint and English translations agree in understanding the word to mean "virgin" in almost every case.[11] Some groups claim that Jesus was an only child. They state that the Mar 6:3 reference to His brothers is mistranslated. They base this on the Greek word for "brother" also translated as "brethren" in passages like Mat 4:18.

Some denominations have generated their own Bible translation to support their theology. What does God think when He sees errant translations? Scripture warns they will get their just rewards now and/or in the hereafter - Deu 4:2, 12:32, Pro 30:5-6, Mat 5:19, Gal 1:8-9, and Rev 22:18. This loose respect for the accuracy of Scripture has led some, who claim to be Christian teachers, to say the Bible is like a library - pick what you read and follow only what you believe applies. That is just as bad as providing new, false revelation.

Some publishers produce a new translation every few years. My wife, Peggy, is a bit frustrated with their wordsmithery.

She had memorized numerous verses in the previous edition. She noticed they changed tenderhearted to compassionate in Eph 4:32 and Counselor to Advocate in Jhn 16:7. It is understandable that some wording would change as older Bible manuscripts and period writings are found and the translation of the Greek, Aramaic, and Hebrew is improved. However, word revisions with no change in meaning are of questionable value.

My TV has a bazillion pixels on the screen. The salesperson said they would eventually stop working. A failed pixel will hardly be noticeable, unless there is a bunch in the same area. The impact of a few glitches in the text of the Bible is like a few failed pixels on our TV. If we see them and obsess over them, then we will likely miss the program we are trying to watch. The Bible in our language is a great blessing. We can study it at length and commit it to our hearts as God intended. This is a privilege that many people did not have for the first 1600 years of Christianity. Some today still do not have that blessing. God's Word is truth, it will accomplish His purposes - Isa 55:11, 2Ti 3:16-17, and Heb 4:12. Paul supports the concept - "Let the word of Christ dwell in you richly, teaching and admonishing one another in all wisdom," (Col 3:16). Applying the concepts discussed in chapter 8, we can know which of the myriad of translations is best.

> Jhn 7:17 If anyone's will is to do God's will, he will know whether the teaching is from God or whether I am speaking on my own authority.

We can have a dozen translations on our shelf and not use any of them as God intended. Translations can enrich our knowledge and understanding of Scripture if approached properly. If abused, they can be a great tool for the devil to get us squabbling among ourselves while the lost remain lost. Bottom line, the best reputable translation to use is the one we will read and obey.

Faith and Works

One of the driving issues in the Protestant Reformation was the debate over the means to salvation - faith or works. Those who say that works are not required for salvation may be wrong. Those who say that faith alone is not enough are also likely wrong. As is usually the case, taking a dogmatic extreme position is quite risky. When two conflicting concepts seem to both be supported by Scripture, we should look for an understanding or circumstances where they are both true.

This is the marquee passage for the faith alone proponents.

> Eph 2:8-9 For by grace you have been saved through faith. And this is not your own doing; it is the gift of God, [9] <u>not a result of works, so that no one may boast</u>.

There are many other passages stating works do not save us - Gal 3:5-6, 2Ti 1:9.

> Jhn 6:28-29 Then they said to him, "What must we do, to be doing the works of God?" [29] Jesus answered them, "This is the work of God, that you <u>believe</u> in him whom he has sent."

Still not convinced? Here are a few more - Gen 15:6; Jhn 3:16; Rom 1:17, 3:12, 4:3-5, 5:1, 10:9; Gal 2:16, 3:11; and Jas 1:21. Before the sola fide (faith alone) crowd starts a victory dance, take a look at the role our works play. At least nineteen of the 27 books of the NT speak of the need for our good works. The passage just after the primary faith alone passage, Eph 2:10, teaches we were "created in Christ Jesus for good works, which God prepared beforehand, that we should walk in them." There is a similar saved by faith for good works pair in Tit 3:4-8. Jesus said, "I chose you and appointed you that you should go and bear fruit and that your fruit should abide" (Jhn 15:16).

The whole of Scripture explains the roles of faith and works. Paul provides a summary in Eph 3:3 - 4:9; we are saved by faith alone. However, there are dozens of passages that indicate our works are proof of our faith - Mat 3:8-10, 7:21, 25:45-46; Mar 4:20; Act 26:20; Heb 6:7-9; 1Jn 3:9; Jas 2:17-18.

Luk 3:8-9 <u>Bear fruits in keeping with repentance</u>. And do not begin to say to yourselves, 'We have Abraham as our father.' For I tell you, God is able from these stones to raise up children for Abraham. [9] Even now the axe is laid to the root of the trees. <u>Every tree therefore that does not bear good fruit is cut down and thrown into the fire</u>."

Jhn 14:23 Jesus answered him, "<u>If anyone loves me, he will keep my word</u>, and my Father will love him, and we will come to him and make our home with him.

The OT has a similar message - God "keeps covenant and steadfast love with those who love Him and keep his commandments" (Dan 9:4), "to <u>one who orders his way rightly</u> I will show the <u>salvation</u> of God!" (Psa 50:23). God accepted eunuchs and foreigners based on their commitment and obedience - Isa 56:4-8. Scripture repeatedly directs us to respond to the calling and faith that God has given us.

Jesus judges the validity of our faith based on our works - Mat 25:41-46. Jesus, John, Peter, Paul and the author of Hebrews have all told us something similar to work out your own salvation with fear and trembling - Pro 10:17, Mat 10:22, Phl 2:12, Heb 6:11, 2Pe 1:9-10. There are passages that clearly link obedience to salvation - Heb 5:9. They fit hand in glove with the faith passages. Our works are the proof of saving faith. It is not a cause and effect but a statement regarding the evidence of faith.

Jhn 8:51 Truly, truly, I say to you, if anyone keeps my word, he will never see death."

Luk 6:46 "Why do you call me 'Lord, Lord,' <u>and not do what I tell you</u>?

195

The good soil (believer), in the parable of the soils, is growing in faith and yielding up to a hundredfold - Mar 4:8. Paul gives great descriptions of the products of our faith being hope and love.

> 1Th 1:3 remembering before our God and Father your work of faith and labor of love and steadfastness of hope in our Lord Jesus Christ.

> 1Co 13:13 So now faith, hope, and love abide, these three; but the greatest of these is love.

How can love be greater than the faith that saves us? To truly express love like our Lord, we must first have the faith and the hope that enables it. If we have that love, we have all three and we are being obedient to the Lord. James supports this too - "But be doers of the word, and not hearers only, deceiving yourselves" (Jas 1:22).

Works finalize our faith, they are inseparable - Jas 2:21-24. Some of us rush to be religious like the priest and Pharisee rather than doing God's ministry like the good Samaritan. Many think believers under the Mosaic Covenant were forgiven their sins by sacrifices. It was not the act, but the faith it displayed that pleased God.

> Isa 1:11, 16 -17 "What to me is the multitude of your sacrifices? says the LORD; I have had enough of burnt offerings of rams and the fat of well-fed beasts; I do not delight in the blood of bulls, or of lambs, or of goats.... [16] Wash yourselves; make yourselves clean; remove the evil of your deeds from before my eyes; cease to do evil, [17] learn to do good; seek justice, correct oppression; bring justice to the fatherless, plead the widow's cause.

This passage, along with Amo 5:21-24, and Mic 6:6-8, tells us it is a heart of obedience that pleases the Lord. Just like in the NT, our obedience validates our faith. Abraham's faith in God in Gen 12:7 enabled him to do the great deeds we see in

Heb 11:8-19. This makes sense; we will be serving our Lord in heaven, too - Rev 7:15, 15:3, 19:5, 10, and 22:6. True joy comes from serving Him.

Rev 20:12-13 and 22:12 also support the concept that actions are a clear reflection of faith. Should we go so far as to say that no works means no faith as James states in Jas 2:17? NO! Judging salvation is God's job - Rom 14:4, 1Co 4:5, and Jas 4:12, 5:9.

The other extreme is just as bad. Works based salvation has wrought many problems. We go past being fruit inspectors to taking God's role of judging other's salvation or prescribing requirements for salvation - Mat 23:4, and Act 15:10.

> Rom 14:13 Therefore <u>let us not pass judgment on one another any longer,</u> but rather decide <u>never to put a stumbling block or hindrance in the way of a brother.</u>

Related to this controversy is the application of grace. Some ignore it, leading their constituents to believe we have to earn our way into heaven. Others want to apply grace to any and everything, leaving no apparent value in godly living. It is like the spiritual counterpart to some education initiatives. Standards are lowered until everyone passes; knowledge gained is of secondary importance. Grace overemphasized with a neglect of other biblical teaching can lead to a shallow walk with a weak witness, or worse. Some denominations, considered cults, have much better service for and attraction to the community than some *accepted* denominations. It is interesting to note the groups that have service expectations have grown more than many of those that do not. Scripture does not tell us to coerce people by telling them their works will save them.

Jesus said our fruit should confirm our faith and thus our salvation. If we do not feel led to do the Lord's bidding then we may not have saving faith - Mar 12:30-31. There are reasons we may not bear fruit in our lives for a season.

Remind everyone, if they are not bearing fruit in their lives for other than a complete restriction (mentally incapacitated), they need to consider the authenticity of their faith. With the right attitude, a bed-ridden person has a powerful platform to proclaim the gospel.

Baptism

There are many hardened beliefs about Baptism. We see a plethora of requirements regarding age, belief, and technique. Some dispensationalists claim baptism is no longer needed. Perhaps the worst is - one must be baptized in our denomination to be saved. How vain! The immediate question is how were people saved before that denomination came into being? The second would be to prove it in Scripture. The Bible does not discuss denominations. Men do not save us.

> Psa 49:7 Truly <u>no man can ransom another</u>, or give to God the price of his life.

What about rebaptism? Some forbid it based on the one baptism mentioned in Eph 4:5. That passage can be read as one valid baptism or one baptism period. Some churches forbid a second baptism for any reason. Others require a rebaptism if they feel the first was done incorrectly, for example, baptized before belief. Act 19:1-5 presents an example of repeating baptism. It is a very specific example and does not support some requirements we see today.

A dispute over the need to rebaptize is a great place to use the bilateral weaker brother mentality ©; lots of empathy, sharing of feelings and prayer because we are not positive who is completely correct according to all Scripture. Then seek the Lord's guidance for the best course of action.

Many refer to Peter and the eunuch in Act 8:37 as requiring believer Baptism. Those who require belief before baptism consider this verse the mandate for their position. Those who support infant baptism favor the older more reliable manuscripts, which do not contain that verse. In or out, it does not resolve the issue. If we shared the gospel with an adult, and they expressed their need to be baptized, we would attempt to ensure they truly believe before we facilitate their baptism. The infant baptism crowd claims this is what Peter was doing in Act 8:37.

In some ways, a believer baptism can be more meaningful than a profession of faith around the age of understanding. It creates urgency for the question of belief that is sometimes not there for people baptized as infants. Conversely, this urgency sometimes causes parents to push children to a profession and baptism at such an early age they have not made a mature spiritual commitment. In that case, there is no other faith defining experience in their life. Is this contributing to over 50% of baptized youth leaving their faith in their late teens and 20s?

Baptism is an important experience in the life of a Christian and those who love them. Some denominations have only adult baptism. That seems to be missing out on a great opportunity to get a commitment from those involved in bringing up a child when they are baptized (christened, etc.) at an early age. Others have infant baptism with no major spiritual expression of commitment in their adult life. Some recognize both spiritual steps to realize both benefits, that makes sense.

Some focus on the many passages in Scripture linking baptism with salvation and state it is required for salvation.

> Jhn 3:5 Jesus answered, "Truly, truly, I say to you, unless one is born of water and the Spirit, he cannot enter the kingdom of God.

Others will reference the exceptions in Scripture like David's son, and the thief on the cross and state that baptism is not required for salvation. They would also note that Scripture states we are saved by faith alone. We cannot put the God of the universe in a theological box. The Catechism of the Catholic Church Vc. §1257 contains the following statement - "God has bound salvation to the sacrament of Baptism, but he himself is not bound by his sacraments." Some may take exception with the wording, but both concepts are biblically sound - Mat 28:19; Mar 16:16; Jhn 3:5; Act 2:38, 10:48, 22:16; Gal 3:27; and Tit 3:5-7.

Take a hypothetical situation; you are an elder (or equivalent) in your church and your board is examining a person for membership in the church. The person relates they were never baptized and do not see the need to. Would you let them join? Or, would you attempt to help them understand the importance of our obedience to God? This is analogous to our works being a reflection of our faith. A priest said it this way, "If you have a chance to be baptized then it is required." It is hard to oppose that position.

John baptized Jesus in the Jordan, not likely a sprinkle. However, some say the Jordan was not deep enough at that time of year for immersion. What about the description of baptism "come up out of the water" (Mat 3:16, Mar 1:10, and Act 8:39)? John went to areas with adequate water to baptize - Jhn 3:23. Scripture does not mention what they did in areas without sufficient water to immerse. In that dry land, there were almost certainly conversions when there was barely enough water to drink. Some contend that pouring and sprinkling began in the second century when there was insufficient water for immersion; over time, these secondary modes came to replace immersion.[12]

There are groups that condemn immersion techniques other than their own. Some of these examples are well documented, others take a little digging to find. Two denominations share similar doctrine except their immersion technique. One goes face first, while the other goes back first. They have little to do with each other. WOW! Some require three immersions: one for the Father, the Son and the Holy Spirit - Mat 28:19.

Jews baptized for centuries before Christ. They used a squat descent.

Today over two billion of the 3+ billion Christians in the world practice some form of sprinkling or pouring. We have borrowed, assembled, filled, and heated water in a loaned baptismal for a requested immersion baptism in our church. Choosing a less involved, symbolic form of baptism is lot easier. Is sprinkling a worse sin than the divisions in the body, criticizing our siblings in the Lord, judging and condemning them as sinners, or even not believers? Immersion may be the more excellent way. Scripture does not say those who pour or sprinkle are not saved.

God may have left the wiggle room for situations where a person can't be immersed - insufficient water, death bed conversions, fox hole conversions, diminished health, people with fear of water, etc. I am confident our loving God will accept a sprinkle or a pour to meet His command to be baptized if that is all that is attainable. We honor God with the heroic efforts needed to immerse a person in a wheel chair. It is our expression of obedience, worship, and emulation.

There have been volumes written on this issue, and unnumbered sermons and debates. If the method or circumstance of baptism were essential, God would have made it clear in Scripture. If we get out of pridefully defending our mode, then we may be able to open our hearts and see it from God's perspective.

There are passages to support various methods and the ages of the participants. We should allow people and churches to follow their heart without criticism or condemnation on the non-essential aspects of baptism. Those that sprinkle children could allow members to wait until their child is a believer and do an immersion baptism if requested. There is a lake or pool available for those who feel that leading. We have done it in our Presbyterian church several times. We should allow them the variation described in Scripture and not contest this any longer.

We have attended many marriage ceremonies - small to giant, modest receptions to sit down dinners, standard vows and custom written. After looking at the pictures a few times, the only thing that matters is living up to the vows. The ceremony does not make the marriage. Scripture tells us to repent from our sins, be baptized, and make a public profession of faith. What does Scripture teach is most important to God: the age, sequence, technique of those three steps, or our obedience to the vows until He calls us home?

Coming to an agreement as the body of Christ on the essentials and freedoms related to baptism would send a clarion call to the Christian and secular world that we R2B1!

Do This In Remembrance Of Me

Mentioned just five times in Scripture (three in the gospels), Communion is another area with many tightly held doctrines. Divisions have taken their toll on famous theologians. Jonathon Edwards and John Calvin were expelled from their churches for their position on the Lord's Supper. The frequency of taking communion varies from every service to monthly or less. Scripture does not prescribe a frequency. There is a variety of methods for administering the Eucharist. There are many understandings of what the elements represent - water, juice, wine or the miraculous change to the body and blood of Christ.

Scripture is clear we are not to partake of Communion if we do not believe.

> 1Co 10:21 You cannot drink the cup of the Lord and the cup of demons. <u>You cannot partake of the table of the Lord and the table of demon</u>s.

Another clear message is that we are not to take our salvation for granted; we are to examine ourselves each time we partake.

1Co 11:28-32 <u>Let a person examine himself</u>, then, and so eat of the bread and drink of the cup. [29] For anyone who eats and drinks without discerning the body eats and drinks judgment on himself. [30] That is why many of you are weak and ill, and some have died. [31] <u>But if we judged ourselves truly, we would not be judged</u>. [32] But when we are judged by the Lord, we are disciplined so that we may not be condemned along with the world.

Some do not allow fellow Christian from a different denomination to celebrate the Eucharist in their church. Can we be so sure we are correct in our doctrine as to exclude others who claim Jesus as their Lord and Savior? Paul directs us to partake as one body.

1Co 10:16-17 The cup of blessing that we bless, is it not a participation in the blood of Christ? The bread that we break, is it not a participation in the body of Christ? [17] Because there is one bread, <u>we who are many are one body</u>, for we all partake of the one bread.

Allow Christians of other faiths to participate in the communion at our church and commend those denominations that practice an open communion. Which of the following is more important to Jesus: our belief about the elements and who we allow to participate, or how the celebration changes our life until the next observance? Do not focus on process at the expense of our Lord's objective to lead us to examine our obedient response to His sacrifice.

Women's Role in Church

This is a highly contested issue in the body. The secular women's movement has likely catalyzed this issue. Why be so adamant for either extreme? Unlike the 30+ passages that speak to unity in the body of Christ, there is not a lot said about this in Scripture.

Paul makes a clear statement in support of male elders and deacons - 1Ti 3:2, 3:12 and Titus 1:6. There are excellent women elders and deacons. We do not know why God did not make future allowance for this in the Word, but He did not. HOWEVER, when men are not qualified, available or willing to serve, the Lord's work must be done. Men accepting the responsibility, but not doing it well, are also a problem - Jdg 4:8-9. A woman serving in church leadership is sometimes analogous to single mothers. Men leave their wives (or the mother of their children) to raise his children alone. The wife has no alternative other than to attempt to fulfill the male role in his absence.

Many men abuse the model of male leadership described in the NT. If we love our wives like Christ loves the church - Eph 5:25, we would never have to quote Scripture to get our wife to do the right thing. Sadly, men's wishes are often not the right thing. If we bathed our differences in prayer, the Holy Spirit would lead us to know the right request of our spouse. If we lived like that, we would have much less criticism about God's leadership model. In fact, we would have women lining up to marry a man that loves her as Christ loved the church. On the other side of the issue, I have seen many churches where the women have taken on most of the leadership in the church and the men sit back doing very little.

It is hard to identify the weaker brother here. If the people are uncomfortable with female leadership and the congregation wants to go with the conservative position, Scripture does not object. To say this is a sin would be wrong. Conversely, many churches have weak education and ministry due to lack of leadership. A woman talented in teaching or in leadership picking up the slack is not a sin. Taking that position would be contrary to the examples in Scripture. There have been many dying churches revived by women pastors.

Many would say Paul's guidance in 1Ti 2:12 was for that day and does not apply now. We cannot say for sure it was intended for that time when women were not educated to teach, or forever.

We must be extremely careful with contextual exclusion, or we end up dismissing Scripture in a way God never intended. We have seen the Lord use women in the male dominated times of the Bible. Is today any different? Deborah led an army in Judges 4-5. Act 2:17 says women prophesy, and Act 18:26 describes Priscilla helping Aquila train Apollos. God uses women to teach for the glory of His kingdom. Nancy Demoss Wolgemuth teaches on Moody Radio. Even though her program is for women, I found her more edifying than some of the male preachers; and they are all inspiring teachers. A Barna Pastor Poll determined the number of Protestant female pastors doubled in the ten-year period ending in 2015.[13] This does not support making it a requirement as some denominations have. Drug abuse and adultery are also gaining popularity. We must never base our standards on public opinion.

One practical reason women should not teach men is the attitude of men. The bias against women teaching men is so strong in some, a woman could present Billy Graham's best sermon and it would do no good. Many will not listen with the intent to learn and some will not even come to class. Some men are so set in their ways, teaching them can be like washing a duck; it all just runs off anyway. It should not be that way; but in many cases it is. Even open-minded men likely resonate more with teaching from men - like athletes mentoring athletes, former addicts counseling addicts, etc. Respect from men in the church may be won without a word by the conduct of their women - concept from 1Pet 3:1.

Another reason to limit women teaching men is the importance of their talent elsewhere. Children are moldable clay, effectively teaching them is critical. Children frequently bond better and feel more comfortable with women teachers. Similarly, in many homes the mother does most of the teaching of the children, so it is vital that the mothers be well prepared in this area. One last practical reason is another facet of the male abdication mentioned above. The person who learns the most in a class is the teacher. If the women are doing all the teaching, they are getting the best learning as well.

This battle has casualties too. In the fervor of our PC world, some see "women's ministry" as a demeaning term for second-class citizens. Efforts to cultivate ministry for and involve women of God has diminished. This is not the first time the children of the King have tried to solve one problem and created another.

Perhaps God, the creator of the male psyche, led Paul's guidance in 1Ti 2:12 to help keep men involved. Male leadership in church does mirror the order of leadership in the family. This mystery will not be resolved this side of heaven. We are likely wrong to take an extreme position on either side of this issue, OR to criticize others for their approach in this area. There are far bigger problems to deal with in the body and in the world.

Trinity

This concept is a divisive doctrine in the body of Christ. Most who support it consider those who do not to be a cult. The OT comprises 76% of our Bible. It speaks extensively about God, His nature, and His dealing with humanity. It only mentions Jesus in about 300 prophesies deliberately shrouded in mystery - Rom 16:25, and perhaps in a few preincarnate appearances. The NT also speaks extensively about God and describes Jesus and the Holy Spirit as being subordinate to the Father - Jhn 5:19, 16:13; 1Co 8:5-6, 11:3, 15:28; Col 1:15-17 and others. Jesus said, "I am ascending to my Father and your Father, to my God and your God" (Jhn 20:17). It is understandable that some would question the concept of the Trinity. The term does not appear in Scripture, but many passages support the concept.

The battle over the nature and identity of Jesus has raged from almost the beginning. Emperor Constantine called the Council held in Nicaea in 325 to settle several disputes including the nature of the Son in his relationship to the Father. Presbyter Arius and two others (out of about 300) supported the position that Jesus was created out of nothing, and therefore had a beginning. While the rest supported the position that Jesus was begotten by the Father from His own being, and therefore had no beginning. The conclusion of the council was the Nicene Creed, which clearly states that Jesus was begotten not made. The dissenting position continues today, referred to as Arianism after Arius.[14] There are two major, and about a dozen smaller, denominations that do not see the Father, Son and Holy Spirit as one Trinitarian being. Non-Trinitarian views differ widely on the nature of God, Jesus, and the Holy Spirit. This diverse perspective might be an indication that they are not on the right track.

The Bible teaches that God is beyond our comprehension - Ecc 3:11, Isa 40:28, Rom 11:34, and 1Co 2:16. We are a lot like the three blind men providing a description of an elephant, each with a limited arm's length perspective (trunk, leg and tail). Our attempts to describe the infinite God fall far short of complete. The belief that Jesus is not God may be blasphemous. Some would consider a biblical understanding of the Trinity to be an essential for salvation. Scripture is clear we are not saved by knowledge of Jesus - Jas 2:19. Saving faith likely includes a proper understanding of how He is qualified to be our Savior.

Appendix D provides Scripture that describe the Father, Son and Holy Spirit. If you struggle with this, ask the Holy Spirit to guide you in reading the Bible front to back focused on passages that give us a diverse picture of the nature of the Father, Son and Holy Spirit. Read a book that deals with this question (Jesus as God by Murray J Harris; or Putting Jesus in His Place by Robert M. Bowman Jr. and J. Ed Komoszewski). This concept is far too important to get it wrong.

Non-Trinitarian denominations usually do not participate in ecumenical councils. They view them as misguided human attempts to establish doctrine and define dogmas by debate rather than by revelation. Before we get on our high horse looking down our nose at those with a different view of the nature of Jesus, we need to ask ourselves if we are being faithful to all of Scripture. We must also ask how we are doing with the "love your neighbor" part. Is our judgmental spirit driving people away from our Lord and the truth of Scripture? Jesus told us to pray, "Our father in heaven, hallowed be your name" (Mat 6:9). The American Standard Version (ASV) 1941 used Jehovah (English form of Yĕhovah) for the name of God 6,781 times. The ASV was the primary text for the development of the Revised Standard Version (RSV) in 1952, which removed them all in favor of LORD even though Yĕhovah appears over 6500 times in the Hebrew text. The KJV uses it four times and other modern translations, none.[15] Some consider this a hostile response to the group that holds the name Jehovah in high regard. "Let him who is without sin among you be the first to throw a stone" (Jhn 8:7).

Peter had a distorted perspective of who Jesus was in Mar 8:32-34. Jesus rebuked him and kept on teaching and loving him. Some believe those holding a different view of the nature of God, Jesus and the Holy Spirit, or differ with their views of essentials are not saved. They are in essence saying no one was saved before that specific doctrine was established. Really?! How could our loving God of grace see it that way? Even if they are not saved, we are to avoid being a stumbling block to them - 1Co 10:32, and 2Co 6:3. If you already see the Father, Son and Holy Spirit as our triune Godhead, do not condemn those who claim Jesus as their Savior and are working hard to spread the gospel and disciple people in the Bible. Love them and lead them to truth as Jesus led Peter.

Some denominations, considered Christian, have accepted doctrine just as wayward to Scripture as the perspective on the Trinity held by the groups considered non-Christian cults. I have read of pastors who preach Jesus was not the product of a virgin birth, and say He is not the Son of God, yet their denomination is considered Christian. A recent *Christian* denominational meeting included a prayer to Allah.

Other Disputed Issues

Should vs. Shall - Nuclear power plants have many, many procedures. They have prescriptive guidance for performing them. Their procedures have steps that *should* be done and others that *shall* be done. A *should* statement had to be done unless not possible and supervision concurred that circumstances prohibited it. Conversely, a *shall* statement must be implemented or stop work and get the procedure conflict resolved. Scripture has a lot of guidance for Christian life. Some appear to be in the form of should and others appear to be a shall. Most of us have intermingled some of the shoulds and shalls, in both directions. Taking a should to a shall comes across as legalistic. If the lost see us as legalists instead of those learning to love like Jesus, we do not draw people to Him, especially the young folks. Changing a shall into a should erodes the authority of all Scripture and starts a movement down the slippery slope into anything goes. There are problems with both deviations. Frequently the children of the strictest parents become wayward, only exceeded in misbehavior by those with little parental oversight.

Christians have dealt with *should* and *shall* doctrine in a variety of different ways. Some have denominational documents that dictate behavior and how to deal with deviations. Some documents specify offenses as well as consequences while others use scriptural guidance for dealing with deviations. Some specify criteria at the denomination level while others allow each church to establish its requirements. It is interesting to note that some have requirements in their church doctrine that time has proven to be invalid. It then becomes quite difficult to remove a requirement that was added based on perceived inspiration. That should be a lesson to us all to be very careful when we establish a shall.

Many of these contested should-shall issues are about Christian life and are not theological essentials. Scripture clearly calls us to be holy, meaning set apart - Eph 5:27, 1Pe 1:15-16, and Rev 22:11. Our approach to being holy is as varied as our theology. There are groups that believe it is a sin to drink alcohol. Alcohol abuse is one of the major societal problems facing the world, but Scripture does not tell us drinking alcohol is a sin. There are several passages in the Bible that would indicate that drinking alcohol in appropriate moderation is not a sin - 1Ti 5:23. Our Lord turned water into wine for guests - Mat 11:19. He will give us aged wine in heaven - Isa 25:6.

Some say those passages are referring to processed grape juice, not a fermented drink. How can processed grape juice gladden the heart of man - Psa 104:15? Paul condemns getting drunk in the celebration of the Lord's Supper - 1Co 11:21. It appears Scripture references to wine deal with a fermented drink.

It is hard to control behavior with mandates. Instilling values and wisdom is far more successful. Studies have shown that alcohol abuse is most frequent by the offspring in the homes of teetotalers (drinking forbidden), next most come from the homes of alcohol abusers, and the least likely from homes of responsible drinkers. There is a place for abstinence. Some people cannot use substances responsibly; it is not in their nature. For them, abstinence is the best policy. Those of us who are around them should abstain in their presence - Rom 14:15.

Publications from Reader's Digest to the New England Journal of Medicine say that drinking a little alcohol is actually good for us. Then we hear Christians say the God that created the universe considers it a sin. What impression is this doctrine having on non-believers? Recent studies have linked drinking in moderation to cancer. Discourage alcohol on a medical or behavioral basis; just do not say the Bible calls it a sin when it does not.

One denomination forbids partaking caffeine from coffee and tea. However, it is acceptable to consume caffeine from sodas and other drinks. Beverages with caffeine elevated far above coffee and tea are acceptable even though they have been linked to health problems and even death. Ask a few non-believers what they think about this guidance. Ask them if the wisdom and logic draws them to our Lord and Savior. How is it benefiting the kingdom of God? It should bring into question the reliability of the source of this requirement.

Paul states in 1Co 7:9 that some people are not made to be single. I would not have done well as a celibate minister. Where is the wisdom in making celibacy for ministers an expectation? Paul did not speak kindly of those who forbid marriage.

> 1Ti 4:1-3 Now the Spirit expressly says that in later times some will depart from the faith by devoting themselves to deceitful spirits and teachings of demons, [2] through the insincerity of liars whose consciences are seared, [3] who forbid marriage and require abstinence from foods that God created to be received with thanksgiving by those who believe and know the truth.

Peter was a founder of the church, and he was married - Mar 1:30, and 1Co 9:5. There have been far too many instances of sexual abuse by celibate clergy. The Bible advises it is good to be single, it does not say leaders are required to be single - 1Co 7:28. Why require something that the Bible does not?

Some groups forbid any religious practice not mentioned in the NT. The use of musical instruments is an example. I saw a church website with one of the main links going to a seven-page article supporting this position. They feel that once we no longer need to find NT support for a position, anything goes. Musical instruments are used extensively in the OT. The NT contains no prohibition for use of instruments. There are musical instruments mentioned in the NT - 1Co 14:7-8. Do these churches have synthetic fiber in their church carpet or upholstery; do they use electric lights and air conditioning in their sanctuary?

Some groups forbid watching movies. There are many movies a Christian should never see. Some recent productions have inspiring biblical values. Our attendance in these good movies supports more being made, and their success may influence some non-believers to watch them. We need to ensure what we forbid is clearly supported by Scripture.

Other forbidden practices seem to go beyond Scripture. Some forbid jewelry based on 1Pe 3:3 while Gen 24:47, and 53 and Luk 15:22 permit it. Some forbid dancing, though the Bible mentions it in several places. We should place this in the category of wisdom and not doctrine. We need to observe the concept, not take the example to an extreme. If these groups reunited, they could continue their conservative practices. For example, no musical instruments at joint activities for the sake of unity in the body.

During a 2015 radio program, Irwin Lutzer, the pastor of Moody Church, shared that his church considers a non-biblical divorce as a disqualification to be an elder. He pointed out it was a local standard. There are positions in the body that are stricter and more lenient. Their interpretation is not wrong; it is what they feel led to do based on guidance in 1Timothy and Titus.

It is good to limit the influence of the world where possible. "You shall be holy, for I am holy" (1Pe 1:15-16). From the Lord's perspective there are probably far more of us falling short on this important element of our Christian walk than there are those overdoing it. Avoiding TV is a challenge; especially once I sit down to watch it. One might look at 1Cor 7:29-31 and say this is a sin. Depending on what I was neglecting or watching, it may be. Healthy food is not a sin; however, eating healthy food to the point of gluttony is. The objective for some denominations limiting outside contact is valid. Time spent pursuing the things of this world do not bring us nearer to our Lord. We may take exception to the extent of their practices. In some cases, they may be missing opportunities to influence the world with the gospel. At the same time, they avoid many of the pitfalls that we encounter getting too close to the world - Jas 3:13-15. They are doing something right. They have far less money problems than other faiths. Some of these groups have 90% of their children remaining in the faith; other Christians cannot approach this success in passing on our faith to our children.

Matthew 6 speaks of fasting in the present tense "when you fast"; it is not if, but when. Fasting is seldom the topic of sermons, though scripture directs us to this significant spiritual blessing. Why do we criticize others for denying themselves worldly distractions such as television, internet, etc? Why do we look down on those who observe Lent? I have denied myself something valued to observe Lent the last several years. Every time I thought about that denial, I considered my relationship with God. That is wonderful!

We need to remember not to apply the same rules to non-believers until they are believers. How we deal with those who violate a *shall* is critical to our obedience to the Lord and the reputation of the body of Christ.

Both theological extremes have problems in how they treat the lost in serious sin. Dealing with them is a lot like raising teenagers. If we judge, ignore, and neglect our teens, they will follow the dominant influences in their life. Most of those are not good. I read of a Christian pastor who threw his unwed, pregnant daughter out of the house for her mistake. He may have broken their relationship for life. What a terrible example to his church and the watching world. The other extreme is to cater to their every whim. Some parents throw keg parties for their minor children and friends saying, "They are going to drink, they might as well do it supervised." Those teens become incapable of doing for themselves. Some claim they are not even responsible for their own decisions; the term used for these afflicted young adults is afluenza. Google defines it as a psychological malaise supposedly affecting wealthy young people, symptoms of which include a lack of motivation, feelings of guilt, and a sense of isolation. Does that definition describe some people going to our churches that claim to be Christian and likely are not? Both parenting extremes deserve the result they get. Jesus will have some choice words for them when they meet Him face to face.

> Mal 2:17 You have wearied the LORD with your words. But you say, "How have we wearied him?" By saying, "Everyone who does evil is good in the sight of the LORD, and he delights in them." Or by asking, "Where is the God of justice?"

The Greek Orthodox Church website has a great statement for dealing with such sin.

> In full confidentiality, the Orthodox Church cares and provides pastorally for homosexuals in the belief that no sinner who has failed himself and God should be allowed to deteriorate morally and spiritually.

We should not be condemning each other for differences in how we feel led to be holy as long as they do not conflict with the Bible. We should learn from each other and pursue what works best for the success of the body of Christ.

Gifts - Spiritual gifts is another area with strongly held differences in the body. God intends there may be no division in the body regarding the use of gifts. Scripture describes the gifts of the Spirit followed by a great description of the united body - 1Co 12:7-25. That passage describes us as one body six times. We should not argue about what Scripture has not made crystal clear. Even if someone is a weaker brother regarding his beliefs about gifts; we are to love them as a brother or sister in the Lord and let God deal with their non-essential beliefs.

Some believe certain gifts of the Spirit ended with the apostolic age; others believe they continue today. We would all agree that God still does miracles. We see many gifts displayed by people in the church every day - hospitality, service, administration, teaching, etc. Paul instructs us in 1Co 12:31 to seek the greater gifts - listed in order in 12:28-30 they are apostles, prophets, teachers, workers of miracles, healing, service, administration, then tongues. The spectrum of attitudes toward speaking in tongues is amazing. It runs from almost forbidden, to expected, or almost required. Those differences are another example where the church is divided and adversarial, and both sides need to apply biblical concepts. The message of speaking in tongues is often a mystery.

> 1Co 15:2 For one who speaks in a tongue speaks not to men but to God; for no one understands him, <u>but he utters mysteries in the Spirit</u>.

Paul advises in 1Co 14:27-28 this application of tongues does not belong in church if there is no interpreter. He also informs us not to forbid speaking in tongues - 1Co 14:39. Tongues is clearly not an essential.

<u>Worship</u> - We all question or even challenge the worship styles of those in a church we have visited or heard about. It could be dress, music style, or physical expressions during worship. We sometimes criticize those in our own church. When we visited a charismatic church, I found myself scanning the room and doing a spiritual critique - "that's Ok," "no that's going too far," "they are just trying to attract attention," and so on. Then it hit me that whatever they were doing in sincere worship was better than my fit of judging when I was supposed to be worshiping the LORD. A good friend of mine is an elder in an evangelical church, a solid Christian and God-fearing man. He attempted to address the frustration of his daughters going to an independent church by visiting there himself on a Sunday night. He said, "I don't know why they put the words to the songs on the screen, they are waving their arms so much you can't see the screen anyway." I asked if there were many people there, and he said it was full. I inquired about the lyrics and teaching, they were biblical. I asked, "So what's the problem?" He paused a moment and said, "Nothing I suppose." The Bible

supports a large spectrum of worship styles. The worship is for God; let Him assess the style and quality.

Sabbath - In the past, many faiths had strict observance of the Sabbath - no work, recreation, etc.; some still do. Others seldom mention any Sabbath observance. As is usually the case, neither extreme is right. Which day is right, Saturday or Sunday? Times were different when everybody observed the Sabbath on the same day. If we eat out, shop, use electricity or water, go to the hospital, watch TV, etc. on our Sabbath day, we are making people work on our Sabbath. Mar 2:27 states the Sabbath is for us not vice versa. Christ Church, in Jerusalem, has services on Friday, Saturday, and Sunday to reach out to people of several former beliefs. Does God still expect us to take a day to rest and fellowship more closely with Him? Absolutely! It is not as important which day we have a Sabbath, as that we do observe one. Lead by imitating Jesus, others will follow.

End Game - Do we go directly to heaven when we die, or do we go to a holding area (paradise, Abraham's bosom, purgatory, etc.)? Some are satisfied with what Jesus told the thief on the cross in Luk 23:43. Those promoting other positions will note that the punctuation in the Bible is not part of the inspired text. If we were to move the comma to after the word today, it opens up other interpretations. Is this worth arguing about? God's plan will be just what we need. What we believe will have no impact on the actual outcome. Those beliefs have no bearing on how we should live our lives until then. As we discussed in chapter 4, there will be a judgment of all believers after death. The mechanics of that are not very clear. The Bible reminds us not to worry. If we live obedient lives, we do not need to be anxious about that judgment. We should direct that energy to being ready and spreading the gospel.

Books and movies have generated a lot of interest in end times. There are many different beliefs about the book of Revelation. Some believe it has all happened already; some believe it is all in the future; and some believe it is unfolding over time.

There are several different beliefs about the rapture relative to the tribulation: pre-millennium, amillennial, and post-millennium. Following a detailed discussion of these beliefs, a former pastor said there is a fourth option, pan-millennium. Many were anxious to hear about this option. He said, "It is very simple, it will all pan out in the end." If we needed to know specifics, He would have had the Scripture writers describe it clearly. It is more likely a glimpse to stimulate our faith and the associated obedience. These discussions are not as important as many other things the Lord has told us to do.

People want to know what to expect; they will ask questions. We should present all related Scripture references not just the ones that support our position. This enables the Holy Spirit to lead people to the correct conclusion - Jhn 16:13. They are likely to conclude this is another mystery. The emphasis in Scripture is for us to be ready at all times; it could be tomorrow - Mat 24:44 and Mar 13:35. When we get to heaven is God going to be more concerned with the accuracy of our eschatology or the effectiveness of our witness and evangelism?

Tolerance

The suggestion to focus on understanding and tolerance in these divisive areas may anger some readers. I pray that is not the outcome.

The death penalty is another divisive issue. The NAE's 2015 Capital Punishment resolution acknowledges the diversity of evangelical views on capital punishment stating, "Evangelical Christians differ in their beliefs about capital punishment, often citing strong biblical and theological reasons.... We affirm the conscientious commitment of both streams of Christian ethical thought." Scripture leaves some matters open to judgment and circumstance. Capital punishment is one of these. Scripture warns that God has given the government the sword to exercise judgment on civil disobedience - Rom 13:4. The Bible also teaches mercy and forgiveness. We should promote our position where appropriate to influence the law of the land, but not condemn other Christians for seeing it a different way.

Our intolerance in sinful beliefs has done incredible harm at times. For example, some southern US churches were opposed to the civil rights movements in the 1960s. In the 1860s, many of the same churches supported slavery with Scripture text.[16] Doctrine **not** fully supported and validated by all Scripture is likely in error. This harms our ministry, the image of the Church, the kingdom, and most importantly, reaching the lost. Do not tell people in a wayward body they are lost, even though they may be. That is God's decision, and we alienate them from our influence. Is there a passage in Scripture that requires our theology to be faultless for our salvation? Take another look at the doctrinal beliefs in Appendix F. Which one(s) would God exclude people from heaven for not getting right? God judges the condition of a person's heart - Act 17:31; Rom 2:16, 14:10; and 2Ti 4:1. He told us not to judge another person's salvation status. We should leave the judging of souls to God and try to grow back together. Love them like Jesus would have. We often treat our cousins in Christ far more harshly than we do non-believers. We might have a more positive influence on them if we treated them like people we want to see in heaven.

Just as we are all sinners, all denominations have some suspect doctrine when challenged by all of Scripture. As discussed earlier, even brothers will have some different beliefs - Rom 14:21, 1Co 8:8-9, and 1Jn 2:10. These must not involve essentials (required for salvation). It is often difficult to determine which of the sinners on this planet are Christians. It is almost as hard to determine which denominations are truly Christian.

> Mar 9:50 "Salt is good, but if the salt has lost its saltiness, how will you make it salty again? Have salt in yourselves, and be at peace with one another."

My study Bible has the following note on that verse - "Strife is resolved and peace restored when we recognize in one another a common commitment to Jesus and the gospel."[17] Seek to influence those with errant essentials by loving them like Jesus would have. If our ministry is without theological error, God will bless it - Jas 1:25-26.

12. WHY NOT?

Commit your work to the LORD, and your
plans will be established. Pro 16:3

I really hope you did not skip to this chapter to see the recommendations. Ecumenical movements have failed in every century since Christ ascended; the preceding chapters provided a compelling motivation to pursue unity with the necessary commitment to achieve success. We have been growing apart for centuries and have seen the adverse consequences. We should not allow this to discourage us from being what Jesus commanded, we R2B1. With a suitable approach, we can grow back together.

Robert F. Kennedy was the US Attorney General, a Senator, and a Presidential candidate (assassinated during the primary season in 1968). One of his famous quotes applies very well to the unity challenge in Christianity. "Some men see things as they are, and ask why. I dream of things that never were, and ask <u>why not</u>."[1]

We must remember the devil is the enemy, **NOT** our brothers and sisters in Christ who espouse different non-essential doctrine. Those that see essentials differently are not our enemy either. They, like us on other matters, need to move back to the Bible in their beliefs. What is the best way to do it? A primary objective of this book is to get us talking and listening to each other.

Forming friendships with people of other denominations (bridging) results in a better understanding of differences It certainly did that for me in the clergy interviews. Jesus reached out to a Samaritan woman who believed quite differently - Jhn 4:7; He would want us to do the same.

The Faith Matters survey of 2006-7 determined a range of 54% to 83% of Christians said that non-Christians could go to heaven, with those who support salvation of the dead being at the upper end. While the clergy stated that faith in Jesus is required for salvation ranged from 57-63% for main line denominations to 98-100% of evangelical denominations. A 1924 survey of High School students in Muncie, Indiana, found 94% felt Christianity was the one true religion, while the same question asked at the same school in 1977, revealed only 38% felt it was.[2] We have the tedious task of identifying our misinterpreted doctrines, and reducing our animosity toward other Christians without losing biblical truth. As you read this chapter, every time you say, "This is obvious," ask yourself "am I doing it?" Then commit to do it.

The following is a great description by J. C. Ryle of our calling as the body of Christ.

> It is a church of which all the members have the same marks. They are all born of the Spirit; they all possess "repentance towards God, faith towards our Lord Jesus Christ," and holiness of life and conversation. They all hate sin, and they all love Christ. They worship differently and after various fashions; some worship with a form of prayer, and some with none; some worship kneeling, and some standing; but they all worship with one heart. They are all led by one Spirit; they all build upon one foundation; they all draw their religion from one single Book—that is the Bible. They are all joined to one great center—that is Jesus Christ. They all even now can say with one heart, "Hallelujah"; and they can all respond with one heart and voice, "Amen and Amen."[3]

If you feel that description is accurate, then the rest of this chapter is achievable. If not, then stop and write a letter to Jesus. Explain what part is objectionable and why. If the letter becomes difficult, then read the rest of this chapter. It may provide a different perspective.

Good Signs

There have been some positive signs of growing unity in recent years. Several denominations have backed away from some tenets that most Christians, and many non-Christians, have found objectionable. It was much easier to be a theological island in the centuries past when these bodies formed. Today people can review doctrine, make belief comparisons, and consult reference material in just minutes. There have been other victories for the single body of Christ. The 1054 mutual excommunication, the Great Schism, between Western (Catholic) and Eastern (Orthodox) branches of Christianity was revoked in 1965 by the Pope and the Ecumenical Patriarch of Constantinople.[4] Both bodies continue to work for unity.

There were major mergers within the Presbyterians and Methodists in the late 20th century. These unions spawned several smaller denominations that could not accept the theology and priorities of the merged bodies. Apparently, they were right; the membership of both united bodies is in a prolonged decline in America. One of those bodies is currently considering a major split.

Some Protestant mergers have been successful. In 1957, four American denominations united to form the United Church of Christ. Those involved were - the Congregational churches, the Christian Church, the Evangelical Synod, and the Reformed Church in the U.S. The body has over a million members, the churches share in support and ministry. By 1985, they established an ecumenical partnership with the Christian Church (Disciples of Christ).

In 1994, Evangelical and Roman Catholic leaders formed a group in the United States known as Evangelicals and Catholics Together (ECT),[5] They approved a joint ecumenical statement culminating an effort started in the early 1970s. The statement was widely criticized for going too far on compromising theological differences. This begs the question, how do we resolve these theological differences unless we come together with that objective, and prayerfully work to that end, trusting God to bless our success and fidelity with truth? The following is an excellent summary about the ECT statement.

> The statement is written as a testimony that spells out the need for Protestants and Catholics to deliver a common witness to the modern world at the eve of the third millennium. It draws heavily from the theology of the New Testament and the Trinitarian doctrine of the Nicene Creed. It does not mention any specific points of theology, and instead seeks to encourage what is known as spiritual ecumenism and day-to-day ecumenism. The document was signed at a time when Protestants and Catholics were still fighting each other in Northern Ireland.

The Anglicans published The Complete Jerusalem Statement in 2008. The 14 tenets provide a great testimony of biblical Christianity, a call to work toward unity, and a challenge to those who have adopted policies that conflict with the Bible to "repent and return to the Lord."[6] Four groups of Anglicans in North America merged into the Anglican Communion of North America.

Appendix A lists 11 different bodies in the Catholic Church group. Renewed ecumenical initiatives resulted in three of those groups now affiliating with the Roman Catholic Church.

Thirteen Reformed and Presbyterian bodies have formed the North American Presbyterian and Reformed Council (NAPARC). The following is the purpose statement from their website; it is a great example of churches in the same faith group working to grow back together.

> We regard this basis of fellowship as warrant for the establishment of a formal relationship of the nature of a council, that is, a fellowship that enables the member churches to advise, counsel, and cooperate in various

matters with one another, and to hold out before each other the desirability and need for organic union of churches that are of like faith and practice.[7]

You may be thinking I do not like what I see in some of these united efforts. Just like us, they have some problems. Do you have a better approach to stem the tide of dispersion in beliefs and be faithful to God's call for unity? If a biblically faithful body formed, God would bless it in a mighty way. If we affiliate with them, we can all begin to pursue theology closer to what God intended.

Dream a Little

Giant coastal redwoods in the Pacific Northwest grow in shallow soil, yet endure extremely high winds. These 300-foot giants stand for a millennium or more with roots in 12 feet of soil or less. They do it by intertwining their roots with the trees around them. Their environment is similar to the circumstances of our denominations - shallow souls and strong winds of adversity. Would the body of Christ be far more effective if we had our roots intertwined with all other Christians? Also similar to the trees, when a storm takes out a big tree, the collateral damage to those nearby is significant. We are the only obstacle keeping Christianity from becoming stronger and more effective.

Consider for a moment what a unified body of Christ could mean to America, to the world, to the lost. Imagine the opposite of all the dysfunction caused by denominationalism described in this book. The benefits of shared ministries would be such a boon for the spread of the gospel, clergy vitality, youth programs, effectiveness, efficiency, etc.

Those who love the Lord with their whole mind, body, and spirit should grow together into an organization with enough influence to make the distinction between Christianity and those who only claim that label but are not living accordingly. Others would see the wisdom and join. That organization could dismiss those committing atrocities in the name of Christ as not Christian with a voice big enough to have the integrity and credibility to influence the media. Unlike today, groups starting a new denomination calling itself Christian would have a hard time defending the basis for a split.

If this new organization was big enough to influence a large portion of God's people, we could establish a new spiritual term for biblical marriage. The new ceremony would only be performed in a church by a spiritual leader who verifies the union is based on the spiritual commitment commiserate with Scripture - Eph 5. The united body could adopt a new term to describe the spiritual union that occurs along with the marriage ceremony to satisfy the laws of the land.

There have been several "great awakenings" in America; most would agree there has not been one since around 1900. Many of us still recite the Apostles Creed, which mentions one catholic (universal) church. It would be great if the true body of Christ were affiliated in one organization. The focus would be on biblical essentials and not on debating non-essential differences. Valued non-essential practices in local bodies could continue. As you read of other potential benefits of uniting the body, may the consensus be, "why not?"

Worthy Objective

Previous problems in establishing a united church are not an indication it is a flawed objective. It only indicates that, like Peter, they took their eyes off the Lord and began to sink.

Chapter 1 presented the compelling reason for us to pursue a unified body of Christ, so that the world may believe - Jhn 17:21. We cannot ignore that mandate.

Why should we continue to split up our dysfunctional family and display this constant vivid deterrent to those who might otherwise find the gospel in our churches? Is there a way we can set aside the divisive non-essential issues and come together in a unified body as Jesus commanded? I have heard and read a lot of material condemning denominations. Some deserve it. Most profess to follow the truth of Scripture; which means, "be reasonable, do it our way." Fallen humanity has been defending flawed positions at the expense of unity for centuries. Committed, Spirit led, Christ followers can find their way back together. Some will say all Christian denominations lead to God. Scripture calls the followers of Jesus the Way not the ways - Act 9:2. Scripture is clear, false teaching can be an indication of the lack of faith required for salvation (see chapter 7). It is highly unlikely that all bodies claiming an affiliation with Jesus are a sound path to heaven.

I read quite a number of blogs and associated responses about the value of denominations. The responses ranged from good to terrible, and everything in between. Some mentioned the benefits of varied worship styles while others pointed to the incredible harm from the evolution of beliefs to embrace the societal value changes. A common thought in several responses was the appearance of no clear truth in the body of Christ. We are not likely to see denominations go away anytime soon. There is just too much loyalty, close fellowship and commitment to tradition. That does not make it impossible to grow back together. What can we do to manage this montage of alleged truth, to present a better perspective to the unchurched, and to improve our impact on the world?

Before saying this will not work, recall the current situation described in chapter 2. Our steady drift in denominational unraveling appears to have no end short of the return of the Lord. Doing nothing is yielding to the problem becoming worse in a time we need Christian unity more than ever. Some feel it is impossible for fallen humanity to come together in one body of Christ.

> Mar 10:27 Jesus looked at them and said, "With man it is impossible, but not with God. For all things are possible with God."

Our religious indoctrination is hard to modify. This is especially true when we mix in a healthy measure of pride, fear of change, and selfishness. It will take time, prayer and great commitment to move to a united body of Christ in the world. One must start every worthwhile journey with one-step. God wants there to be one body of Christ followers; what are we willing to do to bring that about? If we love Him, we will do what He commanded - Mat 16:24, Jhn 14:15. The popular phrase "it is not all about you" applies especially to Christians. How are we going to stop being dividers?

Twelve Steps

This chapter provides 12 steps to conquer that problem. Yes, I manipulated the list to have the 12 steps of Dividers Anonymous (DA). I mean no disrespect for other abuse management programs. Quite the opposite, they are highly effective in what they do. The human characteristics that cause us to embrace divisive doctrine are a part of our fallen nature, just like those leading to addictions. For the most part, church leaders have led us to this dispersion; they need to take the lead in growing back together. There is also a lot we sheep can do from the bottom up.

1. Stop Being a Divider

Christian persecution around the world was the topic on a radio program. The facilitator asked the expert guest what we could do. He said the least we can do is pray and inform others of the extent and severity of their challenges. Then he went on to mention actions that are more involved. What is the least we can do to foster unity within the body of Christ? Stop fueling the fires of denominational battles.

Things are never ideal in a marriage. Focusing on nits is a path to failure. Stop criticizing other groups for their doctrine that is not in conflict with an essential; they are potentially part of the family and certainly closer than atheists are. If we can grow together on essentials, we can reap the benefits for the kingdom. We should use labels such as "evangelical", "main line" and "cult" with care; they promote division. We need to get back to the labels in Scripture - believer and non-believer. That will be tough, and delicate. We should not tell people who claim to be Christians that they are not. However, if their fruit does not indicate saving faith, we should approach them as though they are lost - Mat 7:17-18. Those who think they are a saved Christian and are not, may be worse off than an atheist is.

Jesus condemned judging and exhibiting a critical spirit - Luk 6:39-43. If we criticize other denominations, we alienate them and further divide the body. It often seems doctrinal debates are done for sport; some people enjoy arguing. We are not to slander or speak badly about our brother and do not grumble against him. This would include speaking in and outside the church, especially in the media.

> Jas 4:11-12 <u>Do not speak evil against one another, brothers.</u> The one who speaks against a brother or judges his brother, speaks evil against the law and judges the law. But if you judge the law, you are not a doer of the law but a judge. [12] There is only one lawgiver and judge, he who is able to save and to destroy. <u>But who are you to judge your neighbor</u>?

James continues the thought in 5:9. God hates those who sow discord among brothers - Pro 6:19, not a place I ever want to be. How can we grow back together with someone we are criticizing? Stop referring to differing <u>non-essential</u> beliefs as heresy. A church's website stated that those who believe salvation cannot be lost are heretical. Why take such an extreme position on an issue disputed for centuries? Stop participating in blogs that debate the mysteries in Scripture, many will likely not be solved this side of heaven. Divert that time and talent to reach the lost and build unity. Stop buying and reading books that focus on preferential non-essential doctrine. Resolving partisan non-essentials is NOT one of God's top priorities. Most successful churches do not focus on divisive non-essential theology. However, some denominations have drifted under revisionist interpretation of Scripture. It seems they usually go into decline when they get away from the truth.

> "If you look for truth, you may find comfort in the end; if you look for comfort you will not get either comfort or truth only soft soap and wishful thinking to begin, and in the end, despair." - C. S. Lewis[8]

Do not repeat hearsay about other religions. We all teach classes on other beliefs and tell people all the bad stuff we can dig up to inoculate our folks from ever considering those "heretical" groups. We often have our facts wrong or their beliefs have since been modified. Before criticizing the beliefs of others, get the facts. The best source is their website. Do not repeat hearsay not supported by a reputable source. It is theological gossip. We are better than that - 2Co 12:20.

Look at practices from the perspective of those who possess them; this will frequently reveal a basis for where they are coming from. Another great step in presenting a fair treatment of their beliefs is to talk to one of them.

Stop promoting denominational differences to help ensure our position is secure. Promoting our denominational uniqueness over essentials and mandates of Scripture may be keeping our little church little. The revival that could result from pursuing unity would bring in many new sheep with plenty of opportunities for faithful clergy to minister.

Stop obsessing over non-Christian trends in our society. We are far better known for our ranting than we are for our love. For example, do not obsess about folks saying "happy holidays" insisting they say "Merry Christmas." We cannot force America to be a Christian nation. Do everything in your power to lead it to be one by your example, one person at time.

Stop making theories about God's mysteries into rigid doctrine. Instead, teach and pass on the essentials and mandates of

Christianity that are crystal clear - Deu 29:29, and Phl 3:15-16. It will take a lifetime of prayer and commitment to live out those truths.

2. Forgive Us Our **Sins**

Praying the Lord's Prayer is one of the most confusing moments in Christian worship. When we attend a body of believers from different backgrounds, we hear a muddled mixture of "debts", "trespasses" and a few other terms. It would be a nice show of unity if we all used the same word for the public expression of this all-important prayer. The origin of the use of "trespasses" can be traced to the 1526 Tyndale Bible by way of the 1549 *Book of Common Prayer.*[9] The use of "debts" first appeared in Mat 6:12 in the KJV in 1611 and is used in most reputable translations today including the NABRE. A few contemporary translations use "sins" or "wrongs." The Luke 11 version of the Lord's Prayer uses "sins" (rather than debts or trespasses) in 14 popular translations. We should use "sins". It matches Luke 11 and does not choose sides for the terms currently used. It would be a great statement of support for the unity in the body. It may seem like a small step, but it would say a lot about our intent and provide some momentum for the next 10 steps.

3. Love All Our Brothers and Sisters

The Bible is clear we must love our brothers and sisters in Christ - Jhn 13:35, 15:12; 1Th 3:12; Heb 13:1, 1Pe 1:22; 1Jn 3:10b, 3:15-18, 4:7, 12, 19-21. Currently, there are no active military conflicts between Christians. Scripture teaches that if we hate our fellow Christians, we are **not believers** - 1Jo 2:9. We would surely say we stop short of hating those of other Christian bodies, but not by much. I have heard and read some terrible words from Christians describing other Christians.

We should always have an attitude promoting unity - "And a harvest of righteousness is sown in peace by those who make peace" (Jas 3:18). Is making peace a priority in your ministry? This applies first in our church, then among all believers. The following came from the website of Word Became Flesh Ministries, Mississauga, Ontario.[10]

> As believers, there are certain basic doctrines (essential for salvation) that we must believe, but beyond that there is freedom on how we can serve and worship; it is this freedom where there is diversity not disunity. Diversity allows us to be individuals in Christ; disunity divides and destroys.

"Strive for peace with everyone, and for the holiness without which no one will see the Lord." (Heb 12:14). This requirement for peace and holiness is another example of the evidence in our lives that display the presence of saving faith. The best first step for loving all our brothers and sisters would be to pray for them. It is hard to look down on someone while praying for them. The guidance to love includes groups that call themselves Christian that we think are lost due to their beliefs. Jesus said to love our enemies. Moody professor Dr. Michael Rydelnik has a simple approach to evangelism - "love them until they ask you why." Scripture provides clear guidance on how we are to treat our brothers and sisters - Rom 14:1, 15:1, 1Co 8:11, 9:22. If we do not do it, we are in sin - Jas 4:17, Luk 12:48.

> Jde 1:22-23 And have mercy on those who doubt; [23] save others by snatching them out of the fire; to others show mercy with fear, hating even the garment stained by the flesh.

When others appear to be wrong, be the mature one leaving room for the guiding of the Holy Spirit. Remember, we may be wrong. Do not be so quick to judge others who are following the examples of Jesus and Paul but differ with us theologically. The following is a great statement on growing back together excerpted from an article by Randall Bach, President of Open Bible Churches.[11]

Virtually every stream of evangelicalism has a unique history and some distinctive theological emphases and/or traditions. While those distinctive traits define and brand us, they can also narrow and confine us. By looking at other streams, we are able to learn from and appreciate how God sovereignly works through them. We also gain a deeper appreciation for how much we have in common as we respect our distinctive traits.

This approach will help us weave our threads back into a rope. Jesus would have us include people from many denominations. Seek tolerance on non-essentials, or at least take a position to live and let live. Do it for the sake of the weaker brother - "Accept him whose faith is weak, without passing judgment on disputable matters .... Who are you to judge the servant of another?" (Rom 14:1-4).

We can help lead them to the full truth with our loving example - Tit 2:7-8. If not against us, then they are for us - Mar 9:40. Scripture never directs us to fix the weaker brother on non-essentials - Rom 14:21-22. Criticizing other's religion can be like picking on a weaker spiritual brother. The Bible says it is a sin.

1Co 8:12 Thus, sinning against your brothers and <u>wounding their conscience when it is weak</u>, you sin against Christ.

We should "set an example for the believers in speech, in conduct, in love, in faith, in purity" (1Ti 4:12), and "by the open statement of the truth" (2Co 4:2). In Acts 21 Paul escaped a severe beating by the Jews for telling them to forsake their Jewish customs, including circumcision of their children. His statement was not wrong. Perhaps he could have relayed that truth in a less confrontational manner. At other times, he was far more sensitive to the beliefs of the audience. He had Timothy circumcised in Act 16:3, but did not have Titus circumcised in Gal 2:3. Be sensitive to the weaker brothers in Christ, without adding "#you're a weaker brother."

Consider the churches in Revelation. Jesus chastises all except Philadelphia for problem behavior. Many denominations and churches do not realize they have one or more of these problems. Thus, it is likely we are weaker brothers in some of our beliefs. Approach the non-essential theological conflicts as directed in the Bible: love, turn the other cheek, forgiveness, understanding, and a positive example. All our efforts to correct someone espousing what we see is errant theology must always be filled with grace - Col 4:6, 2Ti 2:24-25.

> 2Co 6:3 <u>We put no obstacle in anyone's w</u>ay, so that no fault may be found with our ministry.

That approach will be far more successful than the loud, condemning, overpowering approach we see modeled in the secular world. It will also make it much easier to concede if we discover **we** were wrong. The following link is to a great article on theological exclusivism - http://nae.net/so-loud-i-cant-hear-you/.[12] We have all sinned in our teaching. We should "Be merciful, even as your Father is merciful" (Luk 6:36). Our approach to correcting other denominations should usually be "Judge not, and you will not be judged; condemn not, and you will not be condemned; forgive, and you will be forgiven" (Luk 6:37). For that matter, we should take the same approach with non-Christians. Our condemnation can prevent an opportunity for sharing truth. Only when all other approaches fail, show them the Scripture that describes their condemnation. Use His words not ours.

Many groups use door-to-door outreach. A tough time to be unity minded is when someone comes to our door promoting their beliefs. Show them the love of Jesus and they may be willing to listen to your perspective on truth. If time permits, invite them in and make them feel welcome. Ask if they mind a time of prayer before starting. Never call them a cult, even if they meet the common definition - Jas 4:12. Do not criticize them or their beliefs; show them and tell them of the truth as Jesus did and would do today. Focus on the essentials, not differences that do not affect salvation.

Apply the following guidance as applicable. Ask them these questions: What must I do to be saved? Who is Jesus? Where did He come from? Why did he come to earth as a man? Compare their answers to the Bible in John 1, Colossians 1, Hebrews 1, and Revelation 1. If they do not believe Jesus is one with God, then show them the Trinity passages discussed in Appendix D. Request they provide answers in a reputable translation of the Bible; share the basis for its validity from chapter 11. If they insist on introducing teaching from their prophet, agree to listen if they will first listen to what the Bible teaches about prophets and new revelation in chapter 3. Ask if any of their prophets have ever been wrong or their decisions changed by a successor. Their denomination likely does worthwhile ministry. Many subscribe to portions of standard Christian doctrine. Their denominations have grown, but so have some very non-Christian groups. They are completely convinced their beliefs are fully correct, just like the rest of humanity. God does love them. We should not give up on them, nor should we tell them their rejection of the essentials of Scripture is acceptable.

Many claim this passage as a basis to be hateful to those promoting a denomination different from ours.

> 2Jo 1:10-11 If anyone comes to you and does not bring this teaching, do not receive him into your house or give him any greeting, [11] for whoever greets him takes part in his wicked works.

Most commentaries feel John was saying do not support bad teaching. Jesus went to the misled to show them the true way, including Pharisees, tax collectors, and the morally deviate. How can we do that if we will not even talk to them? The following passages also support the concept of isolation - Ro 16:17, 1Co 5:11, 1Ti 6:3-7, and 2Ti 3:5. Most of this teaching is guidance for dealing with people in our local church to ensure that they understand the harm they are doing - Mat 18:15-17. Clearly, we are not to support their efforts. However, Jesus would tell us to share the truth with them. If you feel uncomfortable sharing the truth, invite them to come back and arrange for your pastor to join in. If they listen, you have met the call in Rom 10:14; if they do not, you did what you could.

4. Influence Our Church

In some churches, the laity will need to drive the unity initiative. There are those pastors and administrators who do not see a thing wrong with their denomination. Others are happy with the status quo and do not want to rock the boat. Some pastors are independent because they want to be, participation in any organization would be against their nature. In this day of personal expression, some people may want to stay separate. When we get a significant portion of the body of Christ in an association, they will see the blessings and value and want to join us.

The prophets of the OT provided many examples of unfaithful teachers.

> Isa 56:10 - 11 His <u>watchmen are blind</u>; they are all without knowledge; they are all silent dogs; they cannot bark, dreaming, lying down, loving to slumber. [11] The dogs have a mighty appetite; they never have enough. But they are <u>shepherds who have no understanding; they have all turned to their own way, each to his own gain</u>, one and all.

Beyond the guidance for false teaching provided in chapter 6, we should also challenge teachers who are being divisive in their teaching about other denominations. The approach is the same; first make sure we are right through prayer, investigating several sources, and benignly asking others (discuss the issue, not the offender).

Grow where God planted you. Do not go looking for the ideal church; there is not one. Church hoppers contribute to the bad perception of Christianity. Stay there and make a difference.

If the teaching is in error, work through the church leaders to get it fixed.

> 1Co 7:17 Only <u>let each person lead the life that the Lord has assigned to him</u>, and to which God has called him. This is my rule in all the churches.

5. Believe, Repent, and Be Baptized

The Bible teaches that we are to believe the gospel, repent and be baptized - Act 2:38. The early church flourished before the NT was written. Other than repeating the teaching of Jesus and the Apostles, the early church did not have inspired doctrine to affirm before baptism. The concept of denominations did not exist, yet we see in Acts 2 through 22 "the Lord added to their number day by day", and "the number of the disciples multiplied greatly in Jerusalem." There was no mention of a body vetting believers before baptism. We should only require belief in the essentials for salvation and repentance in order to be baptized - as instructed in the Bible. It would be a great show of unity and commitment to our "one Lord, one faith, one baptism" (Eph 4:5). Perhaps that would lead to our numbers increasing instead of losing 3,500 Christians every day in America.[13] If our teaching is sound, and our ministry true, people will still join our fellowships even if it is not required for baptism.

6. Visit Our Cousins

Some people do not consider the other denominations in their faith group to be brothers and sisters in Jesus. We know they could be - Luk 18:27. We share a common history that should help us move toward growing together. When Peggy and I travel, we try to see a variety of other approaches in worship. It helps us see and appreciate them as people with a different way to worship the Lord, yet loving Him as much as we do. We see many neat ideas for worship and ministry. By visiting them we can begin to see areas of agreement, areas of difference where one or both of us need to grow closer to truth, and other differences that are both faithful to Scripture.

It is amazing how many people we know at other churches in our area. Visit their church on occasion. You can establish relationships to open channels of communication and understand their obstacles to growing together. It will give us an opportunity to model our superior Christianity that will draw them to truth. Be open to some influence going the other way where needed. All of this will make it easier to remove barriers, build bridges, and grow closer to God together. Yes, this is like asking someone to visit their ex spouse. There have been cases where a divorced couple have made a second attempt with more wisdom and commitment and have found success. Some will ask why you are visiting their church. Tell them about the Lord's mandate for unity in one body of Christ; tell them about this book.

7. Join an Interdenominational Group

Where do we start? David, Paul and Peter give us a good example and motivation to make progress. Looking at our contributions to this dilemma is a good motivation to do something about it - Rom 12:4-5, 15:5 and Phl 4:2.

> Psa 139:23-24 Search me, O God, and know my heart! Try me and know my thoughts! ²⁴ And <u>see if there be any grievous way in me</u>, and lead me in the way everlasting!

> 1Pe 3:8 Finally, all of you, <u>have unity of mind</u>, sympathy, <u>brotherly love</u>, a tender heart, and a humble mind.

Evangelist Gipsy Smith said, "Lord, please send revival to this community. But, oh God, let the revival start inside this circle. Let it begin in me." Progress will be much easier when believers are open to consider their own theology for errors and intolerance. The first recognition, and needed change, will likely be the hardest.

> Rom 14:19 So then let us <u>pursue what makes for peace and for mutual up building</u>.

We must commit to love each other as Jesus loves us. He would ask us to love those who need to come to true saving faith. With that commitment, the result of our dialogue could be life changing. We may present the truth in a way that they finally see and understand.

Pastors should join or start a fellowship of area pastors. This will provide three great benefits. They can coordinate the ministries of area churches. As relationships build, they will gain an appreciation for the priorities and focus of other groups and help them recognize where they may be off the mark on essentials (if any) - "iron sharpening iron" (Pro 27:17). They can minister to each other in their challenges of leading churches.

There are obvious values in meeting with folks facing the same challenges we are: fellowship, prayer, sharing, mentoring, coordinating ministry plans, fostering a spouse's network, confiding, sharing, prayer and peer guidance. We can share information on planned ministries. We may have someone in our congregation who needs a session of Divorce Care; it would be helpful to know who is offering it. Scheduling a session for the one person in our fellowship that needs it will not provide the healthy interaction of a group that is struggling with the same challenge. Do not be afraid to encourage people to go to other churches for ministries, we R2B1.

This coordinated effort will help avoid several area churches offering a program one season and none during the next. Churches providing coordinated options will supply the whole community more of what it needs. Well-coordinated ministries for relevant groups with well-prepared leaders attract non-believers.

Many pastors operate as an island; they have limited contact outside the congregation. Denominations only meet a few sessions a year with limited time to address pastoral needs. Some groups have churches close enough together to do this within their body, but they are missing opportunities to promote unity. Pastors could present a devotion at association meetings. If agreed, coaching and feedback could be provided. Your sheep will not likely tell you things you need to hear about behaviors that may be having an adverse impression on visitors. The sermon presentation classes in seminary likely left some less than fond memories. Many of the things in life that help us most are not fun. Pastors preaching to pastors has been rewarding to presenter and audience in many denominations. Why not do it more often?

Sermons presented to other clergy will undoubtedly reveal doctrinal differences providing an opportunity to discuss them constructively. This could be very helpful in several ways. It would help us understand where others are coming from and expand our perspective on non-essentials. Some in attendance will espouse theological error; these interactions could help to change their mind. The sharing of truth and the Holy Spirit's enabling can help convince others to move toward biblical truth. We are to plant the seeds of truth, then let the Lord water and grow them. The result should bring our theology and positions to be more biblical and we will be more confident in them. In competitive debates, the participants must argue the position taken by their opponents. If we had to defend our opponent on theological differences, we would fully investigate and empathetically understand the opposing position. Try doing that with divisive beliefs to ensure fidelity with Scripture.

After relationships form, the pursuit of unity could move to the next level. Pastors should agree to share and listen to essential differences with discernment, not judgment. Recognizing that all involved think the others are the weaker brother should cause everyone to listen more carefully; teacher talking to teacher bathed in prayer. Some are saying this will not work. It is far better than the current approach. Most air essential differences using a unilateral and often critical approach. Some use media, which the target audience likely will not read or hear. How often have we read material challenging our theological positions? We often share our condemnation of other beliefs in our preaching, discussions or lectures. The flock might share it with someone from that denomination. Second hand sharing is often misrepresented. Those listening are getting the conflicting party line from their leaders. This indirect approach often teaches disdain for others who may be children of God, now or later. Differences must be addressed closer to the source. Progress will be slow; pray about it. Ask God to help everyone to see truth. Ask Him to help each person to put the pursuit of truth ahead of all other motives.

We have all heard the Paul, Barnabas and Mark concept that we should have a mentor and one or more that we mentor. Many pastors do not have a suitable peer in their denomination close enough for these relationships. Other pastors have valuable experience to share, including things that do not work. Sometimes the mentoring will go upward as well. We can teach old pastors new tricks. Pastor associations will enable these interactions to flourish.

We cannot force people to believe as we do. Peg and I saw this at the Little Big Horn Battlefield in Montana. President Grant directed the army to "Christianize the Indians." That translated into subdue them onto reservations, drive them off, or kill them. In the 19th and 20th centuries, the majority of American Christiandom abused the religions not considered true Christian in the same way Protestants were abused in Europe. They were outcast, and in many cases harassed or worse, until they left. In 1838, the governor of Missouri issued an order that all Mormons were to leave the state or be killed. The extermination order remained on the books until 1976.[14] With this history, it is easy to understand why some have not heard the biblical truth we support. That legacy of mistreatment has resulted in more resentment toward those condemning them than any serious consideration of our teaching. How are they going to hear biblical truth - Rom 10:14-15?

Invite them to an ecumenical meeting. Show them the love of Jesus to earn the respect needed to influence them. Share the essentials of the gospel. Then continue to love them and let the Holy Spirit do the heavy lifting.

Folks in the big churches may feel they do not need any ecumenical support, they may be right. They can sponsor any ministry they feel led to do and have a staff big enough to support the needs of their flock. The small churches do not have the talent and resources to meet all their ministry needs. They can lean on each other, but like most human endeavors, the talent rises to the top. Those best equipped to mentor (experience, success, etc.) are at the larger churches. They could say let them close their doors and come to our big churches. That does not sound like a strategy to grow Christianity - "with all humility and gentleness, with patience, bearing with one another in love, ³eager to maintain the unity of the Spirit in the bond of peace" (Eph 4:2-3). Our Lord designed us to reap great joy and accomplishment from service. Choosing not to get involved in a local ecumenical fellowship may cause you to miss the joy and benefits of uniting the kingdom.

Interdenominational Laity Groups

Laity should form groups also! They should be separate from the clergy. Pastors have special challenges and need to be able to share and minister to each other in appropriate confidence. Organize a cross-denominational Bible study, book review club, or just people from different denominations doing things together. This provides more opportunities for relationships to grow, communication to occur, and the exchange of ideas. Invite some folks to review this book together. Some are thinking this will not happen people just do not change. The early Christians probably felt the Jewish leaders would never change.

> Act 6:7 And the word of God continued to increase, and the number of the disciples multiplied greatly in Jerusalem, and <u>a great many of the priests became obedient to the faith</u>.

Just because women have perfected book studies to an art does not mean it will not be good for men, too. I attend a group on Tuesday mornings that reads and discusses books. It gets me reading good material carefully (underlining for discussion), hearing other perspectives and praying together. It does not get much better than that. Truth can sneak up on us; most good authors do not mention denominations. You would be surprised at the affiliation of many popular Christian writers.

Still not feeling led to meet with folks from other bodies? Review the following concepts from the wisest person of his day. Do any of them hit close to home?

> Pro 15:12 - A scoffer does not like to be reproved; he will not go to the wise.
> Pro 18:19 - A brother offended is more unyielding than a strong city, and quarreling is like the bars of a castle.
> Pro 15:32 - Whoever ignores instruction despises himself, but he who listens to reproof gains intelligence.
> Pro 18:2 - A fool takes no pleasure in understanding, but only in expressing his opinion.
> Pro 10:17 - Whoever heeds instruction is on the path to life, but he who rejects reproof leads others astray.
> Pro 19:2 - Desire without knowledge is not good, and whoever makes haste with his feet misses his way (also Rom 10:1-3).

It is hard to look in the mirror and ask, "Am I being the fool?" I have often figured something out after it was obvious to many others, a much more humbling approach. Remember, our motivation is to share only truth so we do not lead others astray. We may be the fool if we refuse to hear another's perspective and quickly quote our proof texts. We cannot help unless we listen and respond in love. Sharing our perspectives on an essential biblical truth will not likely get immediate agreement. Present and do not argue so we do not destroy our relationship with them. If they are not alienated, our walk and talk can open doors to sharing.

In spite of our most loving attempts to share the truth, some will reject it. How should we respond to them?

> Pro 26:4-5 Answer not a fool according to his folly, <u>lest you be like him yourself</u>. [5] Answer a fool according to his folly, lest he be wise in his own eyes. Their condemnation will be on their own heads.

That does not mean a stern condemnation. Using Scripture; tell them of the benefits, warn them of the consequences if they are wrong, and make sure they know they are always welcome. There will be bumps in the road in these groups. Leaders need to address the concerns, solve the problems and move on - Act 6:1, 5.

8. Shared Communion

As mentioned before, the communion practices of the 19 denominations interviewed ranged from members only, to specific criteria for non-members, to any Christian. Although the latter is a great statement for unity, there are many opinions for what makes a person a Christian. Some denominations and individuals consider themselves Christian, while others would take exception to their claim. It would be great if all believers supported the essentials of a unified body of Christ and could take communion in any member church. It would not be ambiguous, like "Christian" or "Evangelical Christian." It would be a great statement for both unity and theological accord.

9. Merge Where Possible

Several pastors interviewed said they know of denominations that could merge with little or no differences in beliefs. If you feel that way, ensure leaders of those bodies know about it and ask to make it a priority. Then look to resolve obstacles to merging with other groups through discussions, understanding, acceptance of non-essentials, or needed change on essentials. If not a merger, then form an association to promote unity and share ministry.

Denominations that split over racial composition but still share common theological essentials should work to merge back into one, with fully representative leadership. That will involve work and initiative on both sides, but it is what Jesus would want us to do. How can we show the lost we are sharing the love of Jesus when our denominations are as segregated as almost any American institution? Only 13% of Protestant churches say they have more than one predominant racial or ethnic group in their congregation.[15] There are worship and preaching style preferences; being in the same denomination would not affect that. When people of other races or ethnicity visit your church, make them feel more than welcome. Heaven is going to be very diverse - Rev 5:9, why not now? As we grow together, the benefits and efficiencies described throughout this book can begin.

10. Pursue One Body

The Great War, later named World War I, was a human tragedy on the scale humanity had never seen. The League of Nations was formed to attempt to prevent a similar tragedy. Without making this a history lesson, it was not adequate to prevent World War II, a far greater human tragedy. When the conflicts ended, a high priority of the victorious leaders was to form a better body to prevent another similar disaster. The United Nations was the result. It is not a flawless body. Nevertheless, that concept, along with other treaties, alliances, and in some cases military action, have prevented WW III for 72 years and counting. That is a phenomenal accomplishment in view of the corrupt souls of many leaders and the military capability humanity has developed. The UN provides a means to share ideas, concerns, grievances and an oversight body that has significant influence. We need an ecclesiastical organization similar to the UN to help us manage and prevent theological wars before they damage our Lord's Church. The organization needs to involve a significant majority of the Christians. The influence of the UN is limited when dealing with non-member countries. They have power to influence the bad actors, but it is more muted and confrontational. Historically, the Christian answer to bad actors has been to split and divide, which has severely diminished our image in and, our influence on the world.

We were looking for a church to attend in Sedona, Az. None of them listed a denomination in their title. We attended Wayside Chapel, an independent church. We heard an excellent message straight from the Bible. The pastor said he attends a meeting of local pastors every Wednesday to help each other stay faithful to Scripture. There is a refreshing doctrinal harmony among independent churches faithful to Scripture. There is a large core of Christians who believe the Bible is the truth from God and try to follow it without strained and convoluted interpretations. We need an affiliation that is solidly founded on the Bible to help us grow back together and to provide a compass for a united body of Christ.

Many independent bodies would say they don't need a theological compass. Several have ministries that have had a great impact. They have many ideas that could be shared with others. A few have achieved great success in numbers and dollars, but spiritually, not so much. When the founder retires or falls into personal failings, these groups are vulnerable in the selection of new leadership. These churches could contribute to and benefit from an association of committed Christians.

Clearing up our questionable theology so we can come together will not be a one-way street for anyone. As in 99.999% of marital disputes, the fault lies with both parties in conflict. Like marriage, unity is worth far more than winning non-essential battles. As we grow back together we will likely look back and realize we were also moving closer to truth.

Christianity is in a spiritual recession, or depression, in many parts of the world. How long we stay in it depends on God and

His people. He can certainly do what He wants, but usually waits to see if we have the proper attitude and initiative. He then supports us with blessings and provision.

> Hos 10:12 <u>Sow for yourselves righteousness</u>; reap steadfast love; break up your fallow ground, for it is the time to seek the LORD, <u>that he may come and rain righteousness upon you</u>.

Must we let the crisis grow worse before we turn to Him in unity? Will persecution lead us to focus on the kingdom, and not on denominational fiefdoms? What will be the cost of waiting? It will take a strong commitment to resolve differences in favor of biblical truth as we grow together. If we commit to unity over non-essential theological differences, we can reverse the decline of Christianity in the west and expedite the spread of the gospel worldwide. The following is the Conclusion from the Lausanne Conference (1974).[16] Their statement sounds much like the passage that follows.

> "Therefore, in the light of this our faith and our resolve, we enter into a solemn covenant with God and with each other, to pray, to plan and to work together for the evangelization of the whole world. We call upon others to join us. May God help us by his grace and for his glory to be faithful to this our covenant! Amen, Alleluia!"

> Phl 2:1-3 So if there is any encouragement in Christ, any comfort from love, any participation in the Spirit, any affection and sympathy, [2] <u>complete my joy by being of the same mind</u>, having the same love, <u>being in full accord and of one mind</u>. [3] Do nothing from selfish ambition or conceit, but in humility count others more significant than yourselves.

According to Lutheran theologian Edmund Schlink, most important in Christian ecumenism is that people focus primarily on Christ, not on separate church organizations.

In Schlink's book *Ökumenische Dogmatik* (1983), he writes "Christians who see the risen Christ at work in the lives of various Christians or in diverse churches realize that the unity of Christ's Church has never been lost, but has instead been distorted and obscured by different historical experiences and by spiritual myopia."[17]

This body of Christ could function similar to the engineering standards organizations that review, vet, modify and approve standards for most manufacturing, construction and testing. They thoroughly examine proposed revisions and new requirements to ensure they are in the best interest of those involved. The Christian counterpart could apply the same oversight, wisdom, and management to the statement of essential beliefs of the body of Christ. Placing doctrinal differences in categories of essential, non-essential, mystery, and errant beliefs would take years. There will always be social issues not specifically addressed in the Bible. This body could develop a position for the super majority of Christians in the world.

Keep it simple stupid. Most of the growing churches and associations focus on essentials and discipling people in the Lord. They do not have volumes of doctrine and rules. Jesus was direct - "Truly, I say to you, whoever does not receive the kingdom of God like a child <u>shall not enter it</u>" (Mar 10:15). The following statement is from the Greek Orthodox Church; could we all subscribe to this same concept for the whole body of Christ?

> "The Orthodox Church acknowledges that unity does not mean uniformity." However, all the churches are united in the same faith and order.[18]

This association of Christians could provide other functions in addition to theological stability. For example - arbitration services for fellow Christians to solve disputes as instructed in 1Co 6, and Mat 18:17. Currently, who would a Baptist and a Catholic locked in a legal dispute appeal to? Neither would likely be willing to submit to arbitration by the other's leadership. Many denominations in the same faith group have split or want to change affiliation and are suing each other over property. The lawyers make a bundle and we make a terrible witness to the world.

This organization could spread to include Christians worldwide. It would make evangelism and ministry around the world so much more efficient and effective.

It would be great if our affiliation to Jesus was more important than our affiliation to a political party and their agenda? Some say those in the _____ (any party) are not Christians. Both major parties have a large constituency professing Christianity. It would be great if religiosity could cease to be a source of political division.

Based on the last 250 years, that does not seem likely. It is more likely that those who move toward Jesus will be the most successful in the future. That would apply to political parties and denominations. It will be difficult for a large ecumenical organization to remain unbiased relative to politics. Scripture does not direct that. However, putting politics ahead of biblical truth and unity is wrong.

How do we get this one body started? Denominational leaders should join a national ecumenical organization. Independent churches should do the same. There is no ideal ecumenical body. Get involved in one with a good fit and help make it happen. Help ensure that unity in the whole body is a priority. This is not very visible in many ecumenical groups today (Appendix E). Local ministerial associations could affiliate with ecumenical bodies focused on unity. The cream should rise to the top. Ecumenical organizations could form affiliations or even merge. This sustained focus should bring us ever closer to having a body that represents a super majority of true Christians.

Some would say the Evangelicals are all that is needed. We see harmful testimony in the writings and conduct of some who call themselves an evangelical. Those characteristics would include being judgmental, intolerant, and condemning. That sounds like the Pharisees of Jesus' day. Some of those may not fit in. There are many faithful Christians outside the Evangelical tent, working in other bodies as led by the Lord. We should include them. It is highly unlikely that anyone is fully correct regarding all the contested issues in Scripture. If there is, 1Co 13:2 says the one who understands all mysteries is nothing if he does not have love. Loving our Christian family is very important.

11. Establish a List of Essentials for Salvation

It took over 300 years to achieve the canon of Scripture. There were those who wanted more in, and some wanted more out. The Holy Spirit prevailed through all that time to give us the most powerful and influential work ever written. It will take some time to assemble an essentials document that all true Christians can support. With our minds open to Him, we can count on the leading of the Holy Spirit. It will not be easy or fast, especially by today's standards for progress.

Many authors say Christians must be faithful to the essentials of the Bible. Few offered an opinion on what those essentials should be. The opinions on Christian essentials are as diverse as the denominations. These differences must be resolved by people committed to full fidelity with Scripture and not by theological axes to grind. As discussed in chapter 11, some essential positions that appear to be in conflict are not. They represent different perspectives or circumstances, or are not an essential.

We Christians are critical of the Jewish people for not seeing Jesus as the Messiah. They were trained from a young age to look for a Messiah who was going to conquer evil and injustice by ascending the throne; they are looking for a king like David. To accept Jesus as the Messiah they have to turn from the "essentials" their parents and respected religious leaders have taught them. That is quite difficult. It is just as tough for us to turn away from the incorrect essentials we were taught. Keep an open mind and an open Bible.

Representatives from the participating bodies would come together as is intended for the United States Congress. Unfortunately, the current practice in Congress is far too partisan and self-serving. There is no place for that in this new body of Christ's people.

There will be those who will not commit to the essentials of this body; some even opposing unity initiatives. Scripture has many examples of similar opposition - Rom 16:17-18; 2Ti 3:8, 4:14-15; and 3Jn 1:9-10. It will resemble the Israelites rebuilding the wall around Jerusalem, contending with opponents while working together - 2Co 10:5-6. Satan will make every possible attempt to thwart unity from happening - Mat 7:6, even using believers to impede progress. Some in misguided hindrance may need to be excluded.

> 1Co 11:18-19 For, in the first place, when you come together as a church, I hear that there are divisions among you. And I believe it in part, [19] for <u>there must be factions among you in order that those who are genuine among you may be recognized</u>.

Many will claim this verse saying, "We are right, our being a faction is unavoidable." Forgive the repetition, but when two disagree on an essential, at least one is wrong. Are you ready to face Jesus with your version of the essentials? Thankfully, many Christian churches continue to teach the gospel of salvation. Sadly, there are also those who claim to be Christian that do not teach the gospel from the Bible. It can be tough for a seeker to identify those who are genuine among us.

How will the new organization develop this inspired, accurate, complete list of essentials for the body of Christ? There have been many unsuccessful attempts. I am in no way qualified to propose a set of essentials as the starting point. We should learn from previous attempts.

Why have the Nicene and Apostles Creeds lasted for over 1700 years? Catholic, Orthodox, and Protestant churches continue to use them. They contain beliefs supported by all of Scripture. That makes a great starting point.

The World Evangelical Alliance (WEA) has the following statement of faith on their website.[19]

We believe....

- ...in the **Holy Scriptures** as originally given by God, divinely inspired, infallible, entirely trustworthy; and the supreme authority in all matters of faith and conduct...
- One **God**, eternally existent in three persons, Father, Son, and Holy Spirit...
- Our **Lord Jesus Christ**, God manifest in the flesh, His virgin birth, His sinless human life, His divine miracles, His vicarious and atoning death, His bodily resurrection, His ascension, His mediatorial work, and His Personal return in power and glory...
- The **Salvation** of lost and sinful man through the shed blood of the Lord Jesus Christ by faith apart from works, and regeneration by the Holy Spirit...
- The **Holy Spirit**, by whose indwelling the believer is enabled to live a holy life, to witness and work for the Lord Jesus Christ...
- The **Unity** of the Spirit of all true believers, the Church, the Body of Christ...
- The **Resurrection** of both the saved and the lost; they that are saved unto the resurrection of life, they that are lost unto the resurrection of damnation.

The website for Christian Apologetics and Research Ministry (CARM) provides the essentials of the Christian Faith included below.[20] Declaring a belief as required for salvation has incredible potential to help or harm. The article contends that anyone who does not support these beliefs is a non-regenerate person. They might be right; our beliefs do reflect the validity of our faith. They also state there is no Scripture-declared penalty for the denial of some of these - yet they still consider them essential to the Christian faith.[21]

1. Jesus is both God and man - Jhn 1:1,14; 8:24; Col. 2:9; 1Jo 4:1-4
2. Jesus rose from the dead physically - Jhn 2:19-21, 1Co. 15:14
3. Salvation is by grace through faith - Rom 5:1, Eph. 2:8-9, Gal 3:1-2
4. The gospel is the death, burial, and resurrection of Jesus - 1Co 15:1-4, Gal 1:8-9
5. There is only one God - Exo 20:3; Isa 43:10, 44:6,8
6. God exists as a Trinity of persons: Father, Son, and Holy Spirit. (Appendix C for Scripture)
7. Jesus was born of the Virgin Mary - Mat 1:18

The following statement is from the Fellowship of Christian Athletes.[22] It reflects their focus on evangelism and discipleship.

1. We believe the Bible to be the only inspired, trustworthy and true, without error, Word of God. (2 Timothy 3:16-17)
2. We believe there is only one God, eternally existent in three persons: Father, Son and Holy Spirit. (Matthew 28:19)
3. We believe in the deity of Christ (John 1:1), in His virgin birth (Matthew 1:18, 25), in His sinless life (Hebrews 4:15), in His miracles, in His vicarious and atoning death through His shed blood (Hebrews 9:15-22), in His bodily resurrection (1 Corinthians 15:1-8), in His ascension to the right hand of the Father (Acts 1:9-11) and in His personal return in power and glory. (Hebrews 9:27-28)
4. We believe that for the salvation of lost and sinful men (women), regeneration by the Holy Spirit is absolutely essential. (John 3:16; John 5:24; Titus 3:3-7)

5. We believe in the present ministry of the Holy Spirit, by whose indwelling the Christian is enabled to live a godly life. (John 14:15-26; John 16:5-16; Ephesians 1:13-14)

6. We believe in the resurrection of both the saved and the lost, they that are saved unto the resurrection of life and they that are lost unto the resurrection of damnation. (Matthew 25:31-46; 1 Thessalonians 4:13-18)

7. We believe in the spiritual unity of believers in our Lord Jesus Christ. (Philippians 2:1-4)

The EPC adopted the following motto to promote unity in their denomination - "In Essentials, Unity. In Non-Essentials, Liberty. In All Things, Charity; Truth in Love." It would work well for the whole body of Christ. Their essentials document has seven statements, available on their website - http://epc.org/essentials.

A basic set of essentials would move our emphasis away from the 79 trillion possible belief combinations mentioned in chapter 2. It would make sense not to include anything that God would not require for salvation. Otherwise, the essentials might exclude some folks we will see in heaven. How embarrassing.

It sounds like I am promoting compromise. Compromise would mean we surrender valid essentials for the sake of unity - that is not an option. We must have prayer inspired, Spirit directed surrender of theology not completely sustained by all of Scripture. Our submission can garner God's intended essentials. Pray for it.

The obstacles and contentions resolved to gain our Constitution are taken for granted today. The book *Founding Rivals* by Chris DeRose provides an excellent account of that period focusing on Madison and Monroe, two Christian friends on opposite sides of the state's rights spectrum.[23] The Constitutional Convention met several times with little success until George Washington locked them in what is now called Convention Hall with the windows and shutters closed in 90+ degree heat and no air conditioning. This led the delegates to act as a body without interference from the selfish motives of their constituents or the media, which can impede or influence progress at times. Ben Franklin said that he was unsure if the carving on the back of Washington's chair depicting the sun on the horizon was the dawn or sunset of our new nation. The rest of the story is now famous. Likely, the smell alone drove them to consensus. The body of Christ is far more important than our worldly citizenship. We need a convention to establish the essentials (means to salvation) for the body of Christ. Every group who wanted to be in this body of Christ could send an allocation of delegates. Those with no affiliation to a denomination or association could gather ahead of the conference and select representatives. Then lock themselves up with the Holy Spirit and no observers until they came up with a consensus. The essentials document, and the new relationships produced in the meeting would be an amazing step toward unity.

It is asking a lot of God to lead us to a perfect document on the first try. Knowing when to stop and take a victory will be critical. Driven too far in diluting the specifics would result in little value steering the organization into the future. Doggedly clinging to theology not supported by all of Scripture, would result in many backing away. That product would not have the support to become a Christian standard.

As in the past 2000 years, there will always be people seeking to redefine or expand the essentials. This will continue in the future; there has to be an agreed process to consider proposed changes. Otherwise, the culture shifts and other motives might corrupt this document.

12. Everyone Can Do Something

Ever wonder what the migrating geese are honking about as they fly thousands of miles with the changing of the seasons? Some would suspect they were complaining to the leader - "Why are we going this way," "It's going to rain here," "What a terrible head wind," "Look at all the hunters," "There is nothing to eat down there" and so on. No, they are not like pew whiners; they are encouraging the leader to press on. They also share in the challenges of leading. Surely, we have the sense God gave a goose. Encourage everyone involved in this process, and help where you can. There are at least 27 passages in Scripture instructing us in how to treat *one another*. They are extension of the golden rule, telling how to treat others as we would like to be treated. Many of them were included in previous chapters. Here are a few more to consider - Mar 9:50, Rom 15:5, Col 3:13, 1Th 5:13, 1Pe 4:9, and 5:5.

> Rom 12:16 <u>Live in harmony with one another</u>. Do not be haughty, but associate with the lowly. Never be wise in your own sight.

We are all smarter than any one of us. That is especially true for me. That is one of the strengths of the nuclear power industry. They share ideas, far more than any industry I know of. It has paid a great benefit to those power plants and to the customers. In the early 1980s, the capacity factor (percent of the power that could have been generated over a period of time) was below 60%. The capacity factor for 2014 was 91.7% for all plants. That is a huge cost savings. They could have operated with a silo mentality, as we have done in denominations, and not seen much of that improvement.

There are many other great ideas for pursing unity in the body of Christ. Sharing ideas is a great step in the direction of success. Post your ideas, success stories, and commitment to helping grow together at WeR2B1.com.

The focus of this chapter was a commitment to God's guidance for unity. If you are not doing these things, then try to understand why. If you feel unity is a lower priority than other demands on your time, then ask yourself two questions. Is that perspective in accord with Scripture? How are your current priorities affecting the health and growth of your church, and the body of Christ?

What if only two faces represented Christianity? The first believe whatever they choose, while still calling themselves Christian. The second believe the Bible is the inspired word of God, the gospel for the salvation of humanity. It would be a much easier and more relevant choice for the lost to hear and accept the gospel. The more Christians in this united body, the more faithful we are to our Lord's call to unity. Christians taking these 12 steps will create a fertile environment to promote the Church growing back together.

AFTERWORD

He said, "The one who showed him mercy." And Jesus
said to him, "You go, and do likewise." Luk 10:37

"Yet, without true Christians loving one another, Christ
says the world cannot be expected to listen, even when
we give proper answers. Let us be careful, indeed,
to spend a lifetime studying to give honest answers.
For years the orthodox, evangelical church has done
this very poorly. So it is well to spend time learning
to answer the questions of men who are about us.
But after we have done our best to communicate to
a lost world, still we must never forget that <u>the final
apologetic which Jesus gives is the observable love of
true Christians for true Christians</u>." - Francis Schaffer[1]

Who are the true Christians? Of course, it is us! As stated
before, if there was a perfect denomination, God would
be blessing it greatly; and people would flock to it in vast
numbers. Just like their members, all denominations and
independents have their faults. No group is perfect; one option
considered for the name of this book was We Are All Cults.
The earnest pursuit of unity will have a refining effect on us
all, causing us to leave the dross behind to be part of the true
body of Christ. Only together can we meet God's call to unity.
That is a win-win outcome. Pursuing unity is like starting a
fitness program, every little bit helps. We can hurt ourselves
with an improper pursuit of fitness; the unity mission must
be undertaken prayerfully and carefully.

I hope this book was as much a blessing to read as it was to
write. Repeat after me, "God is awesome!" He inspired, guided,
and motivated me throughout. He provided everything needed
to get this done, even when I did not know what I needed.
At the advice from a writer, I read this many times through
before submitting to the publisher. It was very convicting to
see how many times I have not followed the guidance in this

volume. I continue to struggle to work for unity it is not easy. Writing this book brought me new perspective and enhanced motivation.

The last page in this book is a bookmark you can copy or cut out and put in your Bible as a regular reminder to pursue this mandate from our Lord.

If I had a theme song for this book, it would be "The Old Violin." That ballad recounts the auctioning of an aged violin with bids going up to $3. A master musician stepped forward and played the instrument, the bids jumped to $3,000. I am just an old violin the Master used to play something worthwhile. I urge you to go and seek the beautiful song the Master will play with you **IF** you just submit to Him.

Bibliography

Introduction

1. David B. Barrett, George T. Kurian, and Todd M. Johnson, *World Christian Encyclopedia: A Comparative Survey Of Churches And Religions In The Modern World*, Vol. 1, Oxford: Oxford Univ. Press, 2001
2. Frank S. Mead, Samuel S. Hill, and Craig D. Atwood, *Handbook of Denominations in the United States*, 13th edition, Abingdon Press, Copyright © 2010 Abingdon Press, Used by permission. All rights reserved.
3. Samuel G. Dawson, The Harm of Denominationalism, page 1, www.lowcountrychurch.org / uploads/3/0/1/5/3015747/the_harm_of_ denominationalism.pdf
4. Pastor Bo Watson, Chattanooga News Free Press, 3 Jan 2015
5. John V. Farwell, *Early Recollections of Moody*, Forgotten Books, page 21
6. Gerald Procee, Revivals in North America: The Great Revival of 1857 in New York, http://reformedresource.net/ index.php/worldviews/the-hand-of-god-in-history/123-revivals-in-north-america-the-great-revival-of-1857-in-new-york.html
7. Timothy Paul Jones, *Christian History Made Easy*, Rose Publishing, Copyright 1999, page 126
8. What is Essential Christian Doctrine?, Christian Research Institute, www.equip.org/bible_answers/what-is-essential-christian-doctrine/, Article from Hank Hanegraaff, *The Complete Bible Answer Book—Collector's Edition,* Nashville, Thomas Nelson, 2008

Chapter 1 - A Burning Platform

1. Jack Wellman, Why We Are Losing So Many Churches In The United States?, Patheos, 26 Oct 2013, www.patheos. com/blogs/christiancrier/2013/10/26/why-we-are-losing-so-many-churches-in-the-united-states/

2. "Global Index of Religiosity and Atheism" WIN-Gallup International, 27 Jul 2012. Retrieved 24 August 2012, www.wingia.com/web/files/news/14/file/14.pdf

3. Religious Composition by Country, 2010-2050, Pew Research Center, 2 Apr 2015, www.pewforum. org/2015/04/02/religious-projection-table/2010/ number/all/

4. Richard N. Ostling, Researcher tabulates world's believers, Adherents.com, www.adherents.com/misc/WCE.html

5. Monica Anderson, Christianity Poised To Continue Its Shift From Europe to Africa, PEW Research Center, 7 Apr 2015, www.pewresearch.org/fact-tank/2015/04/07/ christianity-is-poised-to-continue-its-southward-march/

6. Walid Shoebat, Christianity Is Dying In Europe:, 13 Jan 2016, http://shoebat.com/2016/01/13/91140/

7. Alan Brownfield, Western Europe's Retreat From Religion Provides Vacuum For ISIS Recruitment, Global News Centre, 11 Jun 2015, www.globalnewscentre.com/ western-europes-retreat-from-religion-provides-vacuum- for-isis-recruitment/#sthash.fPpSTNJ1.zHipNsGt.dpbs

8. "Global Index of Religiosity and Atheism" WIN-Gallup International, 27 Jul 2012. Retrieved 24 August 2012, www.wingia.com/web/files/news/14/file/14.pdf

9. Barna Research Group, Ltd., "Teenagers Embrace Religion but Are Not Excited About Christianity," 10 Jan 2000, www.barna.org.

10. *Yearbook of American & Canadian Churches* 2012, Edited by Eileen W. Lindner, https://books.google. com/books?id=5DWeLz28b88C&pg=PT56&lpg= PT56&dq=jlgeii&source=bl&ots=ANtJPDM-mm&sig= wi7399vrNe3KHfXEKJX-_wYGDds&hl=en&sa=X&ved= 0CCkQ6AEwAmoVChMI0Ni0jbeay*AIVQ5yIChOj_g4l#v= onepage&q=jlgeii&f=fal*se

11. Religious Preference: None, Leonard Allen, Lipscomb University, https://www.lipscomb.edu/bible/blog/ faculty-voices/2014/12/5/religious-preference-none

12. On Apostasy Among Catholics, see Dean R. Hoge, "Why Catholics Drop Out," in Falling from Faith: Causes and Consequences for Religious Apostasy, ed. David G. Bromley (Newbery Park, CA. Sage, 1988), 81-99.

13. Religion Among the Milllennials, Pew Research Center, Feb 2010, www.pewforum.org/files/2010/02/millennials- report.pdf

14. Dr. Richard J. Krejcir, Statistics and Reasons for Church Decline, ChurchLeadership.org, www.churchleadership. org/apps/articles/default.asp?articleid=42346&columnid= 4545

15. America Changing Religious Landscape, Pew Research Center, 12 May 2015, www.pewforum.org/2015/05/12/ americas-changing-religious-landscape/

16. Number of Americans 'Certain" about God falls to 63 Percent, News Max, 3 Nov 2015, www. newsmax.com/Newsfront/US-religion/2015/11/03/ id/700336/#ixzz3qSuYlkVg

17. Key Beliefs of Next Generation Left, Pew Research Center, 26 Jun 2014, www.people-press. org/2014/06/26/appendix-1-typology-group-profiles/ pp-2014-06-26-typology-a1-05/.

18. Larry Kreider, House Church Networks - A Wave Of The Future, Dove International, Jan 2005, www.dcfi.org/ resources/articles/house-church-networks%E2%80% 94a-wave-of-the-future/

19. Thom S. Rainer, Eight Reasons People are leaving Denominational Churches for Non-denominational Churches, 22 Apr 2015, http://thomrainer.com/2015/04/ eight-reasons-people-are-leaving-denominational-churches-for-non-denominational-churches/

20. Record Few Americans Believe Bible Is Literal Word of God, by Lydia Saad, Gallup News, May 15, 2017, http:// news.gallup.com/poll/210704/record-few-americans-believe-bible-literal-word-god.aspx

21. Harold Lindsell, *The Battle for the Bible*, Zondervan Corp, 1980

22. www.goodreads.com/author/quotes/5083573.D_L_Moody

23. Augustine, Covenant Protestant Reformed Church, www.cprf.co.uk/quotes/inerrancyofscripture.htm#. WCW74i0rLb0

24. Timothy Paul Jones, *Christian History Made Easy*, Rose Publishing, Copyright 1999, page 72

25. Amanda Mohdin, Charles Darwin's 'On The Origin Of Species' Voted To Be The Most Influential Academic Text In History, Quartz, 11Nov 2015, http://deadstate.org/ charles-darwins-on-the-origin-of-species-voted-to-be-the-most-influential-book-in-history/

26. Brainy Quotes, www.brainyquote.com/quotes/quotes/b/ blaisepasc133606.html

27. Atheists, Muslims See Most Bias as Presidential Candidate. Gallup News, June 21,2012, http://news.gallup.com/poll/155285/atheists-muslims-bias-presidential-candidates.aspx

28. Timothy Paul Jones, *Christian History Made Easy*, Rose Publishing, Copyright 1999, page 126, page 76

Chapter 2 - The Problem

1. Condition of Society and its only hope is Obeying the Everlasting Gospel, Day Spring Office, 1847, https://books.google.com/books?id=eFxgAAAAcAAJ&pg=PA20&lpg=PA20&dq=denominations+harm+the+gospel&source=bl&ots=FgIL4FXw05

2. Are Denominations Dividing the Church, Beliefnet News, author not posted, www.beliefnet.com/columnists/news/2013/09/are-denominations-dividing-the-church.php

3. Cindy Wooden, Conflicts among Christians harm the body of Christ, pope says, Catholic News Service, www.catholicnews.com/services/englishnews/2013/conflicts-among-christians-harm-the-body-of-christ-pope-says.cfm

4. https://en.wikipedia.org/wiki/Early_Muslim_conquests, Conner, Fred M. (2014). *The Early Islamic Conquests.* Princeton University Press,

5. Image excerpts from Denominations Comparison by Robert M. Bowman Jr., copyright © 2003 by Rose Publishing, Peabody, Massachusetts. Used by permission. All rights reserved

6. Timothy Paul Jones, *Christian History Made Easy*, Rose Publishing, Copyright 1999, page 58

7. https://en.wikipedia.org/wiki/Immovable_Ladder

8. Natasha Rosenstock, Hanukkah Gifts, My Jewish Learning, www.myjewishlearning.com/article/hanukkah-gifts/

9. Frank S. Mead, Samuel S. Hill, and Craig D. Atwood, *Handbook of Denominations in the United States*, 13th edition. Copyright © 2010 Abingdon Press, Used by permission. All rights reserved.

10. Less Divided Over Doctrine, National Association of Evangelicals, Oct 2014, http://nae.net/less-divided-over-doctrine/

11. Patrick Glynn, *God the Evidence*, Prima Publishing, 1997, page 149

12. George Barna, Five Ways Christianity is Increasingly Viewed as Extremist, cfaith, Feb 2016, www.cfaith. com/index.php/article-display/22-articles/christian-living/25344-five-ways-christianity-is-increasingly-viewed-as-extremist

13. https://en.wikipedia.org/wiki/Talmud, https:// creativecommons.org/licenses/by-sa/3.0/

14. A List of the 613 Mitzvot (Commandments), Judaism 101, www.jewfaq.org/613.htm

15. Frequent Reference Question: How Many Federal Laws Are There? by Jeanine Cali, Library of Congress, Mar 12, 2013, https://blogs.loc.gov/law/2013/03/frequent-reference-question-how-many-federal-laws-are-there/

16. The Catechism of the Catholic Church www. catholicsociety.com/catechism/catholic_catechism.htm

17. *Catechism Of The Catholic Church*, Second Edition, Apr 1995, Doubleday

18. Dr. Lewis J. Patsavos, Ph.D., The Canonical Tradition of the Orthodox Church, 2016 Greek Orthodox Archdiocese of America, www.goarch.org/ourfaith/ourfaith7071

19. http://s3.amazonaws.com/orthodox/The_Rudder.pdf

20. Huss and the Church, Online Library of Liberty, http://oll. libertyfund.org/pages/huss-and-the-church

21. A tabular comparison of the 1646 WCF and the 1689 LBCF, www.proginosko.com/docs/wcf_lbcf.html

22. The Average Church Size in America, The Prodigal Thought, 26 Jan 2011, http://prodigalthought. net/2011/01/26/the-average-church-size-in-america/

23. J. Warner Wallace, Are Young People Really Leaving Christianity?, Cold Case Christianity, http://coldcasechristianity.com/2015/ are-young-people-really-leaving-christianity/

24. Ken Ham, Britt Beemer, with Todd Hillard, *Already Gone: Why Your Kids Will Quit Church And What You Can Do To Stop It*, New Leaf Publishing Group/Master Books (2009)

25. David Kinnaman, *You Lost Me: Why Young Christians Are Leaving Church...... Rethinking Faith*, Baker Books, 2011

26. George Barna, Teens and Young Adults Use Porn More Than Anyone Else, 28 Jan 2016, www.barna.com/ research/teens-young-adults-use-porn-more-than-anyone-else/#.V8cRn_krLbl

27. Steve Wright, *reThink, Is Student Ministry Working?*, InQuest Ministries, 2007

28. Changing Denominations Common Among Evangelical Leaders, Dec 2014, National Association of Evangelicals, http://nae.net/changing-denominations-common-among-evangelical-leaders/

29. Are Denominations dividing the Church?, beliefnet News, http://www.beliefnet.com/columnists/news/2013/09/are-denominations-dividing-the-church.php

30. Ed Stetzer, The Rapid Rise of Nondenominational Christianity: My Most Recent Piece on CNN, 12 Jun 2015, Christianity Today, www.christianitytoday.com/edstetzer/2015/june/rapid-rise-of-non-denominational-christianity-my-most-recen.html

31. Nondenominational & Independent Congregations, Hartford Institute For Religion Research, 2015, http://hirr.hartsem.edu/cong/nondenom.html

32. Non-Denominational / Independent Directory of Churches, USAChurches.org, www.usachurches.org/christian/other/non-denominational-independent/

33. Eyder Peralta, Pastor Terry Jones Arrested Before Planned Quran Burning, 11 Sep 2013, the two-way Breaking News From NPR, www.npr.org/sections/thetwo-way/2013/09/11/221528510/pastor-terry-jones-arrested-before-planned-quran-burning

34. In Praise of Denominations, Jason Helopoulos, 28 Dec 2012, The Gospel Coalition, https://blogs.thegospelcoalition.org/kevindeyoung/2012/12/28/in-praise-of-denominations/

35. Elizabeth's Middle Way, www.johndclare.net/KS3/2-3-5.htm

36. The Westminster Assembly Project, www.westminsterassembly.org/

37. Tamara Grdzelidze, "Ecumenism, Orthodoxy" and "In The Encyclopedia of Eastern Orthodox Christianity", edited by John Anthony McGuckin, 208-15. Wiley Blackwell, 2011

38. Timothy Paul Jones, *Christian History Made Easy*, Rose Publishing, Copyright 1999, page 134

39. https://en.wikipedia.org/wiki/Ecumenism

40. https://en.wikipedia.org/wiki/Consultation_on_Church_Union

41. Graymoor Ecumenical Institute, Sample article from Ecumenical Trends, www.geii.org/week_of_prayer_for_christian_unity/to_order/ordering_resources.html
42. National Association of Ecumenical and Interreligious Staff, http://eiln.org/old/aboutnaeis/conferences.htm
43. https://en.wikipedia.org/wiki/Ecumenism
44. The Lausanne Covenant, Lausanne Movement, 1 Aug 1974, www.lausanne.org/content/covenant/lausanne-covenant

Chapter 3 Evolution of Denominations

1. Frank S. Mead, Samuel S. Hill, and Craig D. Atwood, *Handbook of Denominations in the United States*, 13th edition. Copyright © 2010 Abingdon Press, Used by permission. All rights reserved.
2. Thinkexist.com, http://thinkexist.com/quotation/there_is_a_god_shaped_vacuum_in_the_heart_of/166425.html
3. B. A. Robinson, The "Golden Rule" (a.k.a. Ethics of Reciprocity), Religious Tolerance, Dec., 2016, http://www.religioustolerance.org/reciproc2.htm
4. *Spurgeon Memorial Library*, Vol. I., p. 168
5. John Wesley, Universal Knowledge, A Dictionary and Encyclopedia of Arts, Science, History, Biography, Law, Literature, Religions, Nations, Races, Customs, and Institutions, Vol. 9, Edward A. Pace, Editor, New York: Universal Knowledge Foundation, 1927, p. 540
6. Hugh Thomason Kerr, *A Compend of Luther's Theology*, Philadelphia: The Westminster Press, 1943, p. 135
7. Christianity Is No Longer America's Default Faith, 28 Jan 2009, www.barna.org/barna-update/faith-spirituality/15-christianity-is-no-longer-americans-default-faith#.VtgnePkrLb0

Chapter 4 - Begin With the End in Mind

1. Erwin Lutzer, *Your Eternal Reward*, Moody Publishers, 2015
2. Samuel Hoyt, The Judgment Seat of Christ in Theological Perspective, part 2: The Negative Aspects of the Christian's Judgment, Bibliotheca Sacra 137, no. 546 (Apr-Jun 1980): 125-130, www.fbgbible.org/B1543-110115.pdf (page 3)

Chapter 5 - Mysteries and Antinomies

1. Quoteland.com, www.quoteland.com/author/
   Brennan-Manning-Quotes/1805/
2. *The NIV Study Bible*, 10th Anniversary Edition, Zondervan
   Publishing House, 1995
3. Quote from James Weldon Johnson, www.blackpast.
   org/1923-james-weldon-johnson-our-democracy-and-
   ballot#sthash.e7ejmM4p.dpuf
4. https://en.wikiquote.org/wiki/Donald_Rumsfeld, https://
   creativecommons.org/licenses/by-sa/3.0/

Chapter 6 - False Teachers

1. *The NIV Study Bible*, 10th Anniversary Edition, Zondervan
   Publishing House, 1995
2. www.brainyquote.com/quotes/quotes/a/aidenwilso153971.
   html#DgzMfftAvjoXyzWL.99
3. www.goodreads.com/author/quotes/1711.Thomas_Merton
4. www.brainyquote.com/quotes/quotes/s/
   saintaugus148529.html
5. www.goodreads.com/author/quotes/147674.David_
   Crockett

Chapter 7 - Motives for False Teaching

1. www.greatsite.com/timeline-english-bible-history/queen-
   mary.html
2. Andree Seu Peterson, Mental Filibusters, World Magazine,
   14 may 2005, https://world.wng.org/2005/05/mental_
   filibusters
3. Nina Buleigh, Faith, forgery, science -- and the
   James Ossuary, Los Angeles Times,25 Mar 2012,
   http://articles.latimes.com/2012/mar/25/opinion/
   la-oe-burleigh-bible-ossuary-forgery-20120325/2

Chapter 8 - Teaching Biblical Truth

1. www.allaboutgod.net/profiles/blogs/
   the-word-of-god-is-like-a
2. Bob Mumford, *Take Another Look at Guidance: A Study of
   Divine Guidance*, Logos International, 1971
3. author unknown

4. Why is it important to study the Bible in context?, gotQuestions?org, www.gotquestions.org/context-Bible.html

5. Jefferson's Letter to the Danbury Baptists, www.loc.gov/loc/lcib/9806/danpre.html

6. www.goodreads.com/quotes/283520-the-greatest-single-cause-of-atheism-in-the-world-today

7. www.quotes.net/quote/52528

8. www.google.com/webhp?sourceid=chrome-instant&ion=1&espv=2&ie=UTF-8#q=%22Preach+the+gospel%2C+and+if+necessary%2C+use+words%22

9. Blue Letter Bible www.blueletterbible.org/study/misc/quotes.cfm

10. www.brainyquote.com/quotes/quotes/a/aidenwilso153969.html

Chapter 10 - Examination of a Contested Doctrine

1. www.goodreads.com/author/quotes/6188.Georg_Wilhelm_Friedrich_Hegel

2. Is There a "Reformed" Movement in American Churches? Barna Research Group, 15 Nov. 2010, www.barna.com/research/is-there-a-reformed-movement-in-american-churches/

3. National Council of Churches USA, New York, NY, 2011 Yearbook of American & Canadian Churches

4. *The NIV Study Bible*, 10th Anniversary Edition, Zondervan Publishing House, 1995

5. Randy Newman, *Bringing the Gospel Home*, Crossway, 2011, page 195.

6. Arminians Versus Calvinists: Some Surprising Statistics, The Wartburg Watch, 30 Nov, 2011, http://thewartburgwatch.com/2011/11/30/arminians-versus-calvinists-some-surprising-statistics/

7. *The NIV Study Bible*, 10th Anniversary Edition, Zondervan Publishing House, 1995

Chapter 11 - Divisive Issues

1. The "Golden Rule of Interpretation", Bible Truths, Mar 30, 2014, www.bibletruths.org/the-golden-rule-of-interpretation/

2. https://en.wikipedia.org/wiki/Life_Bible-Presbyterian_Church

3. https://en.wikipedia.org/wiki/Carbon_dating_the_Dead_Sea_Scrolls

4. Will Varner, What is the Importance of the Dead Sea Scrolls?, Christian Answers.Net, Associates for Christian Research, 1997, www.christiananswers.net/q-abr/abr-a023.html

5. https://en.wikipedia.org/wiki/Chapters_and_verses_of_the_Bible#Chapters

6. http://cojs.org/apocrypha-_pseudepigrapha-_and_the_dead_sea_scrolls-_lawrence_schiffman-_from_text_to_tradition-_ktav_publishing_house-_hoboken-_nj-_1991-_p-120-138/

7. www.theopedia.com/inerrancy

8. English Bible History, Greatsite.com, www.greatsite.com/timeline-english-bible-history/

9. https://en.wikipedia.org/wiki/King_James_Version

10. English Bible Translations, URl- http://tyndalearchive.com/scriptures/index.htm

11. https://en.wikipedia.org/wiki/Revised_Standard_Version

12. Tom J. Nettles, *Understanding Four Views on Baptism*, Richard L. Pratt, Jr., John H. Armstrong, Robert Kolb, Zondervan, 2007, ISBN 0-310-26267-4, ISBN 978-0-310-26267-1, 222 pages

13. The State of Female Pastors, Ashley Emmert, womenleaders.com, Oct.2015, https://www.christianitytoday.com/women-leaders/2015/october/state-of-female-pastors.html

14. https://en.wikipedia.org/wiki/First_Council_of_Nicaea

15. www.theopedia.com/american-standard-version

16. Sean Michael Lucas; Jim Crow, Civil Rights, And Southern White Evangelicals: A Historians Forum; The Gospel Coalition, 3 Feb 2015, https://blogs.thegospelcoalition.org/justintaylor/2015/02/06/jim-crow-civil-rights-and-southern-white-evangelicals-a-historians-forum-sean-michael-lucas/

17. *The NIV Study Bible*, 10th Anniversary Edition, Zondervan Publishing House, 1995

Chapter 12. Why Not?

1. Brainy Quotes, www.brainyquote.com/quotes/authors/r/ robert_kennedy.html
2. Robert D. Putnam and David E. Campbell, *American Grace*, Simon and Schuster Paperbacks, 2012, page 535
3. J. C. Ryle, The True Church, 1880, www. biblefellowshipunion.co.uk/2002/May_Jun/ TrueChurch.htm
4. https://en.wikipedia.org/wiki/Ecumenism
5. Evangelicals and Catholics Together, Grace to you, www.gty.org/resources/articles/A149/ evangelicals-and-catholics-together
6. The Jerusalem Declaration, contained in The Complete Jerusalem Statement, http://fca.net/resources/ the-complete-jerusalem-statement
7. North American Presbyterian and Reformed Council, www.naparc.org/member-churches/
8. Brainy Quotes, www.brainyquote.com/quotes/quotes/c/ cslewis141015.html
9. Richard Beck, "Forgive Us Our Trespasses", Where Did That Come From?, http://experimentaltheology.blogspot. com/2012/12/forgive-us-our-trespasses-whered-that.html
10. Why There Are So Many Christian Denominations - Part II, Word Became Flesh Ministries, www.wbfmfamily.com/ why-there-are-so-many-christian-denominations-part-2/
11. Randall Bach, President, Open Bible, What Can Your Denominational Tradition Learn From the Others? NAE Article Winter 2014/15, http://nae.net/what-can-your-denominational-tradition-learn-from-the-others/
12. Leith Anderson, NEA, President, So Loud I Can't Hear You, Spring 2009, http://nae.net/so-loud-i-cant-hear-you/
13. Jack Wellman, Why We Are Losing So Many Churches in the United States?, Christian Crier, 26 Oct 2013, www. patheos.com/blogs/christiancrier/2013/10/26/why-we-are-losing-so-many-churches-in-the-united-states/
14. Richard Neitzel Holzapfel and T. Jeffrey Cottle, *Old Mormon Kirtland and Missouri*, Santa Ana, CA: Fieldbrook, 1991
15. Research : Racial Diversity at Church More Dream Than Reality, Bob Smietana, LifeWay Research, January 17, 2014, http://lifewayresearch.com/2014/01/17/research-racial-diversity-at-church-more-dream-than-reality/

16. The Lausanne Covenant, Lausanne Movement, 1 Aug 1974, www.lausanne.org/content/covenant/lausanne-covenant
17. https://en.wikipedia.org/wiki/Edmund_Schlink
18. Rev. Thomas Fitzgerald. The Orthodox Church; An Introduction, The Greek Orthodox Archdiocese of America, 9 Jan. 1996, www.goarch.org/ourfaith/ourfaith7052
19. http://www.worldea.org/whoweare/statementoffaith
20. Matt Slick, What About Different Denominations, CARM 11/21/08, https://carm.org/what-about-different-denominations
21. Matt Slick, Essential Doctrines of Christianity, CARM 11/23/08, https://carm.org/essential-doctrines-of-christianity
22. Fellowship Of Christian Athletes, 27 Oct, 2016, www.fca.org/aboutus/who-we-are/statement-of-faith
23. Christopher DeRose, *Founding Rivals: Madison vs. Monroe, The Bill of Rights, and The Election that Saved a Nation*, Regnery Publishing, 2011

Epilogue

1. Francis Schaffer, The Great Evangelical Disaster, pages. 164-165

Appendix A

1. Frank S. Mead, Samuel S. Hill, and Craig D. Atwood, *Handbook of Denominations in the United States*, 13th edition. Copyright © 2010 Abingdon Press. Used by permission. All rights reserved.

Appendix B

1. The New Strong's Exhaustive Concordance of the Bible, Thomas Nelson Publishers, Copyright 1984.

Appendix C

1. The Thompson Chain-Reference Bible, New International Version, The Zondervan Corporation, 1983

Appendix G

1. Image excerpts from Denominations Comparison by Robert M. Bowman Jr., copyright © 2003 by Rose Publishing, Peabody, Massachusetts. Used by permission. All rights reserved

Appendix A

Faith Groups Professing to be
Christian - from the *Handbook of Denominations
in the United States* 13th Edition.[1]

Orthodox and Oriental Orthodox Churches
African Orthodox Church
Albanian Orthodox Archdiocese in America
American Carpatho-Russian Orthodox Church
Antiochian Orthodox Christian Archdiocese of North America
Apostolic Catholic Assyrian Church of the East, North American Diocese
Apostolic Episcopal Church
Armenian Apostolic Church of America
Armenian Church, Diocese of America
Bulgarian Eastern Orthodox Church
Coptic Orthodox Church
Greek Orthodox Archdiocese of America
Holy Eastern Orthodox Catholic and Apostolic Church in North America
Malankara Orthodox Syrian Church
Mar Thoma Orthodox Syrian Church (Indian Orthodox)
Orthodox Church in America (Russian Orthodox)
Romanian Orthodox Episcopate of America
Serbian Orthodox Church
Syrian Orthodox Church of Antioch, Archdioceses in the U.S.A.
and Canada
Ukrainian Orthodox Church of the U.S.A

Catholic Churches
American Catholic Church in the United States
Apostolic Catholic Orthodox Church
Eastern Rite Catholic / Uniate Churches
Ecumenical Catholic Church USA
Ecumenical Catholic Communion
Mariavite Old Catholic Church, Province of North America
Old Catholic Churches
Polish National Catholic Church of America
Reformed Catholic Church
Roman Catholic Church
Society of Saint Pius X

Episcopal and Anglican Churches
Anglican Communion in North America
Continuing Anglican Churches
Episcopal Church
Evangelical Anglican Church in America
International Communion of the Charismatic Episcopal Church
Reformed Episcopal Church

Lutheran Churches
American Association of Lutheran Churches
Apostolic Lutheran Church of America
Association of Free Lutheran Congregations
Church of the Lutheran Brethren of America
Church of the Lutheran Confession
Evangelical Lutheran Church in America
Evangelical Lutheran Synod
Latvian Evangelical Lutheran Church in America
Lutheran Church – Missouri Synod
Wisconsin Evangelical Lutheran Synod

Reformed, Congregationalist, and Presbyterian Churches
American Waldensian Society
Associate Reformed Presbyterian Church
Christian Reformed Church in North America
Conservative Congregational Christian Conference
Cumberland Presbyterian Church
Cumberland Presbyterian Church in America
Evangelical Association of Reformed and Congregational Churches
Evangelical Presbyterian Church
Korean Presbyterian Church in America
National Association of Congregational Christian Churches
Netherlands Reformed Congregations in North America
Orthodox Presbyterian Church
Presbyterian Church in America
Presbyterian Church (U.S.A.)
Protestant Reformed Churches in America
Reformed Church in America
Reformed Presbyterian Church of North America
United Church of Christ

Mennonite and Anabaptist Churches
Beachy Amish Mennonite Churches

Church Communities International
Church of God in Christ, Mennonite
Conservative Mennonite Conference
Fellowship of Evangelical Churches
Hutterite Brethren
Mennonite Church (USA)
Missionary Church
Old Order Amish Churches
Old Order (Wisler) Mennonite Churches
U.S. Mennonite Brethren Churches

Friends (Quaker)
Evangelical Friends International
Friends General Conference
Friends United Meeting

Brethren and Pietist Churches
Brethren Church (Ashland)
Brethren in Christ Church
Church of the Brethren
Church of the United Brethren in Christ
Evangelical Congregational Church
Evangelical Covenant Church
Evangelical Free Church of America
Fellowship of Grace Brethren Churches
Moravian Church (Unitas Fratrum)
Old German Baptist Brethren Church
Schwenkfelder Church

Baptists
Alliance of Baptist Churches
American Baptist Association
American Baptist Churches in the U.S.A.
Association of Reformed Baptist Churches of America
Baptist General Convention of Texas
Conservative Baptist Association of America
Converge Worldwide
Cooperative Baptist Fellowship
Duck River (and Kindred) Association of Baptists
General Association of General Baptists
General Association of Regular Baptist Churches
Interstate and Foreign Landmark Missionary Baptist Association

National Association of Free Will Baptists
National Baptist Convention of America, Inc
National Baptist Convention, U.S.A., Inc
National Missionary Baptist Convention of America
National Primitive Baptist Convention, U.S.A.
North American Baptist Conference
Old Missionary Baptist Associations
Old Regular Baptists
Original Free Will Baptist Convention
Primitive Baptists
Progressive National Baptist Convention, Inc
Progressive Primitive Baptists
Separate Baptists in Christ
Seventh Day Baptist General Conference
Southern Baptist Convention
Sovereign Grace Baptists
United American Free Will Baptist Church

Methodist Churches
African Methodist Episcopal Church
African Methodist Episcopal Zion Church
Christian Methodist Episcopal Church
Congregational Methodist Church
Evangelical Church of North America
Evangelical Methodist Church
Korean Methodist Church
The Salvation Army
Southern Methodist Church
United Methodist Church
Volunteers of America, Inc.

Native American Christianity
Native American Church

Holiness Churches
Apostolic Christian Churches of America
Apostolic Overcoming Holy Church of God, Inc.
The Christian and Missionary Alliance
Church of Christ (Holiness) U.S.A.
Church of God (Anderson, Indiana)
Church of God (Holiness)
Church of the Nazarene

Churches of Christ in Christian Union
Churches of God, General Conference
Free Methodist Church of North America
New Apostolic Church of North America
Wesleyan Church

Christian and Restorationist Churches (Stone-Campbellite Tradition)
Christian Church (Disciples of Christ)
Independent Christian Churches and Churches of Christ
Christian Congregation, Inc.
Churches of Christ
International Churches of Christ

Adventist and Sabbatarian (Hebraic) Churches
Advent Christian Church General Conference
Branch Davidians
Christadelphians
Church of God (Seventh Day)
Church of God and Saints of Christ
Church of God General Conference
Grace Communion International (Worldwide Church of God)
Jehovah's Witnesses
Philadelphia Church of God
Seventh-Day Adventists
United Church of God

Pentecostal Churches
Apostolic Faith Mission Church of God
Apostolic World Christian Fellowship
Assemblies of God International
Assemblies of the Lord Jesus Christ
Bible Way Church of Our Lord Jesus Christ, World Wide, Inc.
International Fellowship of Christian Assemblies
Church of God (Cleveland, Tenn.)
Church of God in Christ
Church of God of Prophecy
Church of Our Lord Jesus Christ of the Apostolic Faith, Inc.
Church of the Living God, Christian Workers for Fellowship
Congregational Holiness Church
Elim Fellowship
Fire-Baptized Holiness Church of God

Full Gospel Fellowship of Churches and Ministers, International
Independent Assemblies of God, International
International Church of the Foursquare Gospel
International Pentecostal Holiness Church
Open Bible Standard Churches, Inc
Pentecostal Assemblies of the World, Inc.
Pentecostal Church of God
Pentecostal Free Will Baptist Church, Inc.
United Holy Church of America, Inc.
United Pentecostal Church International
Vineyard Churches International

Fundamentalist and Bible Churches
American Evangelical Christian Churches
Baptist Bible Fellowship International
Baptist Missionary Association of America
Berean Fundamental Church
Bible Fellowship Church
Bible Presbyterian Church
Bob Jones University
Grace Gospel Fellowship
Great Commission Churches
IFCA International
Independent Baptist Fellowship International
Independent Fundamentalist Baptist Churches
Plymouth Brethren (Christian Brethren)
Southwide Baptist Fellowship
Thomas Road Baptist Church (Jerry Falwell Ministries)
World Baptist Fellowship

Community and New Paradigm Churches -
Congregations with Over 15,000 Members
Acts 29 Network
Calvary Chapels
Communion of Convergence Churches
Cowboy Churches
Emergent Village
International Council of Community Churches
Lakewood Church
The Potter's House
Saddleback Church
Southeast Christian Church (Christian)

Trinity United Church of Christ
Universal Fellowship of the Metropolitan Community Churches
Willow Creek Community Church
World Changers Ministry

Latter-Day Saints (Mormons)
Church of Christ (Temple Lot)
Church of Jesus Christ of Latter-day Saints
Community of Christ
Fundamentalist Church of Jesus Christ of Latter-Day Saints

Esoteric, Spiritualist, and New Thought Bodies
Church of Christ, Scientist (Christian Science)
Liberal Catholic Church International
Liberal Catholic Church, Province of the United States

Appendix B

Hebrew and Greek Words Translated as "All" or Similar in English.[1]

English	Hebrew/Greek Strong's ref.	Strong's definition	Uses in NASB
all or everyone	Pas G-3956	apparently a primary word; all, any, every, the whole	1410
all nations	Pas Ethnos G1484	probably from G1486; a race (as of the same habit), i.e. a tribe; specially, a foreign (non-Jewish) one (usually, by implication, pagan):—Gentile, heathen, nation, people.	28 - phrase, 163 - G1484
whole world	Holos G3650 Kosmos G2889	a primary word; "whole" or "all", the world (in a wide or narrow sense, including its inhabitants, literally or figuratively)	3650, 2889
any	Tis G5100	an enclitic indefinite pronoun; some or any person or object	479
Whoever	Hos G3739	Which, whom, that, who, whose	1,389
everyone/ whoever	Kol H-3605	the whole; all, any or every, altogether, enough, everyone, whosoever	5411
anyone who dies	MuwthH-4191	Die, dead, slay, death	835

279

Appendix C

<u>Evolution of the English Bible</u>

The information for this simplified graphic came from the Thompson Chain Reference Bible[1] and the website for the modern translations. Many translations of lesser influence were not included. Some aspects of developmental influence are not presented due to complexity.

<u>Format for this table</u>

1963/1971 = year NT published/year OT published
U = Updated Edition
→, ↓, ← = Versions used as input to the next version
Shaded = Catholic Bibles

<u>Notes for the graphic below</u>

[1] Codex Alexandrinus A. D. 450, Codex Vaticanus A. D. 340, Codex Sinaiticus A. D. 400

[2] The Jerusalem Bible is a translation from the Hebrew and Greek rather than the Latin Vulgate. It was influenced by the French translation La Bible de Jerusalem 1956. The following Bibles are also approved for use by Catholics - Confraternity Bible, Douay-Rheims Bible, Good News Bible / Today's English Version - Catholic Edition, New Jerusalem Bible, CTS New Catholic Bible, Knox Bible, New American Bible, New American Bible Revised Edition, New Revised Standard Version Catholic Edition, The Living Bible - Catholic Edition (The Catholic Living Bible).

[3] New English Translation from "best available texts" Published in 2005.

Evolution of the English Bible

5th to 11th Century	Wessex Gospels, Hatton gospels, Old English Hexateuch, Old English Bible translations ↓ ↓			
	Early Copies[1] ↓ → ↓ ↓	Latin Vulgate A. D. 400 ↓		
	Masoretic Text A. D. 500 - 950↓	↓ ↓ Textus Receptus ↓		
12th -15th Centuries	The Wycliffe Bible 1380/1409↓	← ↓	↓ ↓	
	Gutenberg Bible ↓	Luther's Bible 1522 ↓	↓ ↓	
→ ↓ · ↓←	The Tyndale NT 1525, Pentateuch 1530 ↓ →	Coverdale Bible 1535 ↓	↓Douay–Rheims Bible 1582/1610	
The Great Bible 1539 ↓ ↓	← Matthew's Version 1537 ↓	←	↓	
↓ Geneva Bible 1560 ↓	Tavener's Bible 1539 ↓		↓	
↓ The Bishop's Bible 1568 ↓	↓		↓	
↓ (Primary guide) ↓	← (Secondary Influence)		↓	
King James (KJV) or ↓ Authorized Version 1611 ↓ →	→	→	Challoner revision 1749,1750, 1752 ↓	
→ ↓ Revised Version (RV) 1881/1885 ↓ →	American Standard Version (ASV) 1901 →	New American Standard (NASB) 1963/1971,1972, 1973, 1975, 1977, U-1995 →	New World Translation (NWT) 1961, 1981, 1984, 2013	
	↓ →	→ →		
↓ New King James 1982	Revised Standard Version (RSV) 1946/1952, U-1962/1966	→	→RSV Catholic Edition 1946/1952	
↓	↓ ↓		↓ Jerusalem Bible 1966[2]	
New International Version 1973/1978, U-2002, 2005 U-2011	NRSV 1989	English Stand. Version (ESV) 2001, 2007, 2011	↓RSV Second Catholic 2006	
20th Century	41 new translations and paraphrases			
21th Century, by mid 2015	23 new translations and paraphrases, including NET[3]			

(Left margin vertical label: *More Early Copies*)

Appendix D

<u>Scripture Supporting a Trinitarian Understanding of God</u>

All Scripture in this Appendix is from KJV.

This contested concept has been debated back to the early church. There are many books supporting both sides. Differing perspectives are inevitable as we propose a specific description of the infinite Creator of everything. At the center of this dispute is who Jesus is.

If it were simple, the debate would not be active today. Both sides have a lengthy list of proof text passages. The real question is which position fits better with <u>all</u> of Scripture. It is hard to say it is not an essential. Both sides contend it is necessary for our faithful response to the great commandment - Mar 12:30.

Take great care in forming your perspective on the Trinity.

> Mat 10:32-33 Whosoever therefore shall confess me before men, him will I confess also before my Father which is in heaven. [33] But whosoever shall deny me before men, him will I also deny before my Father which is in heaven. - also Mar 8:38, 2Ti 2:12

> Mar 3:29 But he that shall blaspheme against the Holy Ghost hath never forgiveness, but is in danger of eternal damnation:

It is not a surprise the Bible does not use the word trinity. The term evolved several centuries after the Bible cannon. A full understanding of their relationship is beyond our capacity. This Trinitarian Shield depicts that mystery.

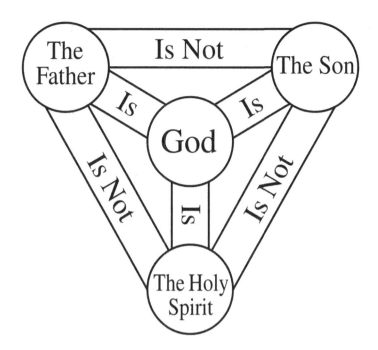

If Jesus is not part of a triune God, then what is He? These passages describe Him the same as God the Father.

Ref	Jesus	Ref	God
Isa 9:6	is the mighty God (el)	Exo 6:3	appeared as God all mighty(el)
Mar 2:5	forgives sin	Mic 7:18	only God forgives sin
Heb 4:15	was without sin	Mar 10:18	No one is good except God alone.
Mat 14:25	he came to them, walking on the sea	Job 9:8	Only God trampled the waves of the sea
2Co 5:10	all appear before the judgment seat of Christ	1Pe 1:7	Father who judges impartially according to each one's deeds
Luk 1:33	and he will reign over the house of Jacob forever	Mic 4:7	LORD will reign over them....forevermore.

Ref	Jesus	Ref	God
Eph 1:23	which is his body, the fullness of him who fills all in all	1Co 15:28	him who put all things in subjection under him, that God may be all in all.
Rom 9:9	You, however, are not in the flesh but in the Spirit, if in fact the Spirit of God dwells in you. Anyone who does not have the Spirit of Christ does not belong to him.		
Phl 2:6-7	though he (Jesus) was in the form of God, did not count equality with God a thing to be grasped, [7] but emptied himself, by taking the form of a servant, being born in the likeness of men.		

The Bible describes all three as being omnipresent: the Father - Act 17:27, Son - Eph 1:23 and Holy Spirit - Act 4:31.

It is hard not to see the triune God in this passage.

> 1Co 12:3-7 Wherefore I give you to understand, that no man speaking by the Spirit of God calleth Jesus accursed: and [that] no man can say that Jesus is the Lord, but by the Holy Ghost. [4] Now there are diversities of gifts, but the **same** Spirit. [5] And there are differences of administrations, but the **same** Lord. [6] And there are diversities of operations, but it is the **same** God which worketh all in all. [7] But the manifestation of the Spirit is given to every man to profit withal.

The following passages use the Spirit of God and Spirit of Christ interchangeably.

> Rom 8:9-10 But ye are not in the flesh, but in the Spirit, if so be that the Spirit of God dwell in you. Now if any man have not the Spirit of Christ, he is none of his. [10] And if Christ [be] in you, the body [is] dead because of sin; but the Spirit [is] life because of righteousness.

284

Gal 4:6 And because ye are sons, God hath sent forth the Spirit of his Son into your hearts, crying, Abba, Father.

All three persons of the Trinity play a part in our sanctification.

Jhn 14:26 But the Comforter, [which is] the <u>Holy Ghost</u>, whom the <u>Father</u> will send in <u>my name</u>, he shall teach you all things, and bring all things to your remembrance, whatsoever I have said unto you.

Eph 3:16-17 That <u>he</u> would grant you, according to the riches of <u>his glory</u>, to be strengthened with might by his <u>Spirit</u> in the inner man; [17] That <u>Christ</u> may dwell in your hearts by faith; that ye, being rooted and grounded in love,

Our baptism is in the name of all three.

Mat 28:19 Go ye therefore, and teach all nations, baptizing them in the name of the <u>Father</u>, and of the <u>Son</u>, and of the <u>Holy Ghost</u>:

Christ is in all ways God.

Col 1:13-20 He has delivered us from the domain of darkness and transferred us <u>to the kingdom of his beloved Son,</u> [14] <u>in whom</u> we have redemption, the forgiveness of sins. [15]Who is the <u>image of the invisible God</u>, the firstborn of every creature: [16] For <u>by him were all things created</u>, that are in heaven, and that are in earth, visible and invisible, whether [they be] thrones, or dominions, or principalities, or powers: <u>all things were created by him,</u> <u>and for him</u>: [17] And <u>he is before all things</u>, and <u>by him all things consist</u>. [18] <u>And he is the head of the body, the church</u>: who is the beginning, the firstborn from the dead; that in all [things] he might have the preeminence. [19] <u>For it pleased [the Father] that in him should all fulness dwell</u>; [20] And, having made peace through the blood of his cross, by him to reconcile all things unto himself; by him, [I say], whether [they be] things in earth, or things in heaven.

They are one.

1Jo 5:7 For there are three that bear record in heaven, the Father, the Word, and the Holy Ghost: <u>and these three are one</u>.

Gen 1:26 And God said, Let us make man in <u>our</u> image, after <u>our</u> likeness:

Isa 9:6 For unto us a child is born, unto us a son is given: and the government shall be upon his shoulder: and his name shall be called Wonderful, <u>Counselor, The mighty God, The everlasting Father</u>, The Prince of Peace.

Jhn 10:30 I and [my] Father are one. (also Jhn 17:11, 17:22)

Jhn 10:38 But if I do, though ye believe not me, believe the works: that ye may know, and believe, that <u>the Father [is] in me, and I in him</u>. (also Jhn 14:10)

Revelation mentions the Father and Son have the same function in heaven. These passages describe God and Jesus together with singular pronouns - His and Him.

<u>Both are the light</u> - Rev 21:23 And the city had no need of the sun, neither of the moon, to shine in it: <u>for the glory of God did lighten it, and the Lamb [is] the light thereof</u>.

<u>Both sit on the same throne</u> - Rev 22:1, 3 And he shewed me a pure river of water of life, clear as crystal, proceeding <u>out of the throne of God and of the Lamb.</u> ³ And there shall be no more curse: but the throne of

God and of the Lamb shall be in it; and **his** servants shall serve **him**:

The Holy Spirit conceived the incarnate Jesus in Mary, the only way Jesus could also be the son of God is if the Holy Spirit is part of God.

> Mat 1:20 But while he thought on these things, behold, the angel of the Lord appeared unto him in a dream, saying, Joseph, thou son of David, fear not to take unto thee Mary thy wife: for that which is conceived in her is of the Holy Ghost.

Jesus has the same image and function as the Father.

> Heb 1:3 Who (*His Son vs. 2*) being the brightness of [his] glory, and the express image of his person, and upholding all things by the word of his power, when he had by himself purged our sins, sat down on the right hand of the Majesty on high;

If you have seen Jesus, you have seen the Father.

> Jhn 14:9 Jesus saith unto him, Have I been so long time with you, and yet hast thou not known me, Philip? he that hath seen me hath seen the Father; and how sayest thou [then], Shew us the Father?

James calls Himself a servant of Jesus and a servant of God in the same passages. If Jesus is not one with God, then this passage conflicts with the 10 commandments "For thou shalt worship no other god" (Exo 34:14). NT authors use the word Kyrios to refer to God - Matt 1:24, 4:7 and Jesus - Jas 1:1 and others.

> Jas 1:1 James, a servant of God and of the Lord Jesus Christ, to the twelve tribes which are scattered abroad, greeting.

If we honor Jesus, we are also honoring the Father.

> Jhn 5:22-23 For the Father judgeth no man, but hath committed all judgment unto the Son: ²³ That all [men] should honour the Son, even as they honour the Father. <u>He that honoureth not the Son honoureth not the Father</u> which hath sent him.

The following passages attribute creation to God and Jesus. Col 1:15-16, and Heb 12:3 also say that Jesus created everything.

> Gen 1:1 In the beginning <u>God created</u> the heaven and the earth.

> Heb 3:4 For every house is builded by some [man]; <u>but he that built all things [is] God</u>.

> Heb 11:3 Through faith we understand that the worlds were <u>framed by the word of God</u>, so that things which are seen were not made of things which do appear.

> 1Co 8:6 But to us [there is but] one <u>God, the Father, of whom [are] all things</u>, and we in him; <u>and one Lord</u> (Kyrios) <u>Jesus Christ, by whom [are] all things</u>, and we by him.

> Eph 3:9 And to make all [men] see what [is] the fellowship of the mystery, which from the beginning of the world hath been hid in <u>God, who created all things by Jesus Christ:</u>

The Father, Son and Holy Spirit work together for our glorification. Why does Peter call Him God the Father if there are not other manifestations of Him?

> 1Pe 1:2 Elect according to the foreknowledge of <u>God the Father (theos pater)</u>, through sanctification of <u>the Spirit</u>, unto obedience and sprinkling of the <u>blood of Jesus Christ</u>:

Jesus exhibits powers that OT only ascribes to God. He casts demons in the abyss - Luk 8:31

Jesus controlled nature, yet Scripture says God controls nature.

> Pro 30:4 Who hath ascended up into heaven, or descended? Who hath gathered the wind in his fists? Who hath bound the waters in a garment? Who hath established all the ends of the earth? what [is] his name, and what [is] his son's name, if thou canst tell?

Also - Psa 148:8; Jonah 1-2, Psa 104:7, 107:23-32.

Jesus has all authority in heaven.

> Mat 28:18 And Jesus came and spake unto them, saying, All power is given unto me in heaven and in earth.

Jesus is in the form of and equal to God.

> Phl 2:6 Who, being in the form of God, thought it not robbery to be equal with God:

We are one being with three parts - body, mind and spirit. The Spirit directs the other two for believers. The following passage describes God as dominant over Jesus and the Holy Spirit. That does not preclude them being members of a Trinitarian being.

> 1Co 15:27-28 For he hath put all things under his feet. But when he saith all things are put under him, it [is] manifest that he is excepted, which did put all things under him. [28] And when all things shall be subdued unto him, then shall the Son also himself be subject unto him that put all things under him, that God may be all in all.

I read several commentaries and they all state this passage is talking about the completion of Jesus' work on earth, because His reign will last forever just like God the Father - Luk 1:31-33 and Mic 4:7.

> Dan 7:14 And there was given him (son of man vs. 13) dominion, and glory, and a kingdom, that all people, nations, and languages, should serve him: <u>his dominion [is] an everlasting dominion, which shall not pass away, and his kingdom [that] which shall not be destroyed</u>.

> Rev 11:15 The kingdoms of this world are become [the kingdoms] of our Lord (Kyrios), and of his Christ; and he shall reign forever and ever.

How can they <u>both reign</u> forever, unless they are two parts of the same being?

This all fits with the rest of Scripture, we see that Jesus surrendered some of His Godly being when He became man; He did it to Himself.

> Phl 2:7 But made himself of no reputation, and <u>took upon him the form of a servant</u>, and was made in the likeness of men:

Some claim that Jesus is the archangel Michael.

> 1Th 4:16 For the Lord himself shall descend from heaven with a shout, with the voice of the archangel, and with the trump of God: and the dead in Christ shall rise first:

Jesus does not change His nature.

> Heb 13:8 Jesus Christ the same yesterday, and today, and forever.

Michael and Jesus are mentioned in the book of Revelation with Jesus appearing last - Rev 12:7, 20:3.

Jesus cannot be an angel, we are superior to angels - Heb 1:1, and He had his own angel - Rev 1:1.

How do we deny that Jesus is God and expect Him to save us from our sins?

> 2Pe 2:1 But there were false prophets also among the people, even as there shall be false teachers among you, who privily shall bring in damnable heresies, even denying the Lord (Despote = Lord or master) that bought them, and bring upon themselves swift destruction.

> 1Jo 2:22-23 Who is a liar but he that denieth that Jesus is the Christ? He is antichrist, that denieth the Father and the Son. [23] Whosoever denieth the Son, the same hath not the Father: [(but) he that acknowledgeth the Son hath the Father also].

They must be one.

Several passages refer to Jesus as our Lord (Kyrios) and Savior - 2Pe 1:11, 2:20, 3:2, 18. While God (Elohiym, Yahwah, Theos) is referred to as our Savior throughout the Bible - 2Sa 22:3, Isa 43:3, 11, 45:21, 49:26, Hos 13:4, Luk 1:47, 1Ti 1:1, 2:3, 4:10, Tit 3:4, Jde 1:25. If They are three in one, then both descriptions make sense. If They are not, then the references to Jesus as Savior are in conflict with the following passage.

Isa 43:11 I, [even] I, [am] the LORD; and beside me [there is] no saviour.

Most reputable translations place the "our" in front of God in the following verses from the KJV. The Bible does NOT tell us to look for an appearing of God the Father. This version is fine if They are one. The second passage also supports a

Trinitarian view; if we got our faith from Jesus, then He must be one with God.

> Tit 2:13 Looking for that blessed hope, and the glorious appearing of the great God and **our** Saviour Jesus Christ;

> 2Pe 1:1 Simon Peter, a servant and an apostle of Jesus Christ, to them that have obtained like precious faith with us through the righteousness of God and **our** Saviour Jesus Christ:

Ecumenical Organization Summary

Organization	Pred.	Founded	Membership	Mission	Theological Unity
National Association of Ecumenical and Interreligious Staff	Association of Council Secretaries	1800s renamed 1940, 1971, 1997	None provided,	Herald for closer ties among all sectors of humankind for mutual benefit and common attack on problems, which threaten the future of all.	Last newsletter was in 2011, last gathering was 2012, the link to join was dead.
The World Communion of Reformed Churches	World Alliance of Reformed Churches	1875, merged in 1970 and 2010	225 member churches in 94 countries	To meet the spiritual needs and foster justice for all in the transformation of the world through the love of Jesus Christ	Several theological initiatives, focused on reformed churches.
National Council of Churches	Federal Council of Churches	1908, renamed 1950	37 faith groups, 100,000 churches, 45 million adherents	recent priority issues include: mass incarceration, international relations with a focus on peace, church authority in the world, nature and mission of the church	Nothing specifically dealing with theological unity. No resolutions over the last 10 years dealt directly with theological unity.

Appendix E

Ecumenical Organization Summary

Organization	Pred.	Founded	Membership	Mission	Theological Unity
National Association of Evangelicals	none	1945	45,000 churches from 40 denoms, also schools, non-profits, businesses	make denominations strong and effective, influence society for justice and righteousness	Strong emphasis to impact public policy for evangelical values. Good articles on theological unity.
World Council of Churches	none	1948	160 denoms. in 110 countries, 500 million; Canada and US involves 31 faith groups with 50 million	Over 50 initiatives with a primary focus of peacemaking, justice and overcoming poverty.	None of the 20 "what we do" areas deal with theological unity.
Churches Uniting in Christ	The Consultation on Church Union	1962, renamed 2002	11 Protestant denominations	ecumenical and racial justice work	Last meeting 2011, calendar badly out of date
National Workshop on Christian Unity	none	1963	16 member national committee,	Roman Catholics, in the context of Vatican II, equip local leadership for ecumenical ministry	Annual conference with diverse speakers and worships.

Appendix E

Ecumenical Organization Summary

Organization	Pred.	Founded	Membership	Mission	Theological Unity
Pontifical Council for Promoting Christian Unity	none	1965	Part of the governing structure of the Roman Catholic Church	Promote an ecumenical spirit in the CC, develop dialogue and collaboration with the other Churches and World Communions, participate in other ecumenical bodies.	engaged in a theological dialogue with 10 Faith Groups and World Communions
Graymoor Ecumenical and Inter-religious Institute	Graymoor Ecumenical Institute	1986, renamed 1991	A ministry of the Franciscan Friars of Atonement	promotes Christian unity and interreligious dialogue in North America.	Publishes periodicals, sponsors workshops to support the ecumenical and interreligious movement.
Christian Churches Together	none	2001, organized 2005	Members represent 39 denominations and organizations	enable churches and national Christian organizations to grow closer together in Christ in order to strengthen our Christian witness in the world.	Great purpose statement, current priorities are US poverty and evangelism.
World Evangelical Alliance (WEA)	The Evangelical Alliance	1846	600 Million in 129 Countries	strengthen the Evangelical alliance at world, regional and national levels	Very sound statement of faith, three events on the 2017 calendar.

Appendix E

Ecumenical Organization Summary

The following are other Ecumenical Bodies with a National Scope

Mission America Coalition (MAC) - alliance of leaders in evangelism and discipleship

Council for a Parliament of World - global interfaith movement to develop respect and appreciation for other religions

Catholic Association of Diocesan Ecumenical and Interreligious Officers (CADEIO) - promote programs that further the work of Christian unity and interreligious cooperation

Church Women United (1941) - theologically inclusive, no effort to resolve/address theological differences

Church World Service (CWS) (1946) - mission is to feed the hungry and help those in need

North American Interfaith Network (NAIN) - builds communication and understanding among diverse religious groups in North America

Pentecostals & Charismatics for Peace & Justice - promotes peace, justice, and reconciliation work, last meeting 2008

There are church councils or similar bodies in at least 34 states.

A more complete listing of ecumenical and interfaith associations, with contact information is available in the latest edition of the *Yearbook of American and Canadian Churches*, an annual publication of the NCC's research department.

Appendix F

<u>Tenets Harvested from 20 Statements of
Beliefs or Covenant Documents</u>

- Jesus is both God and man
- Jesus rose from the dead physically
- Salvation is by grace through faith alone in Christ's death for our sins
- The gospel is the death, burial, and resurrection of Jesus
- There is only one God
- God exists as a Trinity: Father, Son, and Holy Spirit
- Jesus was born of the Virgin Mary
- Scripture is the inspired word of God
- Scripture is infallible
- Jesus is the son of God
- Humans are utterly void of that holiness required by the law of God
- Jesus is the only way to God the Father
- For the salvation of lost and sinful people, regeneration by the Holy Spirit is absolutely essential
- God's election is perfectly consistent with the free agency of men
- The present ministry of the Holy Spirit by whose indwelling the Christian is enabled to live a godly life
- True believers endure to the end
- Visible church - All Believers, Baptized Believers, additional criteria (member of specific denomination)
- There is an eternal heaven awaiting those who trust in Christ
- There is an eternal punishment awaiting those condemned by God
- The Second Coming: Jesus will one day personally return to the earth to rule and judge
- Salvation is available to all
- Jesus lived a sinless life

- Each church is independent and must be free from interference by any ecclesiastical or political authority
- Resurrection of the body of the dead
- Baptism by Immersion is required for salvation
- Transubstantiation of Communion elements
- Must be a believer to be baptized
- Communion by members only
- Rapture (Pre Trib, A millennial, Post Trib)
- Jesus descended into Hell
- Speaking in Tongues is evidence of the baptism of the Holy Spirit
- Healing is provided for all in the atonement
- Salvation is available for those who died without faith in Jesus
- Marriage is between one man and one woman
- Sabbath is the seventh day of the week
- Christians may swear an oath to civil government
- Service can wipe away sin
- Praying to Mary
- Marriage of clergy allowed
- Women clergy allowed
- Dietary requirements (shall)
- All possessions held in common
- Abortion is acceptable for birth control
- Gay clergy acceptable
- Young earth - 6,000 years old

Choices - 45

Possible combinations - 79,164,837,199,872

Appendix G

Sample of Rose Publishing Denominations Comparison[1]

Denominations Comparison Pamphlet
Information is from official documents, websites, or catechisms of each denomination, as well as from encyclopedias and directories of various denominations. The descriptions on this chart are necessarily short and only generally representative of each denomination. There is diversity within each movement by location, local leadership, and individual personality.

Official Web Sites for the Major Denominations
Catholic Church: http://www.vatican.va/phome_en.htm
Greek Orthodox Archdiocese of America: http://www.goarch.org/
Episcopal Church USA (Anglican): http://www.ecusa.anglican.org/
Evangelical Lutheran Church in America: http://www.elca.org/
Lutheran Church—Missouri Synod: http://www.lcms.org/
Presbyterian Church—U.S.A.: http://www.pcusa.org/
United Methodist Church: http://www.umc.org/index.asp
Southern Baptist Convention: http://www.sbc.net/
United Church of Christ: http://www.ucc.org/
Churches of Christ: http://church-of-christ.org/
Seventh-day Adventist Church: http://www.adventist.org/
Assemblies of God: http://www.ag.org/top/

General References Online
Advocates (statistics for all religions): http://www.adherents.com/
Barna Research (what people actually believe): http://www.barna.org/
Creeds of Christendom: http://www.creeds.net/

Other Helpful Gateway Web Sites for the Major Traditions
Catholicism: http://www.catholic.net/
Orthodoxy: http://www.orthodox.org/
Calvinism: http://www.reformed.org
Mennonites: http://www.mennolink.org/

Other Sources Consulted
Balmer, Randall. *Encyclopedia of Evangelicalism.* Louisville, KY: Westminster John Knox Press, 2002.
Burgess, Stanley M., and Edward M. van der Maas, eds. *The New International Dictionary of Pentecostal and Charismatic Movements.* Revised and expanded ed. Grand Rapids: Zondervan, 2002.
Hastings, Adrian. *The Oxford Companion to Christian Thought.* Oxford: Oxford University Press, 2000.
Linder, Eileen W., ed. *Yearbook of American and Canadian Churches 2002.* Nashville: Abingdon Press, 2002.
Melton, J. Gordon. *Encyclopedia of American Religions.* 6th edition. Farmington Hills, MI: Gale Research, 1999.
Newman, William M., and Peter L. Halvorson. *Atlas of American Religion: The Denominational Era, 1776-1990.* Walnut Creek, CA: Rowan & Littlefield Publishers, 2000.

Reference Books
Burgess, Stanley M., ed. *The New International Dictionary of Pentecostal and Charismatic Movements.* Grand Rapids: Zondervan, 2002.
Campbell, Ted A. *Christian Confessions: A Historical Introduction.* Louisville: Westminster John Knox Press, 1996.
Hart, D. G., and Mark Noll, eds. *Dictionary of the Presbyterian & Reformed Tradition in America.* Downers Grove, IL: InterVarsity, 1999.
Lindner, Eileen W., ed. *Yearbook of American and Canadian Churches 2000: Religious Pluralism in the New Millennium.* 68th ed. Nashville: Abingdon, 2000.
Mead, Frank S., and Samuel S. Hill. *Handbook of Denominations in the United States.* 11th ed., rev. by Craig D. Atwood. Nashville: Abingdon, 2001.
Melton, J. Gordon. *Encyclopedia of American Religions.* 7th edition. Detroit: Gale, 2002.
Wardin, Albert W., ed. *Baptists around the World: A Comprehensive Handbook.* Nashville: Broadman & Holman, 1995.

Acknowledgements
Author: Robert M. Bowman Jr., M.A., Fuller Theological Seminary, President, Apologetics.com, Inc.; Instructor, Biola University.
Research Consultant: Eric Pement, Moody Bible Institute.

Other teaching aids from Rose Publishing:
Denominations Comparison chart (439L)
PowerPoint® Denominations Comparison (486X)
Christianity, Cults, and Religions chart (403L)
The Trinity chart (435L)
The Trinity pamphlet (410X)

Presbyterian Churches

When was it founded and by whom?	1536: John Calvin writes *Institutes of the Christian Religion.* 1643-49: Westminster Standards define Presbyterian doctrine. 1789: Presbyterian Church (USA) first organized (see below).
How many adherents in 2000?	Some 40-48 million worldwide; 3-4 million, USA
How is Scripture viewed?	Historic view: Scripture is inspired and infallible, the sole, final rule of faith. PCUSA: Scripture is "the witness without parallel" to Christ, but in merely human words reflecting beliefs of the time. The standard Protestant canon is accepted.
Who is God?	The one Creator and Lord of all, existing eternally as the Trinity (Father, Son, and Holy Spirit).
Who is Jesus?	The eternal Son incarnate, fully God and fully man, conceived and born of the virgin Mary, died on the Cross for our sins, rose bodily from the grave, ascended into heaven, and will come again in glory to judge us all.
How are we saved?	We are saved by grace alone when God imputes to us his gift of righteousness through faith alone (*sola fide*) in Christ, who died for our sins. Good works are the inevitable result of true faith, but in no way the basis of our right standing before God.
What happens after death?	The souls of believers upon dying go immediately to be with Christ. At Christ's return, their bodies are raised to immortal, eternal life. The souls of the wicked begin suffering immediately in hell.
What is the church?	The church is the body of Christ, including all whom God has chosen as his people, represented by the visible church, composed of churches that vary in purity and corruption. Christ alone is the head of the church. Congregations choose elders to govern them. Regional groups of elders (presbyteries) meet in denomination-wide General Assemblies.
What about the sacraments?	Baptism is not necessary for salvation but is a sign of the new covenant of grace, for adults and infants. Jesus' body and blood are spiritually present to believers in the Lord's Supper.
What are other beliefs and practices of note?	Conservatives affirm the "five points of Calvinism": humans are so sinful that they cannot initiate return to God; God chooses who will be saved; Christ died specifically to save those whom God chose; God infallibly draws to Christ those whom he chooses; they will never fall away.
What are the major divisions or trends today?	The Presbyterian Church (USA), or PCUSA, is the mainline church. The Presbyterian Church in America (PCA) is the largest doctrinally conservative church body.

Appendix H

<u>Sample Independent Statement of Faith</u>

The Bible - We believe that the Scriptures of the Old and New Testaments are the Word of God, fully inspired without error and the infallible rule of faith and practice. The Word of God is the foundation upon which this church operates. We believe that the Word of God supersedes any earthly law that is contrary to the Holy Scriptures.

Father - We believe that there is one living and true GOD, eternally existing in three persons: The Father, the Son, and the Holy Spirit. This triune God created all, upholds all, and governs all things. We believe in the person of God the Father, an infinite, eternal, personal Spirit, perfect in holiness, wisdom, power and love; that He concerns Himself mercifully in the affairs of men; that He hears and answers prayer; and that He saves from sin and death all those who come to Him through Jesus Christ.

Jesus - We believe in the person of Jesus Christ, God's only begotten Son, conceived by the Holy Spirit. We believe in His virgin birth, sinless life, miracles and teachings, his substitutionary atoning death, bodily resurrection, ascension into heaven, perpetual intercession for His people and personal, visible return to earth.

Holy Spirit - We believe in the person of the Holy Spirit, Who came forth from the Father and Son to convict the world of sin, righteousness, and judgment, and to regenerate, sanctify and empower for ministry all who believe in Christ. We believe the Holy Spirit indwells every believer in Jesus Christ and that He is an abiding helper, teacher, and guide. We believe in the present ministry of the Holy Spirit and in the exercise of all biblical gifts of the Spirit according to the instructions given in Scripture.

Sin / Salvation - We believe that all people are sinners by nature and, therefore, are under condemnation; that God saves and regenerates based upon faith, those who repent of their sins and confess Jesus Christ as Lord and Savior.

After Death - We believe in a literal Heaven and a literal Hell and that all those who place their faith, hope and trust in Jesus Christ will spend eternity in Heaven with the Lord, while those who reject Jesus' free gift of salvation will spend eternity separated from the Lord.

The Church - We believe in the universal church, the living spiritual body, of which Christ is the head and all who are born again are a part of the body of Christ.

Sacraments - We believe that the Lord Jesus Christ instituted two ordinances for the church: full immersion water baptism of believers, and the Lord's Supper. We practice an open communion for any believer in attendance.

Glossary

antinomy - a contradiction between two beliefs or conclusions that are in themselves reasonable, a paradox

Christian - someone who claims Jesus as their Lord and Savior; their life should confirm it - Mat 3:8-10, 7:21; Mar 3:35, Act 26:20; Heb 6:7-9; 1Jn 2:4,10, 3:9 and Jas 2:17-18

the church - used generically for all Christian bodies

cult - a group with misplaced or excessive admiration for a particular person or thing

denomination - a group of religious congregations united under a common faith and name and organized under a single administrative and/or legal hierarchy

essential (doctrine) - a basic, indispensable, or necessary element to be saved

evangelical - believers who emphasize Christian unity, the unique authority of Scripture, salvation by grace through faith, and evangelism

non-essential (doctrine) - interpretations of scripture that is not required for salvation (examples in chapter 11). It does not include beliefs that conflict with scripture

mystery - a passage of Scripture that does not have a broad consensus of interpretation

pastor and clergy - used generically to apply to the teachers from all faith groups - bishop, minister, preacher, priest, lay leader, etc.

reputable translation - those widely accepted in Christianity that are not distorted as described in chapter 11

Book mark - copy or cut out and place in your Bible.

WeR2B1

Twelve steps we can take!

1. Stop Being a Divider

2. Forgive Us Our **Sins**

3. Love All Our Brothers And Sisters

4. Influence Our Church

5. Membership not required for baptism

6. Visit Our Cousins

7. Join An Interdenominational Group

8. Shared Communion

9. Merge Where Possible

10. Pursue One Body

11. Establish A List Of Essentials For Salvation

12. Everyone Can Do Something

Taken from chapter 12 of the book WeR2B1
